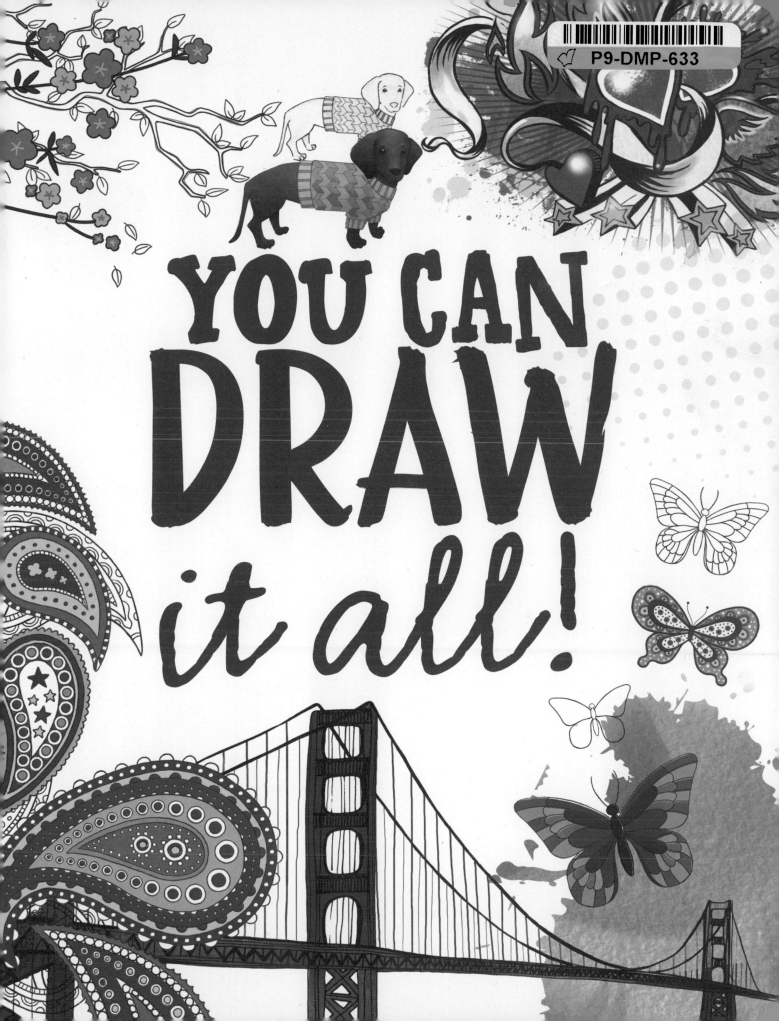

YOU CAN DRAW it all!

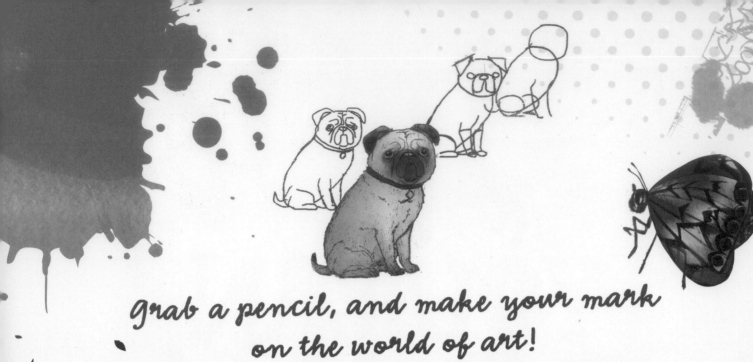

grab a pencil, and make your mark on the world of art!

Flick through the pages of this book to find the things you want to draw, then follow the steps to transform simple shapes into magical masterpieces.

But don't just stop there! Be inspired to draw everything around you, using the tips and techniques you pick up along the way.

And remember, the more you practice, the more your confidence will grow, and the more you'll be ready to DRAW IT ALL!

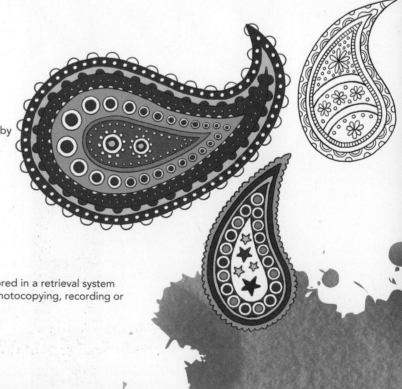

This edition published by Parragon Books Ltd in 2014 and distributed by Parragon Inc.
440 Park Avenue South, 13th Floor
New York, NY 10016
www.parragon.com

Copyright © Parragon Books Ltd 2014

Illustrated by Si Clark, Paula Franco, Alex Hedworth, Steve Horrocks, Julie Ingham, Tom McGrath, David Shephard, and Yasuko
Photographs from Shutterstock, Inc.

ISBN 978-1-4723-5491-4

Printed in China

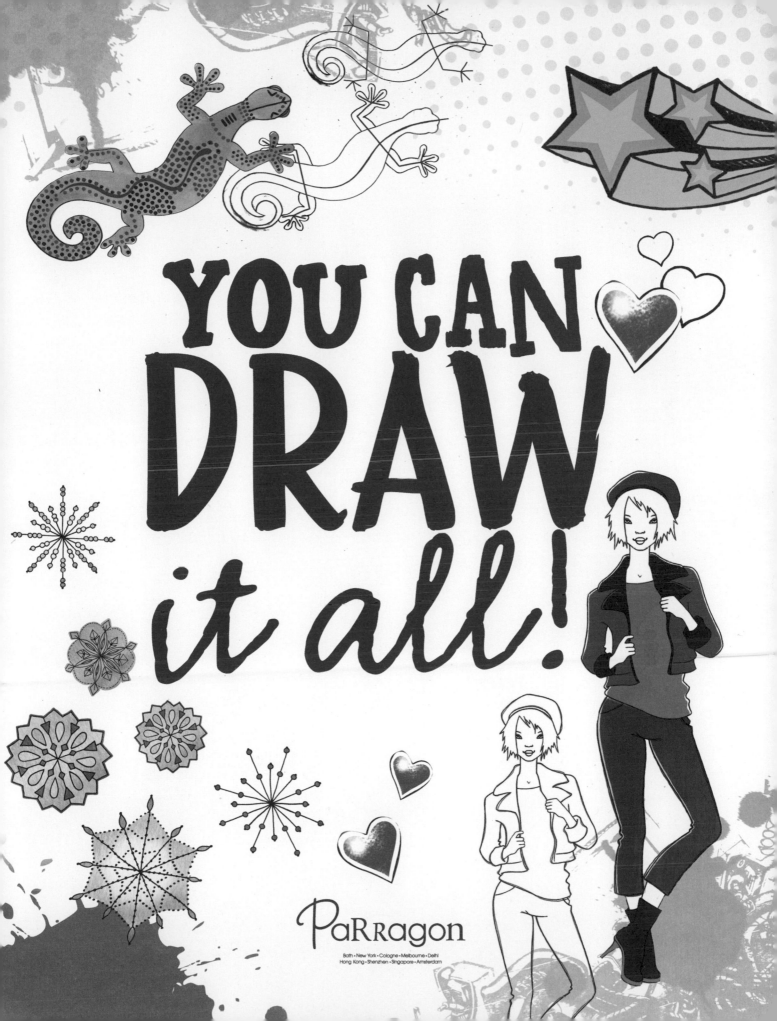

CONTENTS

MATERIALS

ALL YOU REALLY NEED TO DRAW IS A PENCIL AND SOME PAPER, BUT OTHER MATERIALS CAN HELP TRANSPORT YOUR ARTWORK TO ANOTHER LEVEL.

PAPER
Different kinds of paper and pencils can dramatically alter the appearance of your drawing.

Copy paper is great for sharp pencil lines, heavy drawing paper gives a softer effect, and watercolor paper keeps the color of ink and watercolor paints brilliant. To copy or print objects, use transparent (tracing) paper to transfer images onto plain paper.

PENCILS
For thin, fine pencil lines, choose an H (hard) pencil or an HB pencil (a little softer). For shading and blending, go for B (soft). These come in numbered degrees of hard and soft.

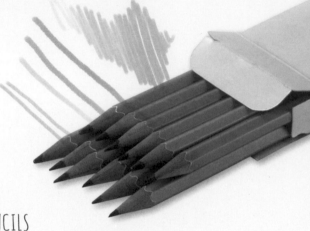

ERASERS
Erase mistakes or unwanted guidelines with an eraser. Also use it to create highlights by sweeping it across your drawing.

PEN AND INK
For line art, to go over outlines, or to make objects stand out from their backgrounds, try a fountain pen, dip pen and ink, or even a fine-tipped brush and ink.

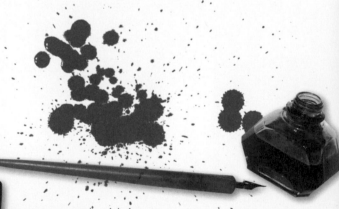

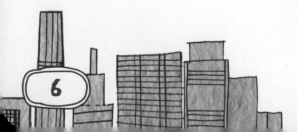

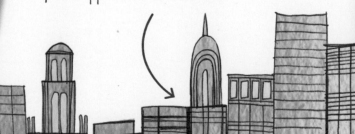

WATERCOLOR AND COLORED PENCILS

Watercolor pencils use water to help blend different colors and shades together. Regular colored pencils are great for creating animal fur and feathery textures.

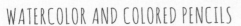

PAINTS AND BRUSHES

For a soft, blending effect, try watercolor paint, and for a heavier, more opaque finish, try gouache paint. For a thick, vibrant appearance, try acrylic or opaque paint—it's great for smooth, solid objects. You can also create these painting techniques digitally.

Experiment with round brushes for washes and general painting, pointed brushes for fine detail, and flat brushes to sweep an even amount of color on bigger areas.

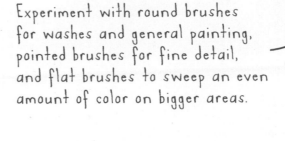

CRAYONS AND PENS

Crayons are great for adding texture to your picture ...

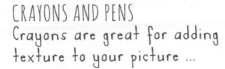

... and felt-tip pens make objects pop out from their backgrounds. You can also use felt-tip or marker pens to outline your work and draw attention to individual elements of your drawing.

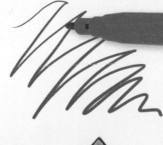

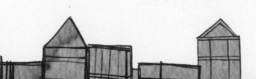

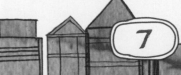

TECHNIQUES

EXPERIMENT WITH DIFFERENT DRAWING TECHNIQUES TO FIND THE RIGHT APPROACH FOR YOU AND YOUR WORK OF ART!

SHAPES AND SYMMETRY

Break objects down into simple shapes to help get the proportions right from the start. Then draw around the shapes to join them together for the object's outline.

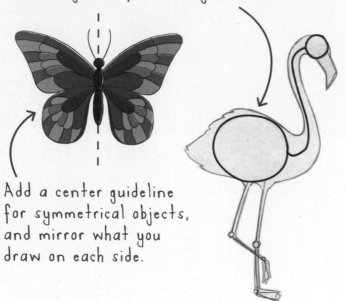

Add a center guideline for symmetrical objects, and mirror what you draw on each side.

DEPTH, DISTANCE, AND DIMENSION

Make your drawing appear realistic by turning basic shapes into 3D objects and using perspective to provide a clear foreground and background in your picture. Objects in the foreground are bigger and normally brighter.

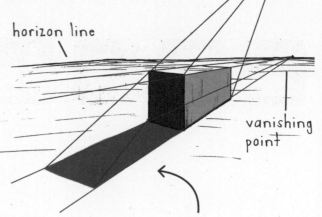

light source

horizon line

vanishing point

Shadows also suggest depth and distance. The higher the light source, the shorter the shadow. Use a light source and vanishing point for accurate shadows.

LINES AND SHADING

For shaded areas, rub the side of a pencil on paper with varied pressure, or use the tip of the pencil to draw lines—the closer the lines, the darker the shading.

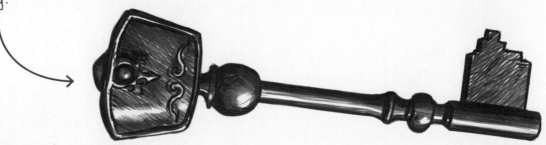

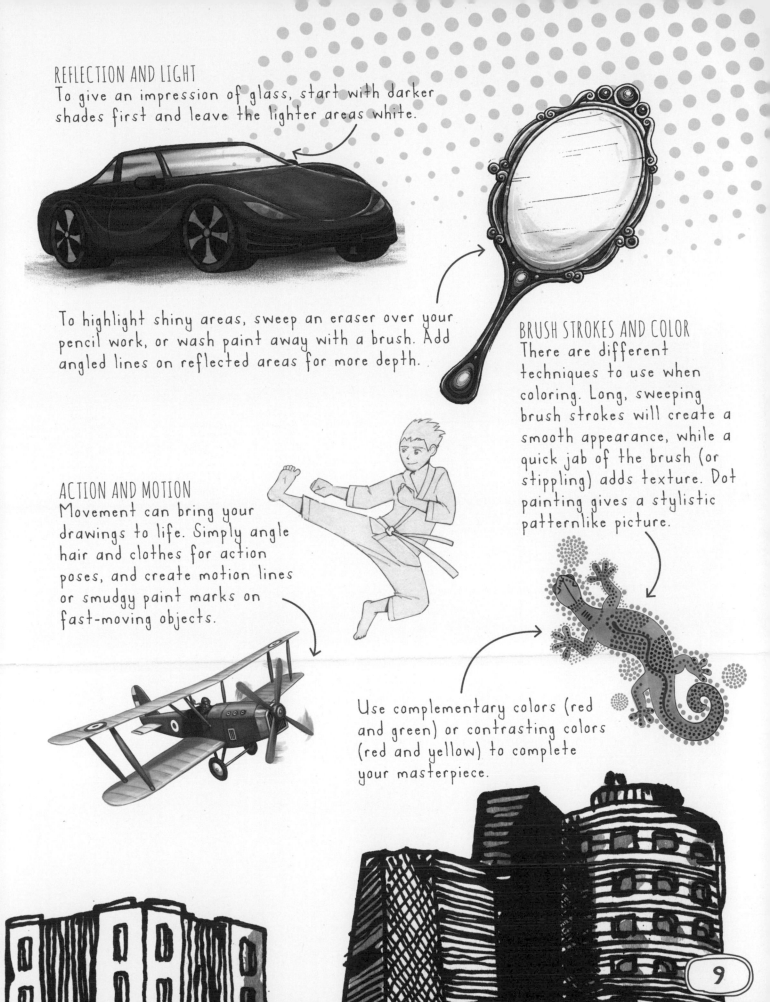

REFLECTION AND LIGHT
To give an impression of glass, start with darker shades first and leave the lighter areas white.

To highlight shiny areas, sweep an eraser over your pencil work, or wash paint away with a brush. Add angled lines on reflected areas for more depth.

BRUSH STROKES AND COLOR
There are different techniques to use when coloring. Long, sweeping brush strokes will create a smooth appearance, while a quick jab of the brush (or stippling) adds texture. Dot painting gives a stylistic patternlike picture.

ACTION AND MOTION
Movement can bring your drawings to life. Simply angle hair and clothes for action poses, and create motion lines or smudgy paint marks on fast-moving objects.

Use complementary colors (red and green) or contrasting colors (red and yellow) to complete your masterpiece.

PEOPLE

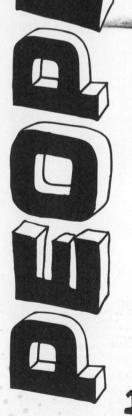

DRAWING PEOPLE IS A GOOD SKILL FOR ARTISTS TO DEVELOP. BREAK THEM DOWN INTO SIMPLE STEPS.

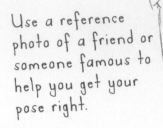

Use a reference photo of a friend or someone famous to help you get your pose right.

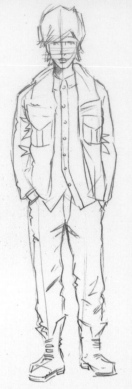

1 SKETCH A STICK FIGURE TO GET THE BASIC POSE. THINK ABOUT WHETHER YOU WANT IT TO BE RELAXED OR DYNAMIC.

2 DRAW A ROUGH OUTLINE OF THE BODY SHAPE AROUND YOUR GUIDE. FOCUS ON GETTING THE PROPORTIONS RIGHT.

3 SKETCH SURFACE DETAIL ON THE CLOTHES, DRAWING JAGGED LINES FOR THE FOLDS. ADD FACIAL DETAILS, TOO.

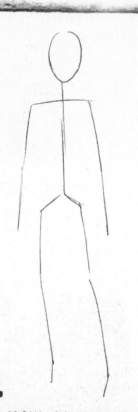

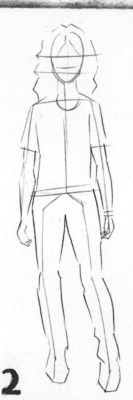

Experiment with different hairstyles and clothing on your people.

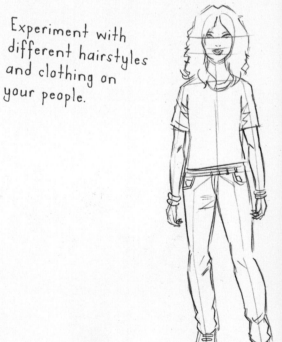

1 AS ABOVE, SKETCH A SIMPLE STICK FIGURE. WORK FROM A PHOTO OR GET SOMEONE TO POSE FOR YOU, IF YOU CAN.

2 OUTLINE THE SHAPES OF THE HAIR AND CLOTHES. THIS POSE IS RELAXED, SO ONE SIDE LOOKS A LITTLE LOWER THAN THE OTHER.

3 WORK ON ADDING MORE SURFACE DETAIL. MAKE SURE THE GIRL'S EXPRESSION MATCHES HER LAID-BACK POSE.

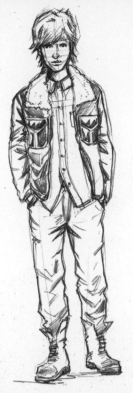

5

ADD SOME SCENERY IN THE BACKGROUND, THEN GO OVER YOUR DRAWING IN BLACK INK. USE WATERCOLORS IN DIFFERENT SHADES TO CREATE A FEELING OF DEPTH.

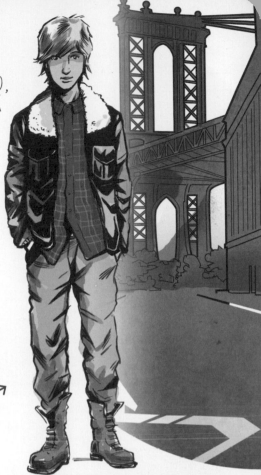

Use pale washes and muted colors for the background. These will help your figure stand out.

4

REFINE YOUR PENCIL LINES, AND CONCENTRATE ON ADDING FINE DETAIL. USE SHORT LINES TO ADD PATCHES OF SHADING FOR THE SHADOWY AREAS.

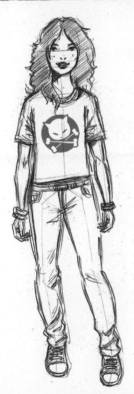

5

SKETCH SOME SCENERY, AND THEN INK IN YOUR DRAWING. CHOOSE COLORS FOR YOUR FIGURE THAT HELP HER STAND OUT FROM THE BACKGROUND.

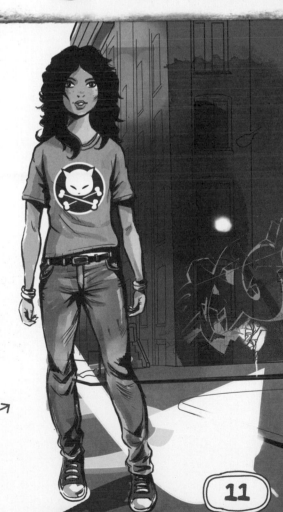

Add subtle areas of shading when you color your picture. It really helps sell the idea that the figure is in 3D.

4

NOW ADD THE FINE DETAILS. THINK ABOUT THE WAY THE FOLDS IN THE JEANS FALL, THEN SKETCH IN CREASE LINES. THESE WILL HELP EMPHASIZE THE OVERALL POSE. SHADE IN THE HAIR.

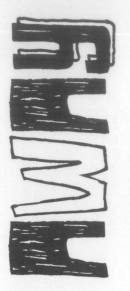

LOTS OF PEOPLE STRUGGLE TO DRAW BACKS OF PEOPLE AND HEADS. LEARN HOW HERE!

Draw a center line, then add a circle on top for the head. Sketch the ears, neck, and shoulders beneath it, like this.

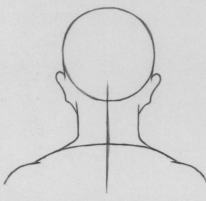

Create a shaggy shape around the head for hair. Add wavy lines inside it. Then draw two curved lines for the T-shirt.

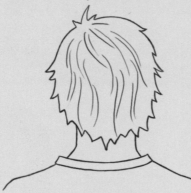

When coloring, use light and dark shading on the hair to give it depth and movement.

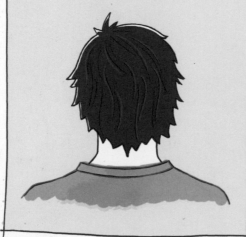

Try drawing the whole body from the back. Create creases on the hood and jacket, and color the drawing in light and dark shades.

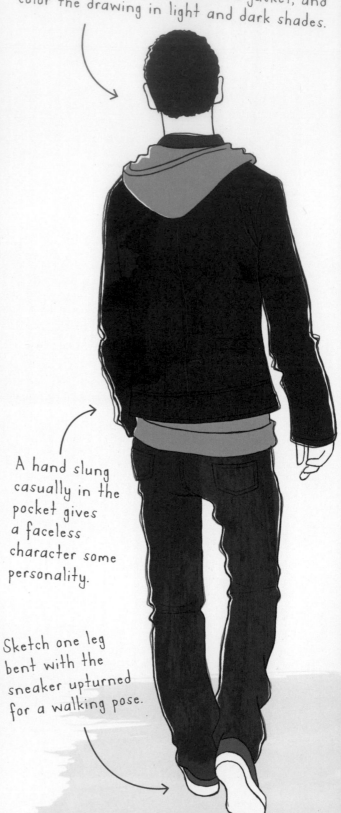

A hand slung casually in the pocket gives a faceless character some personality.

Sketch one leg bent with the sneaker upturned for a walking pose.

For a ponytail, sketch curved lines leading to a semicircular shape. Then draw loose, longer strands down the back.

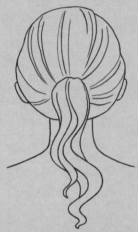

To create soft curls, sketch long wavy lines, flowing in different directions.

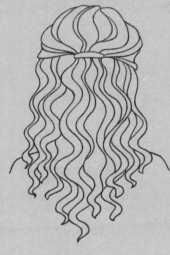

Start a bun like a ponytail, but draw short, curved lines for the actual shape of the bun.

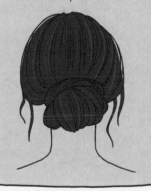

Add fine details to clothes and purses, such as belts and buckles. Then create more meaning to your artwork. Hidden arm gestures and matching leg and feet positions suggest these characters are perfectly in tune.

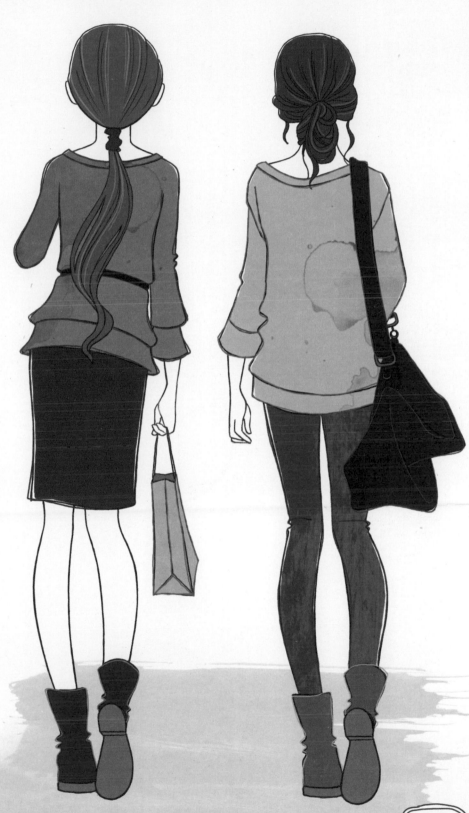

MOST THINGS CAN BE BROKEN DOWN INTO SHAPES. LEARN TO DRAW THE BASICS HERE.

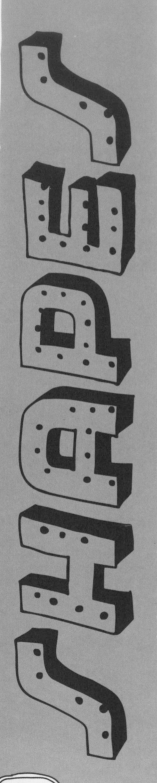

CIRCLE TO SPHERE

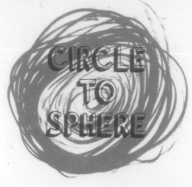

Start with a simple circle. Draw it by hand or with a compass.

Decide where the light source is coming from, then add shading on the opposite side of the circle, following the curved line.

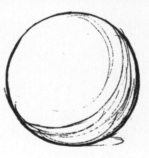

Add color, then create a circular highlight with an eraser to make a sphere. Paint darker marks on the sphere for texture.

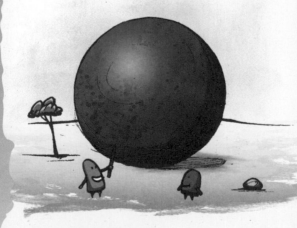

SQUARE TO CUBE

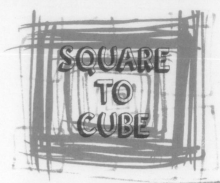

Draw a square, making sure each side is equal in length.

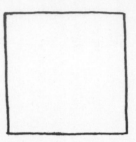

Sketch or trace an overlapping square on top of the original, as shown. Draw lines to connect the two squares.

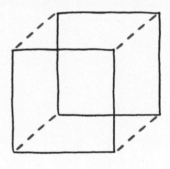

For a 3D effect, sketch darker shadows on the side and front of the cube, with lighter shades on top.

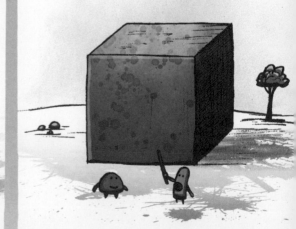

TRIANGLE TO PYRAMID

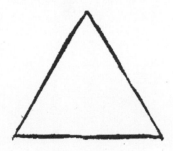

First sketch an equal-sided triangle, like this.

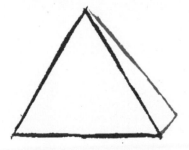

Draw a short diagonal line out from the bottom right corner and a longer line linking up to the tip of the triangle.

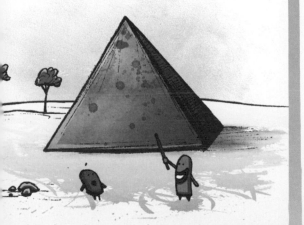

Create depth with your shading and color by making the side of the pyramid darker than the front.

CONE AND CYLINDER

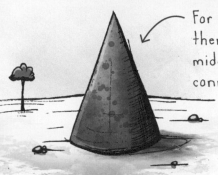

For a cone, draw an oval base, then a line leading up from the middle. Add lines down the sides, connecting the top to the base.

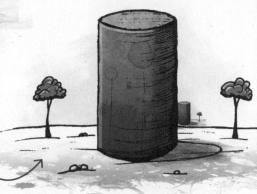

To make a cylinder shape, sketch two parallel ovals on their sides, joined together by two parallel vertical lines and shading.

DRAWING WITH SHAPES

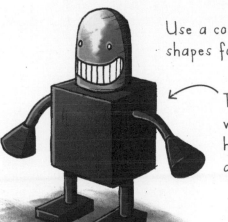

Use a combination of simple shapes for more complex drawings.

Try a cube-shaped robot with cylinders for the head, legs, and arms, and cone-shaped hands.

A tennis ball is easy when you know how to draw a sphere!

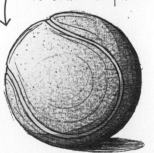

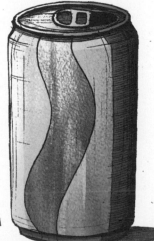

Design your own can of pop from a cylinder.

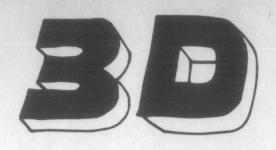 **3D** MAKE YOUR DRAWINGS EXTRA REALISTIC BY DRAWING IN THREE DIMENSIONS: LENGTH, DEPTH, AND WIDTH. START BY LEARNING TO DRAW A BUILDING IN THIS WAY.

1 SKETCH RECTANGLES FOR EACH FRONT-FACING SECTION OF THE BUILDING, AS SHOWN. ADD THE BASIC SHAPE OF THE STEPS.

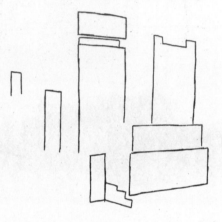

2 NOW DRAW THE SAME SHAPES FARTHER AWAY, AT A DIFFERENT ANGLE, LIKE THIS.

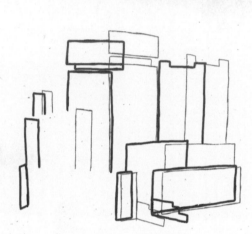

3 CONNECT THE CORNERS OF THE REPEATING SHAPES TOGETHER FOR THE 3D EFFECT.

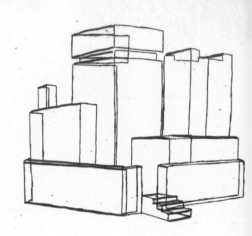

4 TO ADD DETAIL, SKETCH SQUARES AND RECTANGLES FOR WINDOWS, AND CURVED LINES FOR PIPES. ADD OVALS TO THE NECK OF THE BUILDING.

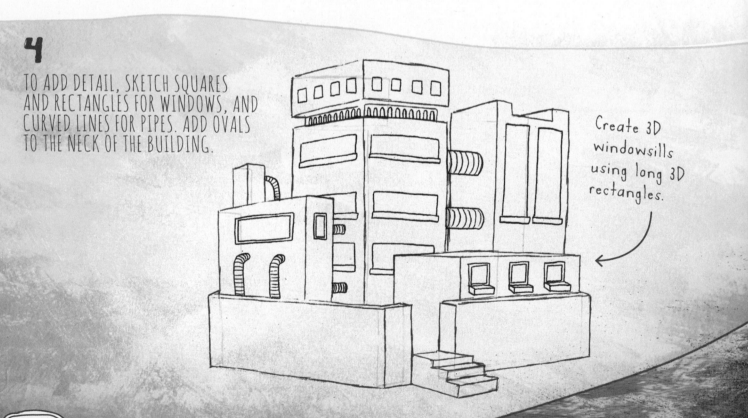

Create 3D windowsills using long 3D rectangles.

3D STEPS

Create an outline of the steps, as shown. Repeat the step shape farther away. Then sketch parallel lines to join each step together. Add light and dark shading, and color the steps in.

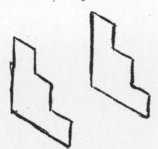 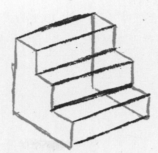 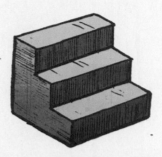

5 CHOOSE THE DIRECTION OF YOUR LIGHT SOURCE. THEN KEEP THE PARTS OF THE BUILDING FACING THE LIGHT BRIGHTER THAN THE AREAS ON THE OTHER SIDE, WHICH SHOULD BE DARKER. ADD COLOR TO FINISH YOUR 3D BUILDING.

Add diagonal lines on the windows to give an impression of glass.

Sketchy lines give the walls of the building a rough-looking texture.

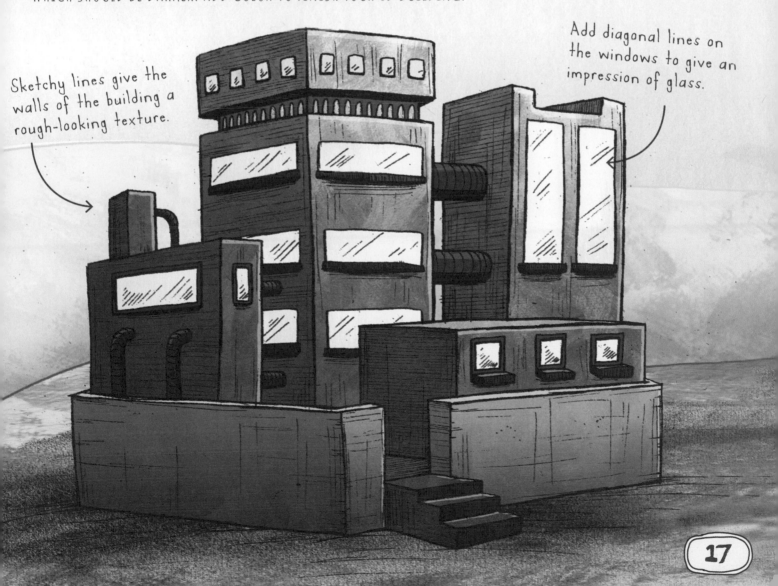

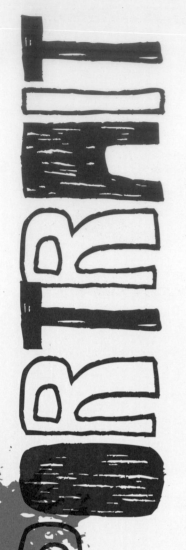

1 SKETCH AN ANGLED OVAL SHAPE. DRAW A CURVED, VERTICAL LINE AND THREE HORIZONTAL GUIDELINES, LINING UP WITH THE EAR AS SHOWN. ADD NECK LINES.

2 USE THE GUIDELINES TO POSITION THE FACIAL FEATURES. NOTICE HOW THE EYES ARE LEVEL WITH THE TOP OF THE EAR AND THE MOUTH WITH THE BOTTOM.

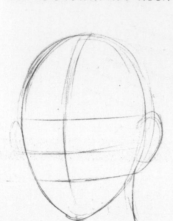

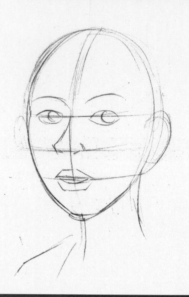

5 DEFINE THE HAIR SHAPE, PARTICULARLY WHERE IT MEETS THE COLLAR. ADD LIGHT PATCHES OF SHADING FOR TEXTURE. ADD CLOTHING DETAIL.

6 FIGURE OUT WHERE THE SHADOWS SHOULD BE, AND SHADE IN THOSE AREAS. REFINE THE DETAIL OF THE EYES, NOSE, MOUTH, AND HAIR.

Keep your wrist relaxed as you draw. It will make it easier to sketch nice, smooth curves.

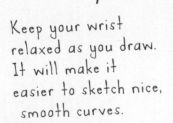

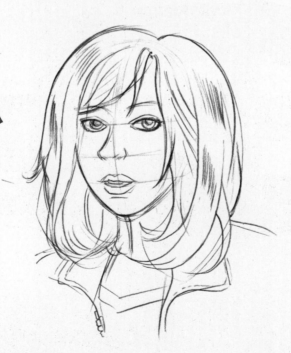

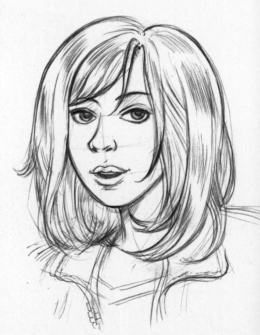

3 SKETCH THE OUTLINE OF THE HAIR USING LONG, SWEEPING CURVES. REMEMBER JUST TO FOCUS ON THE OVERALL SHAPE AT THIS STAGE.

4 ADD A LITTLE MORE DETAIL TO THE FACIAL FEATURES, AND USE MORE CURVED LINES TO SHOW HOW THE HAIR FALLS ACROSS THE FACE.

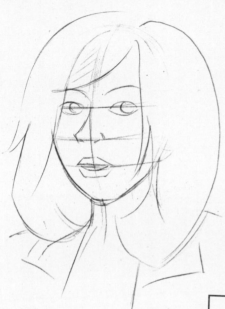

Stick with a light pencil until you're happy with the overall shape of your portrait.

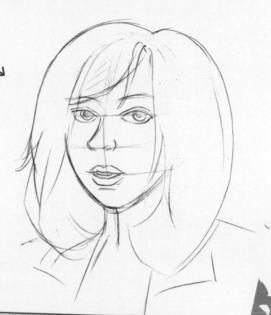

7 PAINT YOUR PORTRAIT USING WATERCOLORS. CHOOSE A BASE TONE FOR THE SKIN, THEN ADD BOTH LIGHTER AND DARKER SHADES ON TOP TO EMPHASIZE THE SHAPES OF THE FEATURES.

Try to keep your painting technique fairly loose. It will help give your final portrait more life and character!

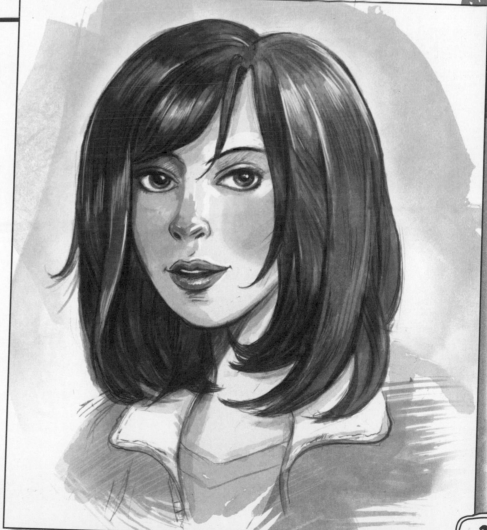

SHADOWS

LEARN ABOUT LIGHT SOURCES AND THE SHADOWS THEY CREATE TO TURN YOUR FLAT DRAWINGS INTO REALISTIC 3D.

ADDING SHADOWS IN PERSPECTIVE CAN LOOK TRICKY, BUT THESE SIMPLE TIPS WILL HELP YOU LEARN TECHNIQUES YOU CAN USE AGAIN AND AGAIN.

light source

vanishing point

Mark a vanishing point in the distance. Draw guidelines to sketch a cuboid shape in perspective.

Now add a light source above the cuboid. Draw lines leading down from the middle of the light to the far corners of the cuboid.

For the shadow, shade the areas where the light source lines meet the vanishing point lines.

A light source positioned higher up will result in a shorter shadow, while a light lower down gives a longer shadow.

SHADING EFFECTS

With a soft B pencil apply pressure to the paper, gradually easing off toward the end for a dark-to-light effect.

To shade using crosshatching, draw lines in opposing diagonal directions over the area you want to darken.

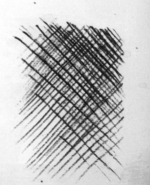

CASTING SHADOWS

USE A SIMILAR TECHNIQUE TO CREATE EFFECTIVE SHADOWS IN OTHER DRAWINGS, LIKE A TREE, HOUSE, OR EVEN PEOPLE!

light source

light source

light source

light source

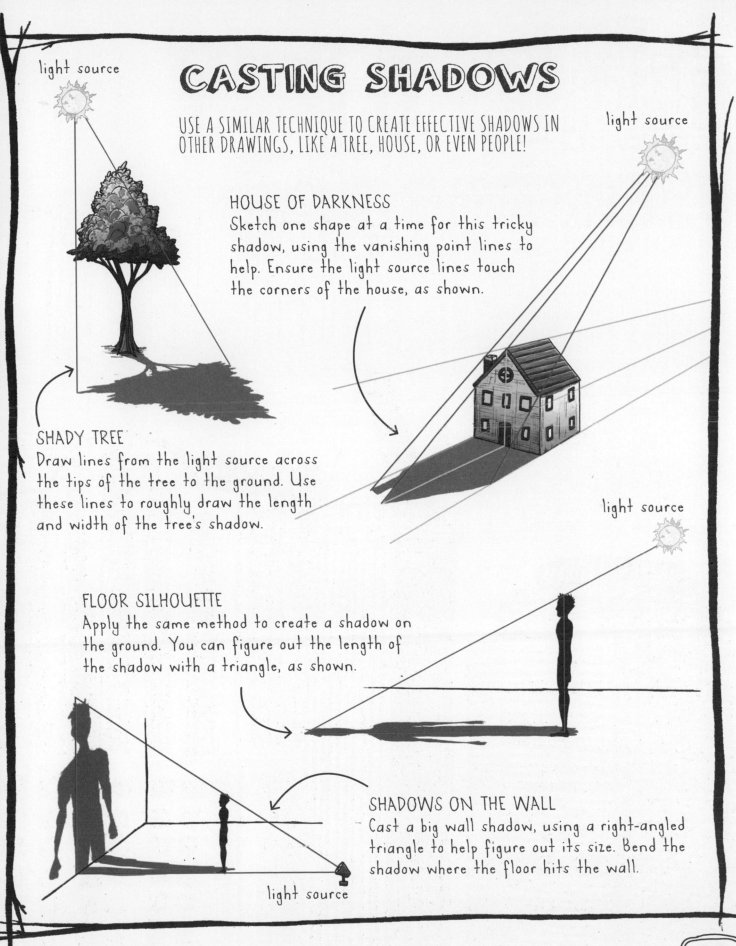

HOUSE OF DARKNESS
Sketch one shape at a time for this tricky shadow, using the vanishing point lines to help. Ensure the light source lines touch the corners of the house, as shown.

SHADY TREE
Draw lines from the light source across the tips of the tree to the ground. Use these lines to roughly draw the length and width of the tree's shadow.

FLOOR SILHOUETTE
Apply the same method to create a shadow on the ground. You can figure out the length of the shadow with a triangle, as shown.

SHADOWS ON THE WALL
Cast a big wall shadow, using a right-angled triangle to help figure out its size. Bend the shadow where the floor hits the wall.

THE CITY

CREATE A CITY LANDSCAPE USING ONLY LINE ART: A COMBINATION OF DIFFERENT LINE STYLES.

START WITH A 3D OUTLINE OF YOUR LANDSCAPE. USE A MIXTURE OF RECTANGULAR, TRIANGULAR, AND CYLINDRICAL SHAPES, LIKE THIS.

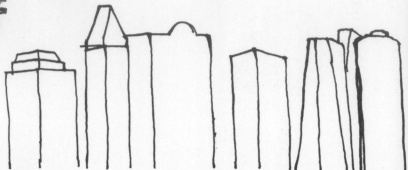

Apply different line effects on each building for a cool, varied city look. Try crosshatching on one side of the building and a mixture of horizontal and vertical lines on another.

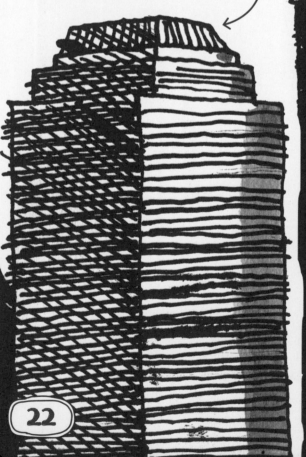

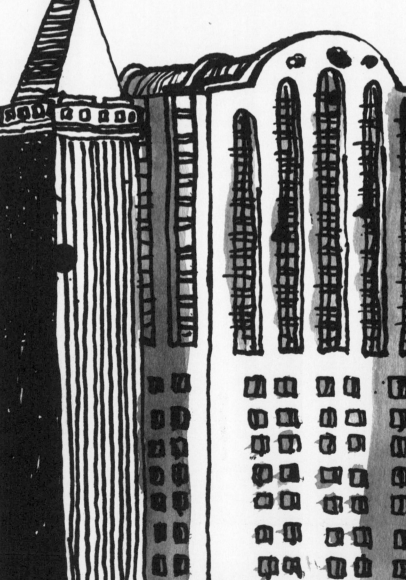

INK LINE STYLES

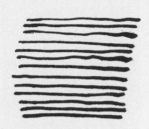 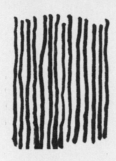 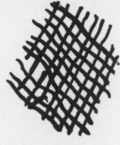 

Horizontal lines highlight the width of a building and give a sense of space.

Vertical lines elongate buildings, leading the eye up to the sky.

Crosshatching is overlapping lines in opposite directions to create shading.

Build up crosshatching for flat black, going over and over the same area.

Lines drawn close together give a darker shading effect than those drawn farther apart. For more depth, add flat, black shading to buildings in the background.

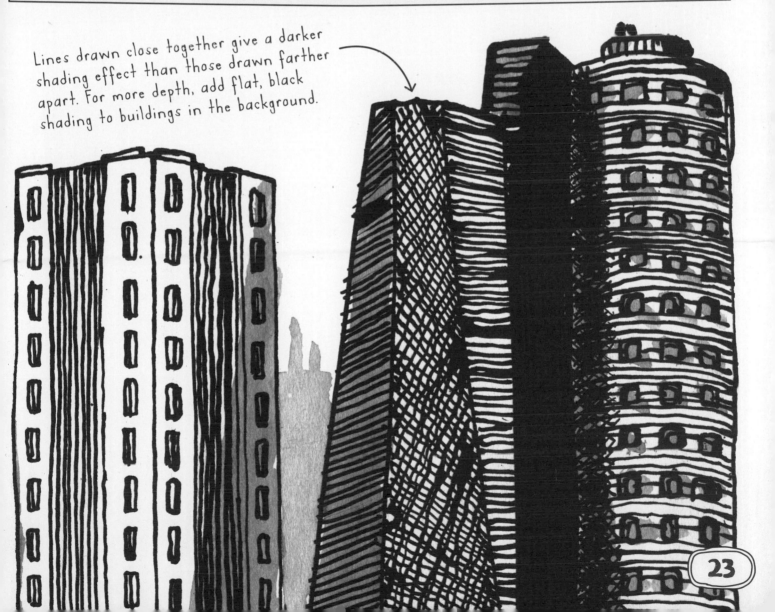

FLOWER POWER

FLOWERS COME IN ALL SHAPES AND COLORS. TRY THESE TECHNIQUES IN YOUR OWN FLORAL DRAWINGS.

1
TO DRAW A POPPY, FIRST SKETCH THE HEAD USING SIMPLE, WAVY SHAPES FOR THE PETALS, AS SHOWN.

2
DRAW A RECTANGLE SHAPE IN THE MIDDLE OF THE HEAD. ADD SMALL, THIN STICKS WITH TINY LEAFLIKE SHAPES ON TOP.

3
LIGHTLY DRAW LINES ON THE PETALS FOR TEXTURE. ADD TWO LONG LINES BENEATH THE FLOWER HEAD TO CREATE A STEM.

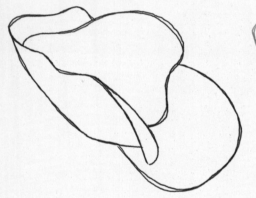

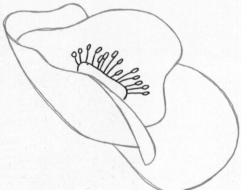

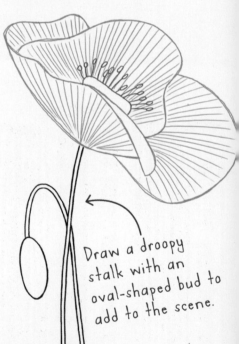

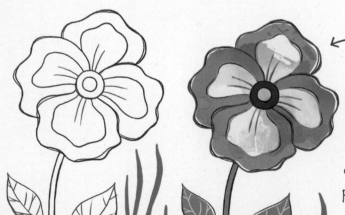

Sketch borders and crease lines in the petals. Then use complementary colors to finish this pretty plant.

Draw a droopy stalk with an oval-shaped bud to add to the scene.

4

GO OVER YOUR DRAWING WITH INK.
ERASE ANY PENCIL MARKS, AND
COLOR THE POPPY HEAD A DEEP RED.

For a rose in bloom, start with
small petals in the center, and
make them bigger as you work
your way out.

Use vibrant colors to finish your
blossoms. The brighter the better!

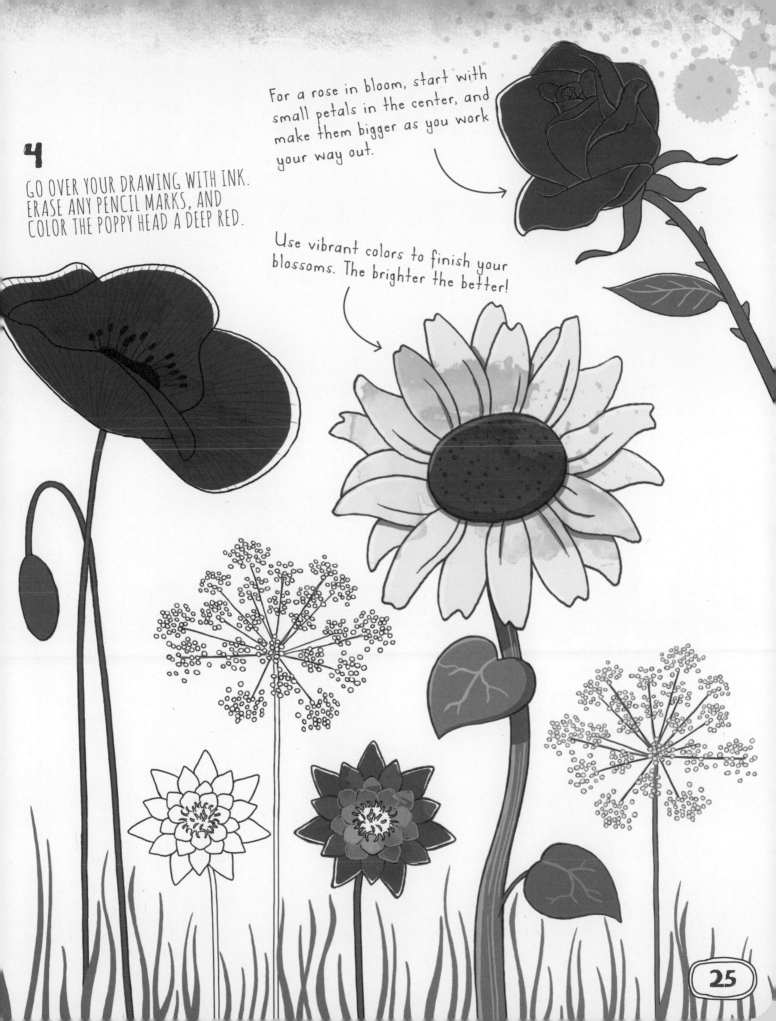

FRUIT BOWL

A MUST-LEARN FOR ANY BUDDING ARTIST!

1 USING A PENCIL, DRAW A SIMPLE BOWL SHAPE SIDE ON. GIVE IT A ROUNDED BRIM WITH A SHALLOW BASE AT THE BOTTOM.

2 LOOSELY SKETCH THE SHAPES OF DIFFERENT FRUITS.

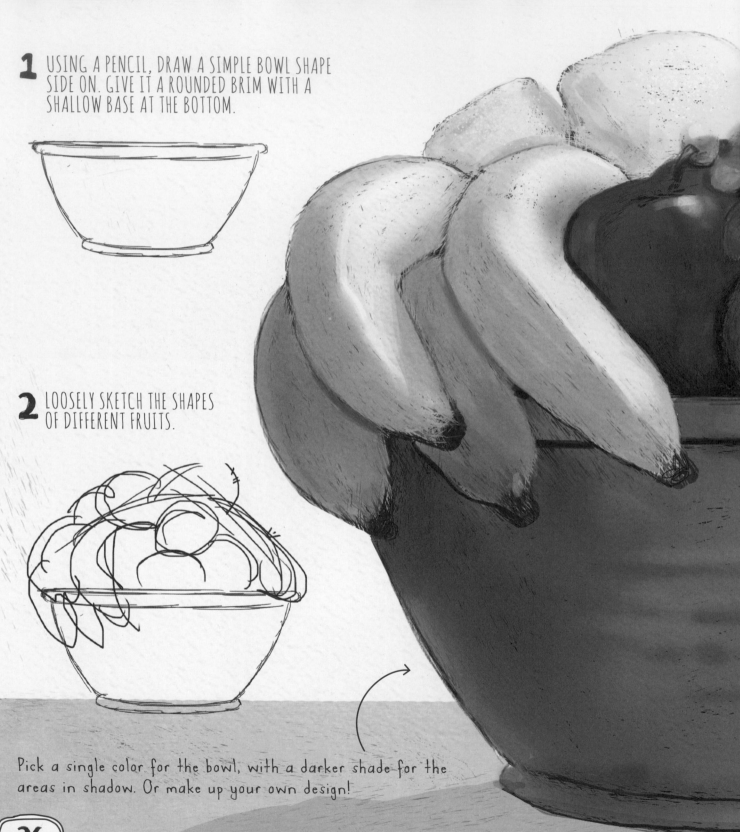

Pick a single color for the bowl, with a darker shade for the areas in shadow. Or make up your own design!

3

START REFINING YOUR OUTLINES, ADDING SMALLER FRUIT SHAPES HERE AND THERE, TOO. ERASE YOUR ROUGH GUIDELINES.

4

DECIDE WHERE THE LIGHT IS COMING FROM IN YOUR DRAWING, THEN ADD SOME SHADING TO THE AREAS THAT ARE IN SHADOW.

Light source

6

WHEN COLORING YOUR DRAWING, THINK ABOUT HOW THE SHINY FRUIT PEEL WILL REFLECT THE LIGHT. CREATE HIGHLIGHTS BY LEAVING SOME AREAS WHITE.

Shiny objects will slightly reflect the color of whatever is near them. So, add a red tinge to the fruit that's next to the bright red apple.

5

REALLY WORK UP THE FRUIT SHAPES, AND FOCUS ON MORE SUBTLE SHADING TO MAKE THE FRUIT LOOK MORE ROUNDED. THIS WILL ALSO HELP ADD DEPTH TO YOUR PICTURE.

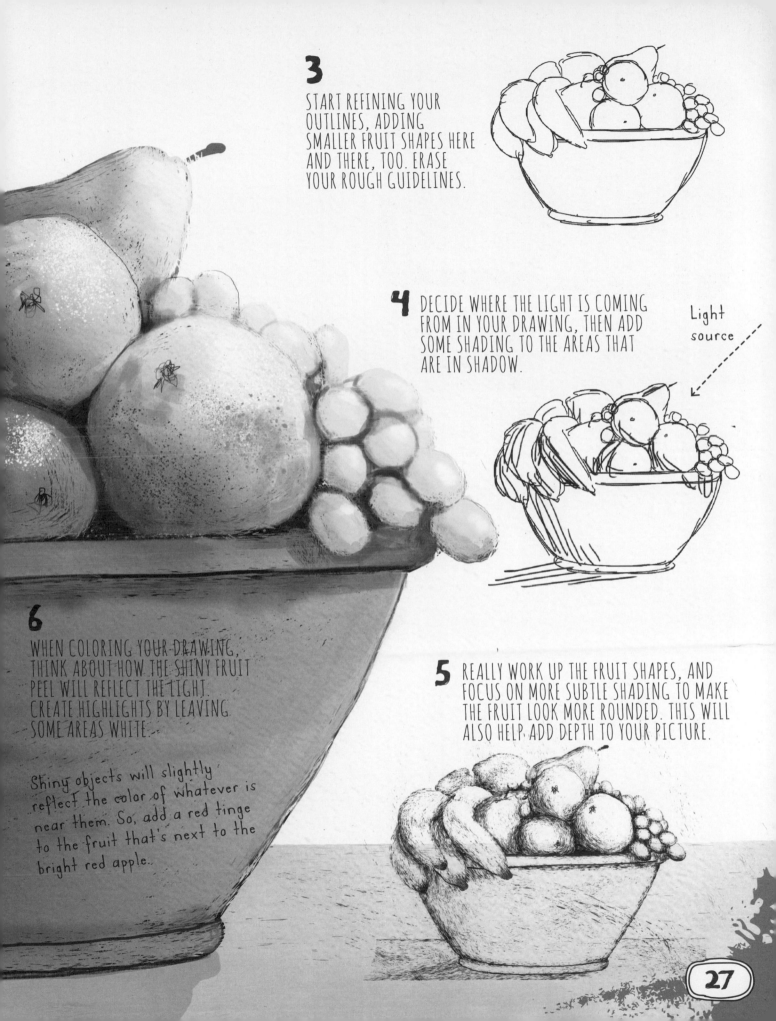

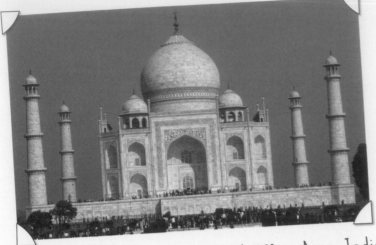

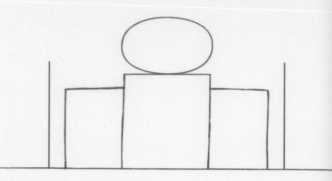

The Taj Mahal was built around 1653 in Agra, India, and is an admired work of art! Find a photo of this famous landmark for your drawing reference.

1

START WITH SIMPLE SHAPES TO BUILD YOUR MONUMENT: LIGHTLY SKETCH A HORIZONTAL LINE, TWO VERTICAL LINES, THREE RECTANGLES, AND AN OVAL, AS SHOWN. USE A RULER IF YOU LIKE.

TAJ MAHAL

Work on smaller sections at a time to help you focus on the line work.

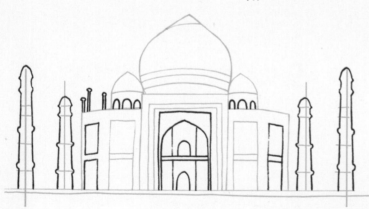

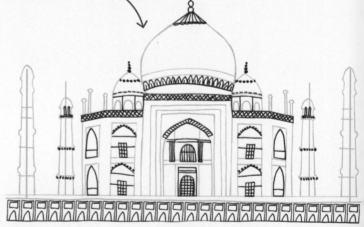

4

START WORKING UP THE FEATURES, SUCH AS ARCHES, DOORS, WINDOWS, AND PILLARS. USE A FINE INK PEN TO DRAW OVER THE TOP OF YOUR PENCIL SKETCH.

5

USE A MIXTURE OF TINY CRISSCROSS LINES, OVALS, DOME SHAPES, AND CIRCLES TO CREATE THE DECORATIVE DETAIL. ERASE ANY PENCIL MARKS.

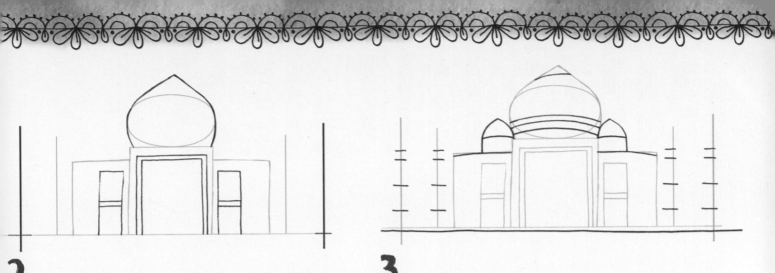

2

DRAW A DOME SHAPE AROUND THE OVAL, THEN USE A RULER TO ADD SMALLER RECTANGLES TO THE BUILDING, AS SHOWN. NOW DRAW TWO MORE VERTICAL LINES ON THE OUTER EDGES.

3

SKETCH FOUR SHORT HORIZONTAL LINES ON EACH OF THE FOUR VERTICAL LINES TO PREPARE FOR DRAWING THE PILLARS. DRAW CURVED LINES WITHIN THE DOME SHAPE, THEN ADD TWO SMALL DOMES ON EITHER SIDE.

6

FINALLY, ADD A WASH OF COLOR INK OR WATERCOLOR PAINT OVER THE MONUMENT AND SKY. DRAW THREE SIMPLE BIRD SHAPES WITH YOUR PEN TO FINISH.

Use light and dark shades to suggest shadow and depth.

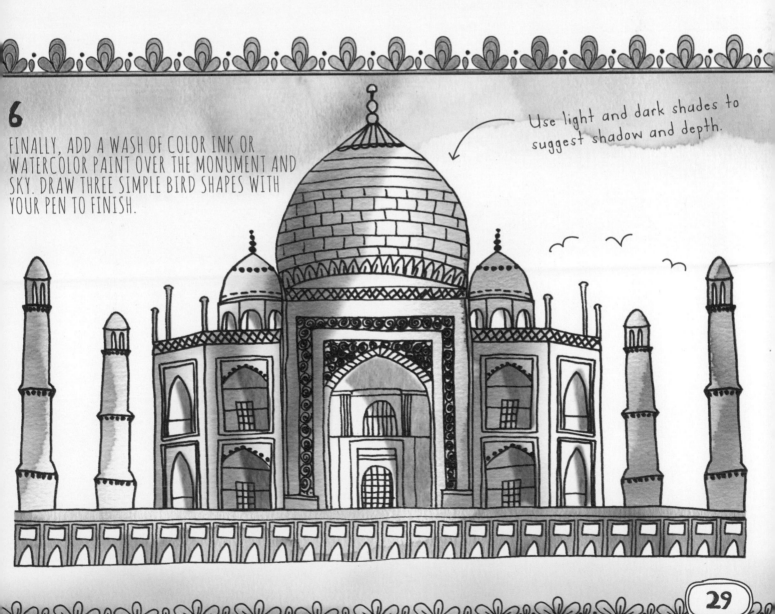

PROFILES

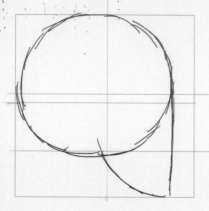

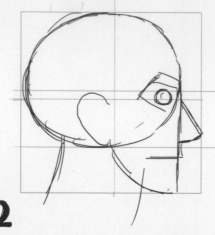

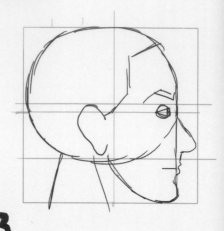

1

DRAW A LARGE SQUARE, AND DIVIDE WITH HORIZONTAL LINES AND A LINE DOWN THE MIDDLE, AS SHOWN. SKETCH AN OVAL FOR THE HEAD AND A POINTED SHAPE FOR THE JAW.

2

USING YOUR GUIDES, DRAW BASIC SHAPES FOR THE EYES, EYE SOCKETS, NOSE, MOUTH, AND EARS. NOTICE HOW THE EYE IS SET BACK A LITTLE FROM THE BRIDGE OF THE NOSE.

3

REFINE THE SHAPES OF THE VARIOUS FACIAL FEATURES A LITTLE. ADD A JAGGED LINE FOR THE HAIRLINE, RUNNING FROM THE TOP OF THE FOREHEAD DOWN TO THE EAR.

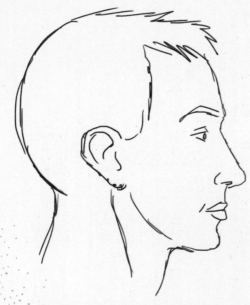

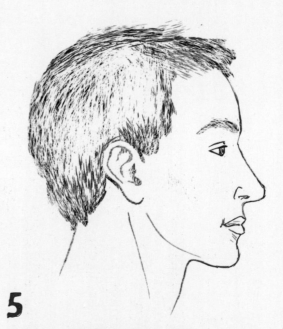

4

ERASE YOUR GUIDELINES, AND WORK ON THE FINER DETAILS. DRAW THE SHAPE OF THE HAIR AND ADD DETAIL TO THE EYES, NOSE, AND MOUTH.

5

USING A PEN OR SHARP PENCIL, GIVE THE EYEBROWS AND HAIR MORE TEXTURE. MAKE LOTS OF FINE LINES USING SHORT STROKES.

6

PAINT THE FACE WITH A MIX OF RED, WHITE, AND BROWN TO MAKE THE RIGHT SKIN COLOR. USE DIFFERENT TONES TO SHOW CONTOURS OF THE FACE, AS WELL AS AREAS OF LIGHT AND SHADE.

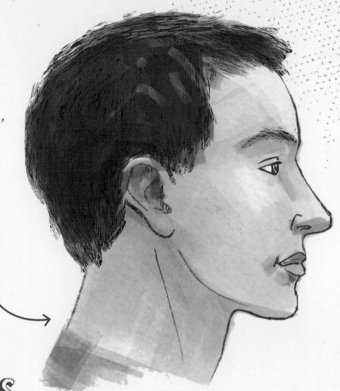

To make the skin look smooth, try to fade gradually between the lighter and darker tones.

PROFILE FEATURES

NOSES

Have fun drawing different nose shapes. Perhaps you could ask your family and friends if you can sketch them in profile?

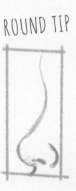
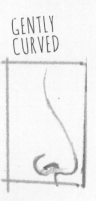
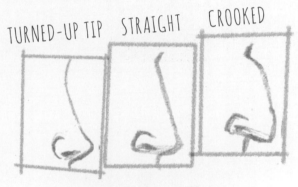

ROUND TIP   GENTLY CURVED   TURNED-UP TIP   STRAIGHT   CROOKED

HEADS

People's head shapes can vary a lot, too. Notice the differences in bone structure and how someone's hairstyle also changes the overall shape of their head.

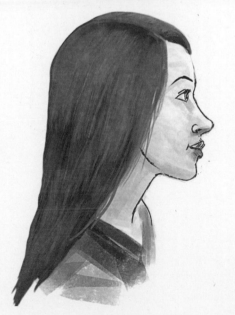
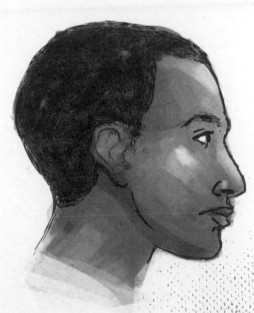

31

BAGS

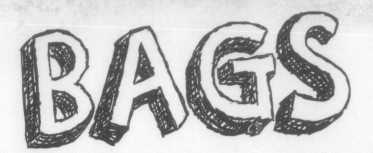

LEARN TO DRAW COOL BAGS AND PURSES, SO THAT YOU CAN ADD EXTRA STYLE TO YOUR DRAWINGS OF PEOPLE!

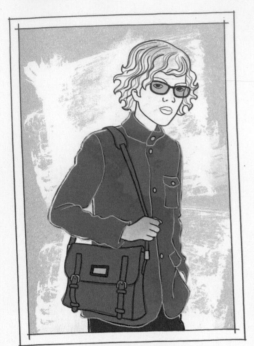

TODAY, THERE ARE MORE BAG STYLES FOR BOYS THAN EVER BEFORE! BE INSPIRED BY FASHION MAGAZINES, OR GO ONLINE FOR THE LATEST LOOKS. TRY DRAWING A BAG AT AN ANGLE TO GIVE IT MORE INTEREST.

MESSENGER BAG

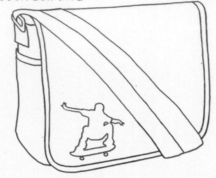

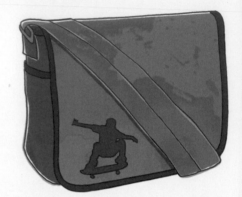

Draw an angled rectangle with a side panel for depth. Add a strap, side pocket, and skateboarder shape.

Use tones of the same color for depth. You could also try a shorter flap with straps and buckles for a vintage look.

KNAPSACK

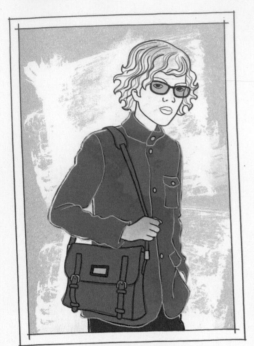

ZIPPERED MESSENGER BAG

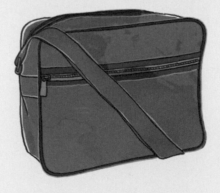

BACKPACK

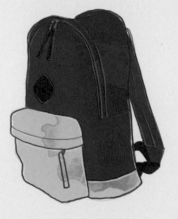

It's all in the extras with this bag! Draw a wobbly rectangle, then sketch pockets, straps, buckles, tassels, and a handle.

For the zipper, draw two long horizontal lines joined by lots of tiny vertical lines, then add a small rectangular zipper pull.

Too cool for school? Use weirdly complementary colors to create an eye-catching effect that grabs attention.

PURSES FOR GIRLS

TOTE, HANDBAG, SATCHEL ... WHAT WILL IT BE? LEARN TO DRAW THE VARIOUS STYLES, THEN TRY DIFFERENT PATTERNS FOR EXTRA DETAIL.

TOTE

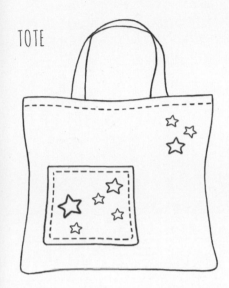

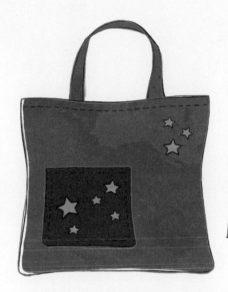

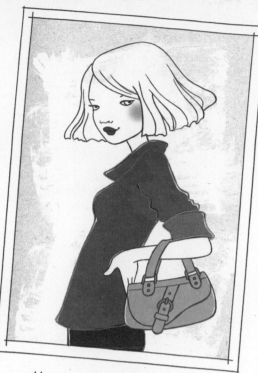

Draw a square, then add two arches for the handle. Draw dashed lines for stitching, a pocket, and some stylin' stars.

Make your star pattern pop by coloring the stars and pocket in lighter or darker shades of the main color.

Have fun creating unique details like this clutch's asymmetrical flap. Stick to a basic color for a sophisticated design.

BUCKLED SHOULDER BAG

SATCHEL HANDBAG

CARPETBAG

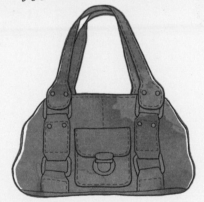

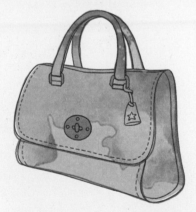

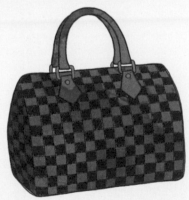

Draw chunky straps and buckles for easy-going elegance. Add a cute pocket and clasp as a finishing touch.

Create clasps and key rings out of circles and rectangles, making an ordinary design feel a little more special.

A carpetbag doesn't need a carpet pattern! Draw lines going down and across to achieve a checkered look.

DOGS, DOGS, DOGS!

FAT OR FURRY, SHORT OR SHAGGY—HERE'S HOW TO DRAW THE PERFECT POOCH!

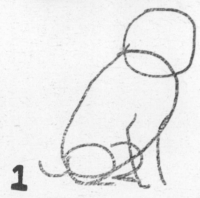

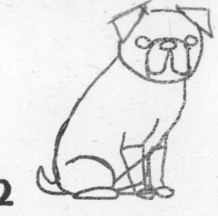

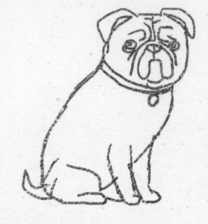

1 SKETCH A BIG OVAL FOR THE BODY, WITH A ROUGH CIRCLE FOR THE HEAD. USE CURVED AND STRAIGHT LINES TO SKETCH THE LEGS AND TAIL.

2 DRAW TRIANGLES FOR THE EARS AND OVALS FOR THE EYES AND NOSE. FLESH OUT THE SHAPES OF THE LEGS, PAWS, AND TAIL.

3 START ADDING DETAIL. DRAW EXTRA LINES ON THE FACE FOR THE DOG'S WRINKLY SKIN. ADD THE MOUTH AND A COLLAR.

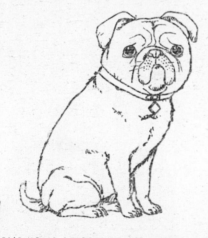

4 REFINE YOUR PENCIL LINES, THEN USE SHORT PENCIL STROKES TO CREATE A FUR TEXTURE. ADD LOTS OF PENCIL DOTS AROUND THE MUZZLE.

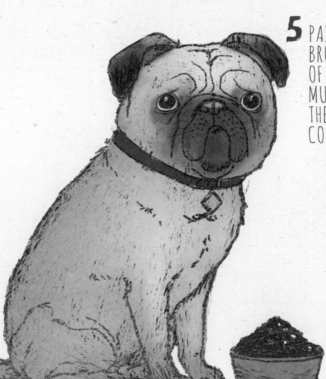

5 PAINT THE COAT A PALE BROWN, ADDING PATCHES OF GRAY TO THE EARS AND MUZZLE AREA. PICK OUT THE COLLAR IN A BRIGHT, CONTRASTING COLOR.

Draw a dinner bowl or other doggy object to add interest to your picture.

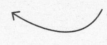

NOW TRY SOME OF THESE DOGS AND STYLES!

FUR AND HAIR

Use fine, squiggly lines to draw the texture of a terrier's shaggy coat. Use shorter pencil strokes for its furry face.

TERRIER

POODLE

Use rounded shapes and tiny pencil strokes to create the neatly groomed outline and look of a poodle. Color using white and off-white tones.

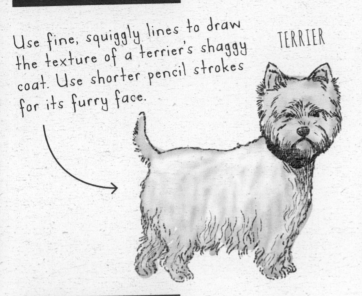
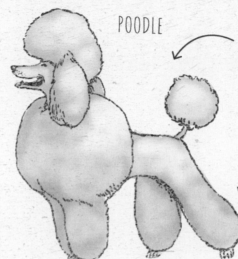

MARKINGS

Draw large patches on the dog's body, and add shading using crosshatching.

BASSET HOUND

Use short pencil strokes for these markings. Follow the contour of the body, emphasizing its shape.

BULLDOG

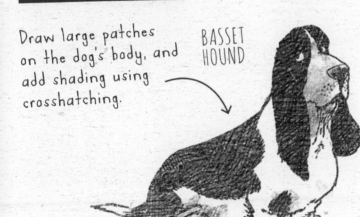

SILHOUETTES

Practice sketching dogs in silhouette. It'll help you get better at drawing different poses.

SCOTTIE DOG

CHIHUAHUA

Silhouettes help you think about different doggy shapes. This one's ears are huge compared to its body!

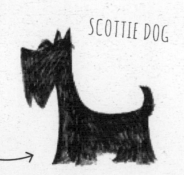

MirrOrs and GLAss

LEARN HOW TO CREATE MIRRORED AND REFLECTIVE SURFACES
TO ADD DIMENSION AND DEPTH TO YOUR DRAWINGS.

1

SKETCH AN OVAL, THEN DRAW
A FRAME AROUND IT, LIKE THIS.
ADD DARK SHADING ON ONE
SIDE OF THE MIRROR.

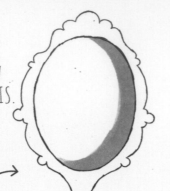

When creating the
appearance of glass, it's
best to start with the
darkest shades first.

2

SKETCH CIRCLES AND SWIRLY LINES
ON THE FRAME FOR DECORATION.
NOW ADD A LIGHTER LAYER OF BLUE
SHADING ON THE MIRROR.

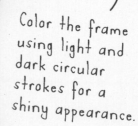

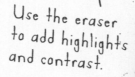

Use the eraser
to add highlights
and contrast.

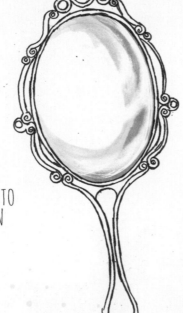

3

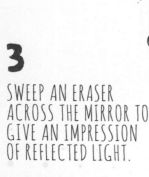

SWEEP AN ERASER
ACROSS THE MIRROR TO
GIVE AN IMPRESSION
OF REFLECTED LIGHT.

4

ADD LIGHTER SHADING TO THE
MIRROR WITH A SWIRLING
MOTION. DRAW DIAGONAL
LINES FOR A MORE 3D EFFECT.

Color the frame
using light and
dark circular
strokes for a
shiny appearance.

REFLECTION

DRAW A MIRROR, THEN ADD THE REFLECTION OF YOUR CHARACTER INSIDE IT. SKETCH THE BACK OF THE CHARACTER OUTSIDE OF THE MIRROR.

Add light and dark shading to the mirror, using the same technique as before. Color the reflected character slightly lighter than the actual one.

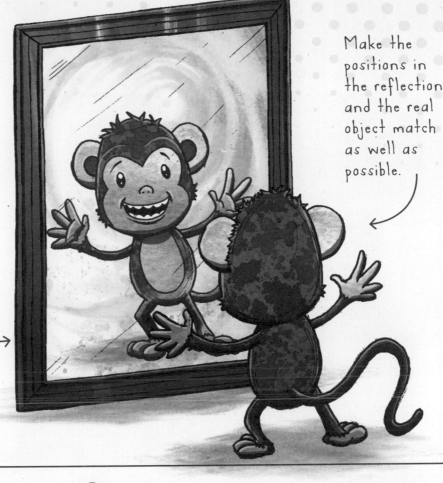

Make the positions in the reflection and the real object match as well as possible.

GLASS

USE A SIMILAR APPROACH WHEN DRAWING GLASS-BASED OBJECTS, LIKE A MARBLE OR A DRINKING GLASS.

1

FOR THE MARBLE, SKETCH A CIRCLE, THEN DRAW SEVERAL SWIRLY LINES ACROSS THE CENTER, AS SHOWN.

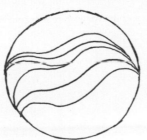

2

ADD LINES AND SHADING AROUND THE MARBLE AND ON EACH SHAPE INSIDE IT. USE AN ERASER TO CREATE HIGHLIGHTS ON THE GLASS.

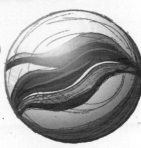

1

DRAW A CYLINDER SHAPE FOR THE GLASS, WITH A FLATTENED OVAL SHAPE IN THE MIDDLE FOR THE WATER. ADD THE STRAW.

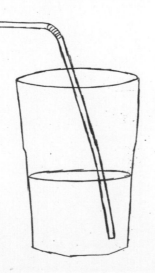

2

USE DARK SHADING AROUND THE BASE OF THE GLASS AND TO CREATE VERTICAL LINES FOR THE RIDGES. ADD HIGHLIGHTS WITH AN ERASER.

Draw a wobbly straw outline beneath the water for a distorted effect.

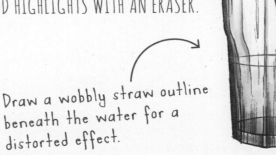

WEATHER

DIFFERENT ELEMENTS CAN GIVE THE SAME SCENE A VERY DIFFERENT FEEL!

RAIN

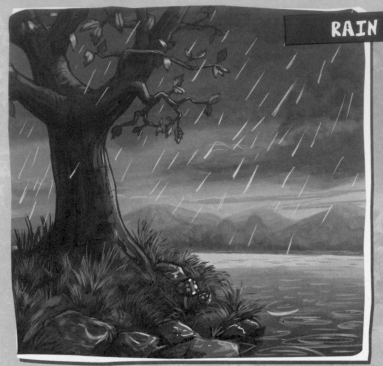

DRAW LONG, SLOPING LINES TO CREATE RAIN. PAINT THEM A LIGHT COLOR TO MAKE THEM STAND OUT AGAINST DARK STORM CLOUDS.

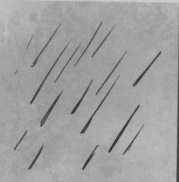

PAINT THE TREE AND GRASS WITH DARK TONES.

DRAW RIPPLES ON WATER BY SKETCHING CONCENTRIC CIRCLES THAT RADIATE OUTWARD AND MERGE INTO EACH OTHER.

WIND

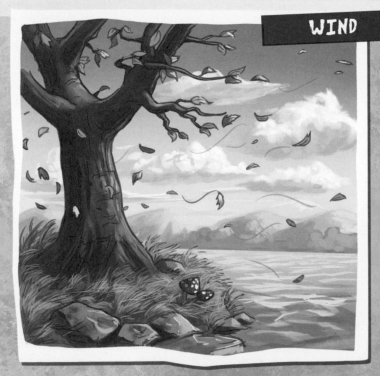

THE WIND MAKES THE TREES, FLOWERS, AND GRASS BEND IN THE SAME DIRECTION.

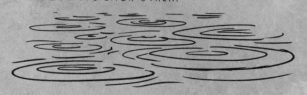
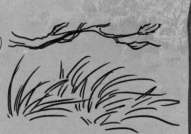

USER BRIGHTER COLORS FOR THE TREE AND GRASS FOR A SUNNY BUT BLUSTERY DAY.

DRAW LEAVES DANCING IN THE AIR TO GIVE THE IMPRESSION OF A STRONG BREEZE. GIVE SOME OF THEM WAVY TRAILS TO ADD MOVEMENT.

ELECTRIC STORM

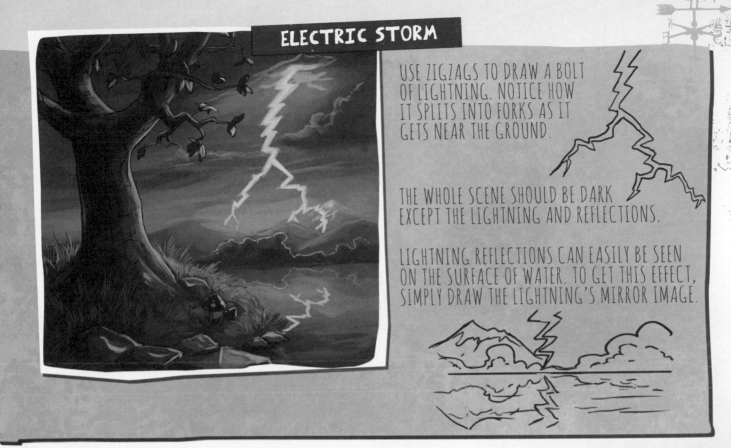

USE ZIGZAGS TO DRAW A BOLT OF LIGHTNING. NOTICE HOW IT SPLITS INTO FORKS AS IT GETS NEAR THE GROUND.

THE WHOLE SCENE SHOULD BE DARK EXCEPT THE LIGHTNING AND REFLECTIONS.

LIGHTNING REFLECTIONS CAN EASILY BE SEEN ON THE SURFACE OF WATER. TO GET THIS EFFECT, SIMPLY DRAW THE LIGHTNING'S MIRROR IMAGE.

SNOW AND ICE

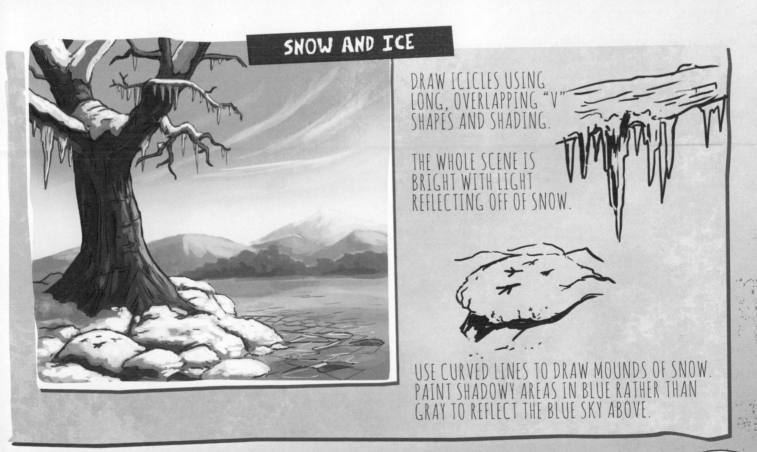

DRAW ICICLES USING LONG, OVERLAPPING "V" SHAPES AND SHADING.

THE WHOLE SCENE IS BRIGHT WITH LIGHT REFLECTING OFF OF SNOW.

USE CURVED LINES TO DRAW MOUNDS OF SNOW. PAINT SHADOWY AREAS IN BLUE RATHER THAN GRAY TO REFLECT THE BLUE SKY ABOVE.

HAND

Draw a horizontal line halfway up the hand to help you position the thumb correctly.

1

FOR THE KNUCKLES, SKETCH A ROOF SHAPE WITH THE POINT POSITIONED AS SHOWN. FOR THE HAND, DRAW BULGING SIDES AND A HORIZONTAL LINE.

2/3   1/3

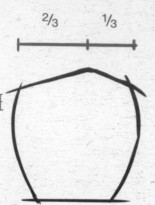

2

ADD VERTICAL LINES FOR THE WRIST, A SEMICIRCLE FOR THE THUMB, AND SHORT GUIDELINES ON THE KNUCKLES FOR THE FINGERS.

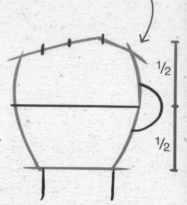

1/2

1/2

3

SKETCH GUIDELINES FOR THE FINGERS AND THEIR JOINTS, USING THE KEY FOR SCALE BELOW. DRAW LINES FOR THE THUMB AND A CIRCLE FOR ITS JOINT.

4

DRAW AN OUTLINE AROUND THE HAND TO JOIN THE SHAPES TOGETHER, LIKE THIS. LOOK AT YOUR OWN HAND FOR REFERENCE.

5

ERASE THE GUIDELINES, AND ADD COLOR AND SHADING. ADD OVAL-SHAPED NAILS AND CREASE LINES ON THE FINGER JOINTS.

FINGER JOINT KEY:

1/2

1/3

2/3

1/2

1/2

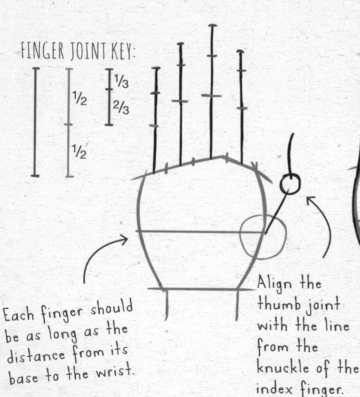

Each finger should be as long as the distance from its base to the wrist.

Align the thumb joint with the line from the knuckle of the index finger.

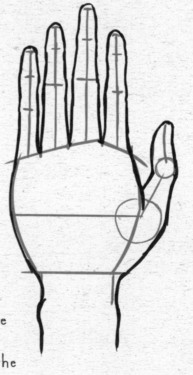

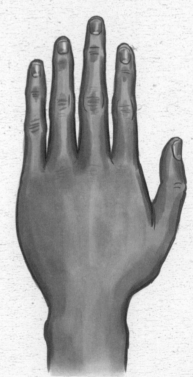

STRIKE A POSE!

TRY EXPERIMENTING WITH DIFFERENT HAND POSITIONS, AND LEARN HOW TO ALTER THE SKIN, JOINTS, AND MUSCLE TONE WITH EACH NEW SHAPE YOU MAKE.

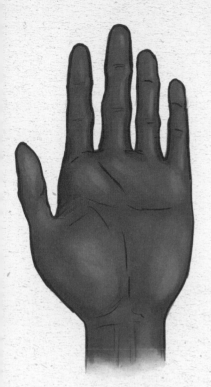

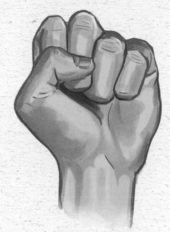

DRAW THE PALM IN A SIMILAR WAY TO THE BACK OF THE HAND, BUT HIGHLIGHT THE MUSCLES WITH CURVED LINES AND SHADING.

FOR A CLENCHED FIST, DRAW A BUMPY LINE WHERE THE JOINTS PUSH TOGETHER. ADD LINES AND SHADING ON THE PALM TO SUGGEST WRINKLED SKIN.

CREATE A SIDE-ON VIEW, WITH THE MIDDLE FINGER HIDING THE SMALLER DIGITS BEHIND IT. GIVE THE HAND A SLIGHTLY CURVED SPADE SHAPE.

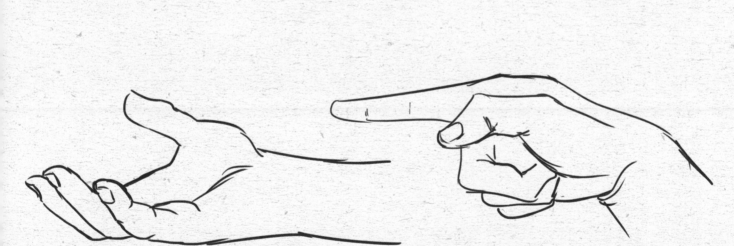

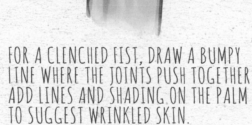

TO DRAW AN OPENED-OUT HAND, REFER TO MODELS AND PICTURES OF SKELETONS. A GOOD UNDERSTANDING OF HOW BONES AND JOINTS WORK TOGETHER WILL HELP WHEN YOU GO ON TO DRAW PEOPLE AND ANIMALS.

FOR A POINTING POSE, IMAGINE THE FINGERS ARE BOX-SHAPED RATHER THAN ROUND. VIEW THE JOINTS LIKE DOOR HINGES. IF YOU KNOW WHERE THEY BEND, YOU CAN POSITION THE FINGERS MORE ACCURATELY.

FLAMINGOS

1
START WITH CIRCLES FOR THE HEAD AND BODY, STRAIGHT LINES FOR THE LEGS, AN "S" SHAPE FOR THE NECK, AND TRIANGLES FOR THE FEET. ADD A HOOKED, POINTY BEAK.

2
CONNECT THE BASIC SHAPES TOGETHER WITH A STRONGER OUTLINE. USE STEP 1 AS A GUIDE TO HELP YOU GET THE PROPORTIONS RIGHT.

3
ADD MORE DETAIL TO YOUR DRAWING: AN EYE, A NOSTRIL ON THE BEAK, FEATHERY WINGS, AND WEBBED FEET, AS SHOWN.

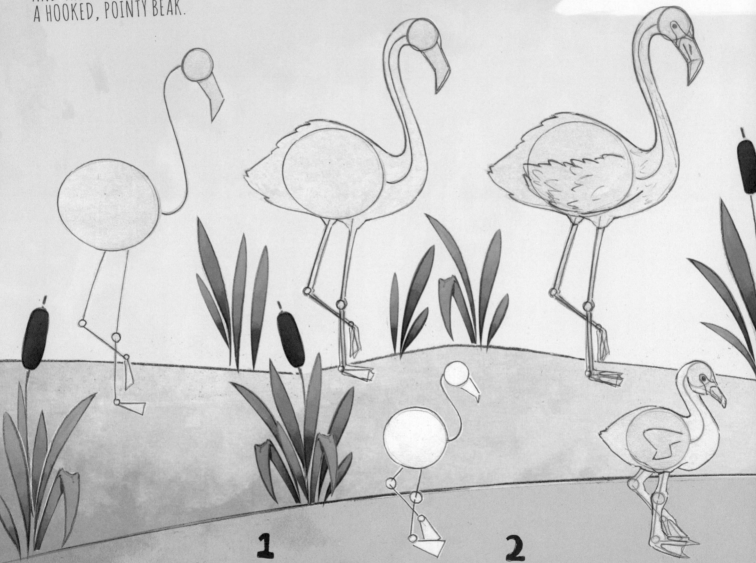

1
SKETCH A BABY FLAMINGO IN A SIMILAR WAY TO THE ADULT ONE, BUT MAKE THE SHAPES SMALLER AND SHORTER, APART FROM THE FEET.

2
GO AROUND THE GUIDELINES, AS BEFORE, BUT THIS TIME, MAKE THE LEGS A BIT THICKER AND THE WINGS STUBBIER. ADD IN FACIAL FEATURES.

4

CAREFULLY ERASE YOUR GUIDELINES TO REVEAL YOUR FLAMINGO DRAWING.

5

COLOR WITH WATERCOLOR PENCILS. CREATE A FEATHERY TEXTURE WITH THE DIRECTION OF YOUR STROKES AND A 3D EFFECT WITH LIGHT AND DARK SHADES.

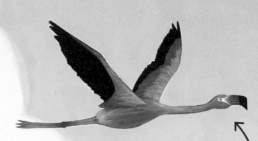

Try drawing a flying flamingo with wide, open wings and a straight, horizontal body line.

Try another flamingo pose, with the head and neck down. Add cattails to build up the setting.

3

ERASE YOUR GUIDELINES TO LEAVE JUST THE OUTLINE AND FEATURES OF YOUR BABY FLAMINGO.

4

APPLY LIGHT GRAY SHADING ON THE BODY. CREATE THE EFFECT OF FLUFFY FEATHERS BY USING SHORT PAINT STROKES. COLOR THE LEGS, FEET, AND BEAK WITH LIGHT AND DARK SHADING.

EYES

MASTER THIS FACIAL FEATURE, THEN CREATE ALMOST ANY MOOD OR EMOTION YOU LIKE JUST BY VARYING THE SHAPE!

FRONT-ON

1

DRAW A CURVED LINE AND BIG CIRCLE AS GUIDES. DRAW A POINTED EYEBALL AND ARC WITHIN THE CIRCLE.

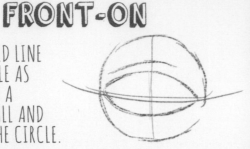

2

ERASE THE BIG CIRCLE AND LINE. DRAW ANOTHER CIRCLE FOR THE IRIS AND A SMALLER ONE FOR THE PUPIL.

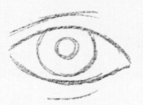

3

USE PENCIL FLICKS TO DRAW EYELASHES. SHADE AROUND THE EDGE OF THE IRIS, AND ADD A CIRCULAR HIGHLIGHT.

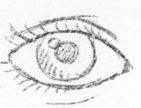

4

TO PAINT THE IRIS, USE DIFFERENT SHADES OF THE SAME COLOR TO SHOW THE EYE'S REFLECTIVE QUALITY.

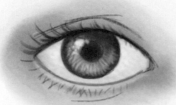

IN PROFILE

1

DRAW A BIG CIRCLE FOR THE EYEBALL, BUT THIS TIME, SKETCH THE VISIBLE PART AS A BIG TRIANGLE.

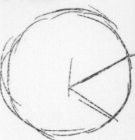

2

DRAW THE UPPER EYELID, WHICH STICKS OUT A LITTLE. ADD A CURVE TO FORM THE IRIS.

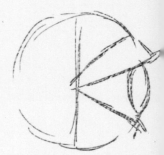

3

ERASE THE EYEBALL GUIDELINES AND SKETCH SOME EYELASHES. ADD A THIN OVAL FOR THE PUPIL.

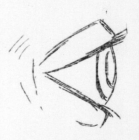

4

ADD PENCIL SHADING TO DEFINE THE SHAPE OF THE EYE SOCKET. PAINT THE IRIS AS BEFORE IN DIFFERENT SHADES OF THE SAME COLOR.

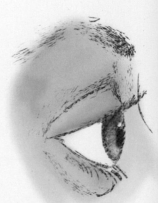

Creating Expressions

SURPRISE

Draw the eye wide open, so that the iris is fully visible. The eyebrow needs to be raised quite high above the eye.

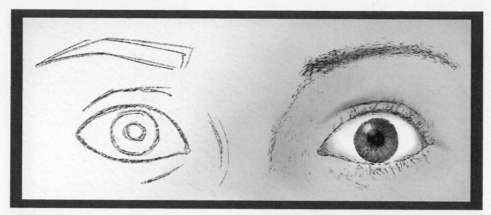

ANGER

Draw the eyelids much closer together, and add crease lines to show tension. Sketch the inner part of the eyebrow much closer to the eye.

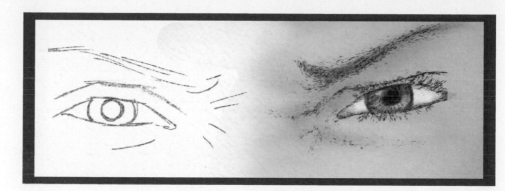

HAPPY

Draw the lids close together, but make the lower lid slightly curved, as shown. Add some curved crease lines around the eye and a relaxed brow.

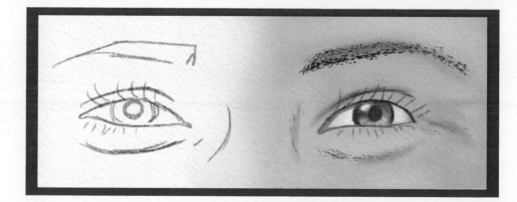

SAD

Draw the eyelids so that most of the iris is visible. Sketch the inner part of the eyebrow high up, to convey a frown. Add a dripping tear, too!

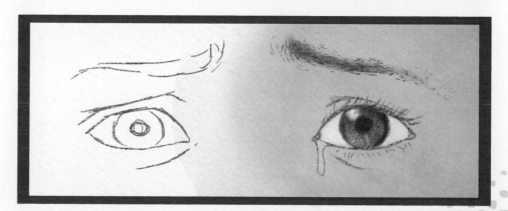

CLOUDS

THERE ARE LOTS OF DIFFERENT TYPES OF CLOUD.
LEARN DIFFERENT TECHNIQUES TO DRAW THEM ALL!

CUMULUS

1

Draw uneven, overlapping circle shapes, then add wavy horizontal lines for the base of the clouds.

2

Paint the shape of the cloud in a bluey-gray color. Then add white and blue reflections from the sun and sky. Paint shadows underneath in warmer hues.

LENTICULARIS

Sketch thin oval shapes piled up on top of each other. Paint the darkest part first, then add highlights, with opaque or acrylic paint.

CIRROCUMULUS
Use quick, short jabs or strokes (called stippling) of transparent paint with a rough flat brush to create flecks of clouds. Layer the paint into thicker and thinner areas.

CIRRUS
With a thin brush, gradually build up layers of transparent paint. Fade out the ends to give a wispy cloud effect.

NACREOUS
Paint the background white, then sweep layers of transparent paint over the top with a round brush for a colored "mother-of-pearl" effect.

CUMULONIMBUS
Layer up lots of cumuluslike circles into a big, towering structure, which mushrooms out over the top. Use dark paint to make ominous, gloomy-looking shadows.

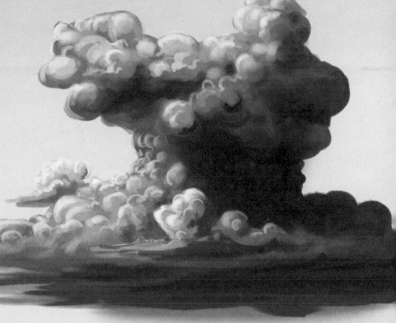
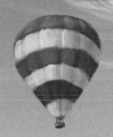

RUNNER

1

DRAW OVALS FOR THE HEAD AND FEET, LINES FOR THE NECK, BODY, ARMS, AND LEGS, AND CIRCLES FOR THE HANDS AND JOINTS, AS SHOWN.

2

SKETCH A MIXTURE OF CIRCLES AND ROUGH SAUSAGE SHAPES TO BUILD UP THE LIMBS. DRAW CURVED LINES FOR THE NECK AND TORSO.

3

JOIN THE LIMB SHAPES TOGETHER WITH MORE DISTINCT OUTLINES TO BRING OUT THE CURVES AND CONTOURS OF THE BODY.

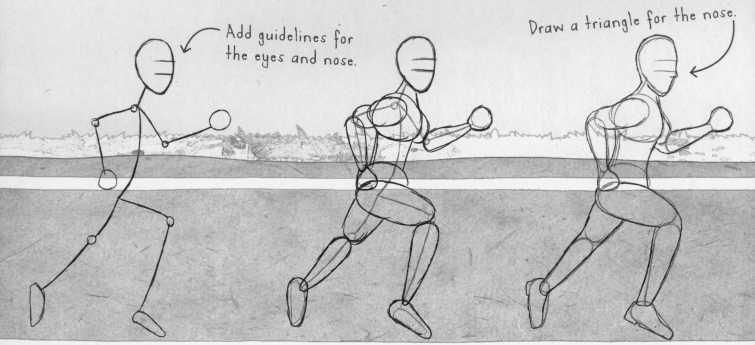

Add guidelines for the eyes and nose.

Draw a triangle for the nose.

4

SKETCH SMALL LINES ON THE ARMS AND LEGS TO SUGGEST MUSCLE TONE. START ADDING IN THE HANDS AND FACIAL FEATURES.

5

NOW FOCUS ON THE FINER DETAILS. DRAW THE RUNNER'S CLOTHES, SNEAKERS, HAIR, EYES, AND EYEBROWS.

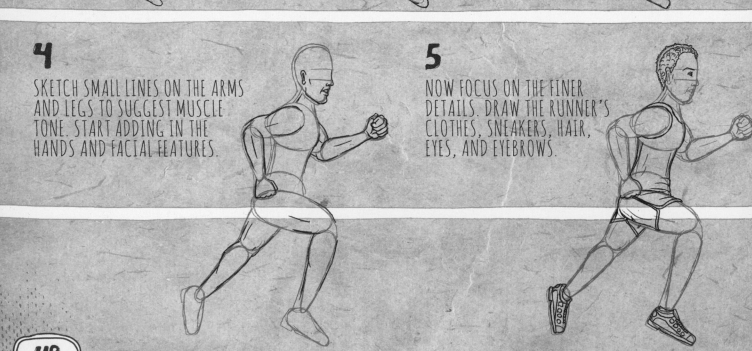

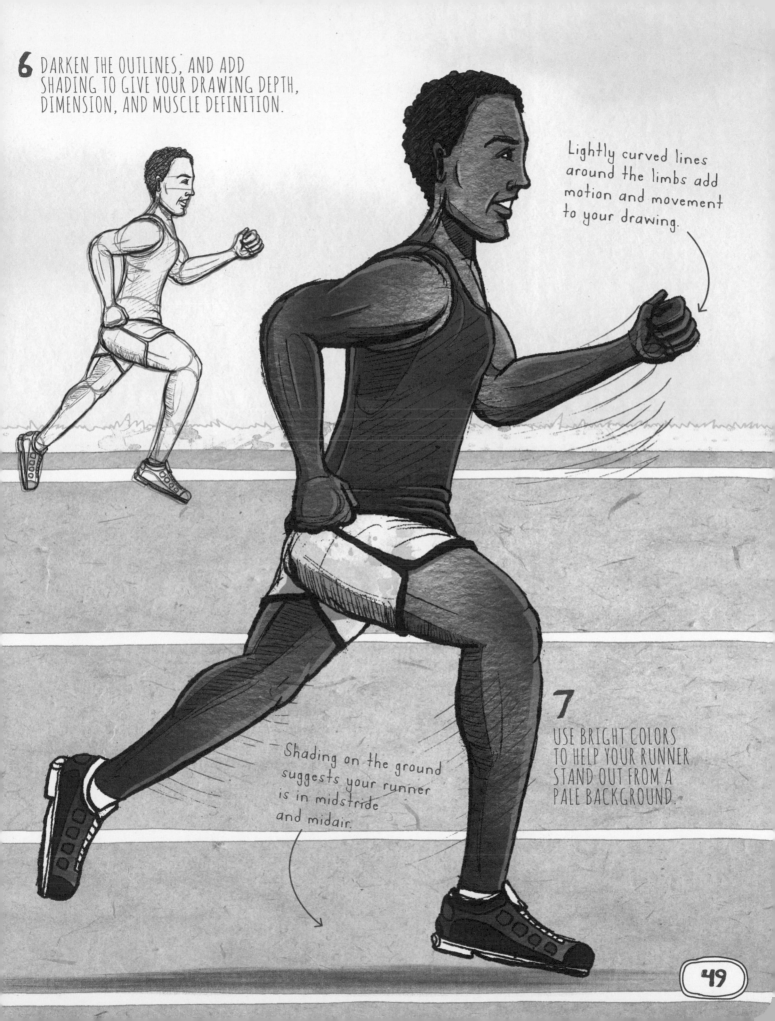

6 DARKEN THE OUTLINES, AND ADD SHADING TO GIVE YOUR DRAWING DEPTH, DIMENSION, AND MUSCLE DEFINITION.

Lightly curved lines around the limbs add motion and movement to your drawing.

7 USE BRIGHT COLORS TO HELP YOUR RUNNER STAND OUT FROM A PALE BACKGROUND.

Shading on the ground suggests your runner is in midstride and midair.

BUTTERFLIES

BUTTERFLY WING PATTERNS CAN LOOK COMPLEX, BUT THEY ARE EASY TO DRAW IF YOU USE SYMMETRY. TRY THESE, THEN CREATE YOUR OWN!

1

START BY DRAWING A CIRCLE ON TOP OF TWO OVALS TO CREATE THE HEAD AND BASIC BODY SHAPE OF A BUTTERFLY.

2

SKETCH A TOP WING ON EITHER SIDE OF THE BODY. THEN ADD A TEARDROP ON EACH SIDE FOR THE SMALLER WINGS, AS SHOWN.

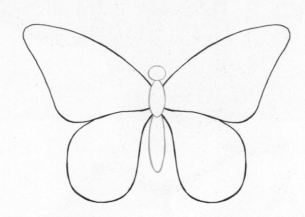

3

DRAW A SYMMETRICAL PATTERN ON THE WINGS, MIRRORING OVAL AND RECTANGLE SHAPES ON EACH SIDE. ADD TWO LINES FOR THE ANTENNAE.

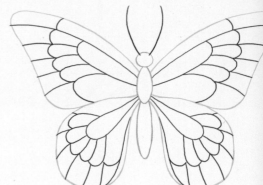

4

USE MORE SYMMETRY WHEN YOU COLOR THE BUTTERFLY, MAKING SURE BOTH WINGS ARE A MIRROR IMAGE OF EACH OTHER.

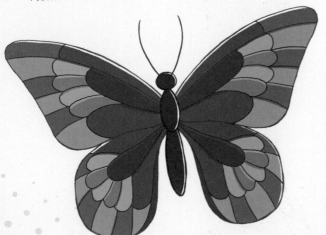

Try drawing different-shaped wings. Start with one side, then just repeat on the other!

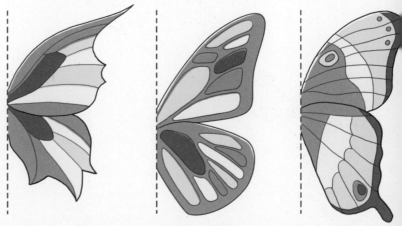

Vary the patterns, trying circles, ovals, and rectangles. Try mixing shapes together for new patterns.

50

EXPERIMENT WITH MORE ELABORATE PATTERNS ...

SPOTTED

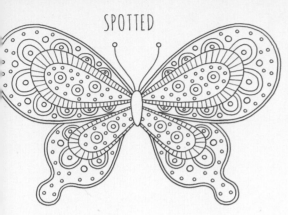

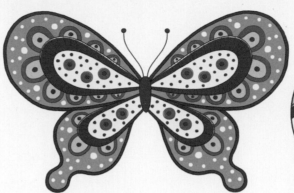

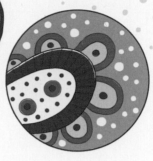

Decorate the wings with different-sized spots, circles, and stripes.

Use only three colors, but use different shades of each for depth.

Add outlines around some shapes to make them stand out.

SWIRLY

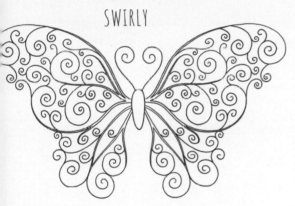

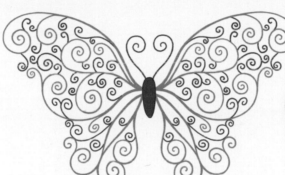

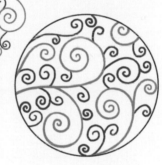

Draw darker, swirly lines inside light pencil wing shapes.

Trace around the swirls in colored pens. Erase any pencil marks.

Color big swirls in one color and small swirls in another.

STRIPY

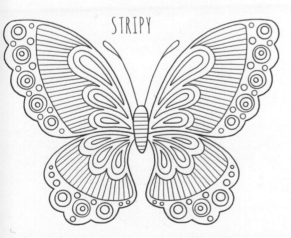

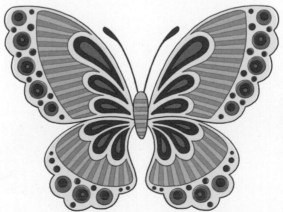

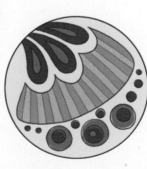

Try spots, stripes, and teardrops on wavy-edged wings.

Color the pattern in a mixture of complementary shades and colors.

Draw a thin border around some of the pattern for emphasis.

MOUTHS

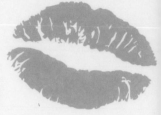

Drawing a mouth front on

1 SKETCH A RECTANGLE, THEN ADD A VERTICAL AND HORIZONTAL LINE AS SHOWN. USE THESE GUIDES TO DRAW A BASIC MOUTH SHAPE.

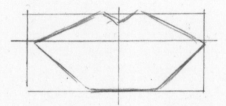

2 SKETCH A CURVED MOUTH SHAPE OVER YOUR GUIDELINE. THE TOP LIP IS A BIT LIKE THE LETTER "M," THE BOTTOM LIKE A WIDE "U."

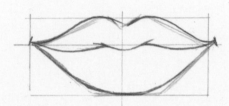

3 ADD SHADING AND COLOR TO YOUR LIPS. THE SHADING NEEDS TO LOOK SLIGHTLY CURVED TO MAKE THE LIPS LOOK 3D.

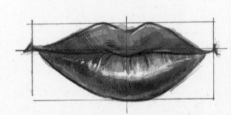

Drawing at an angle

Lips are a surprisingly complex shape, which is more noticeable when you draw them at an angle. The top lip tends to stick out slightly more than the bottom one, while the lower lip curves under smoothly.

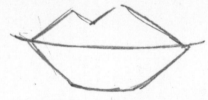
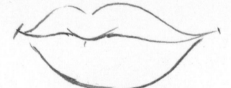
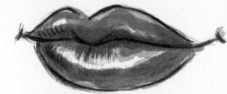

When someone's mouth is slightly open, you'll see the full, rounded shape of the lips.

To sketch a mouth that's fully open, make the lips look thinner since they would be stretched tighter across the teeth.

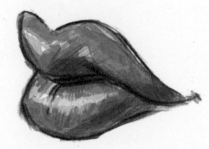
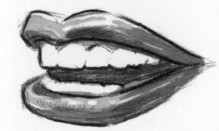

Creating Expressions

HAPPY
The top lip looks like a shallow "M" shape with turned-up corners. The teeth can be close together or slightly apart.

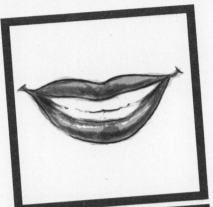

WORRIED
OR CONFUSED
Sketch the upper teeth biting part of the lower lip. One corner of the bottom lip should also droop down.

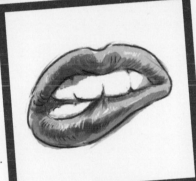

POUTING
To draw a pout, make the top lip thin, with the lower lip jutting out, full and rounded.

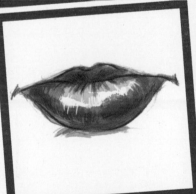

PUCKERED
The lips look as if they've been squashed in from the sides, making both of them full in shape.

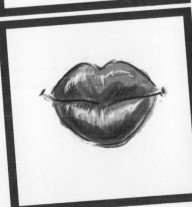

ANGRY
The teeth and gums are visible, and the top lip looks stretched out.

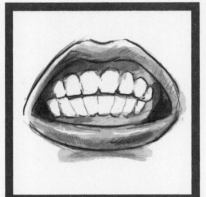

TALKING
The lips are relaxed, and the overall mouth shape is squarer. The teeth and tongue are slightly visible.

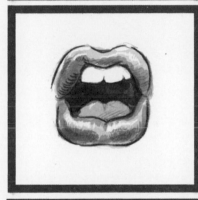

SHOUT
Draw both the top and bottom lips in a stretched position, with the teeth wide apart.

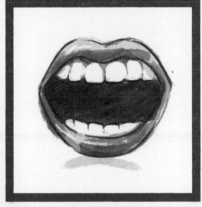

SCREAM
Sketch an "O"-shaped mouth with the lips stretched very thin. Draw the tongue and tonsils, too!

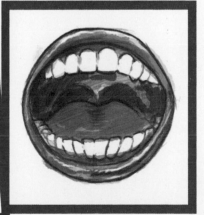

BLIMPS

1

SKETCH A STRAIGHT HORIZONTAL LINE. DRAW AN OVAL SHAPE AROUND IT, TAPERING OFF ONE END TO FORM A POINT.

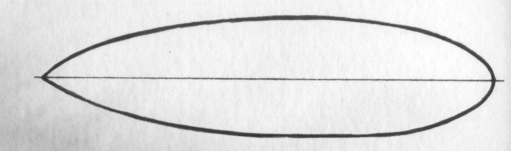

2

ADD THE TAIL FINS AT THE END OF THE BLIMP. DRAW THE PASSENGER CAR BENEATH THE OVAL, AS SHOWN.

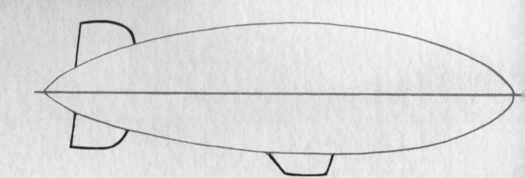

3

DRAW ANOTHER TAIL FIN AT AN ANGLE. SKETCH CURVED GUIDELINES ON THE BLIMP, AS SHOWN. ADD DETAIL TO THE CAR.

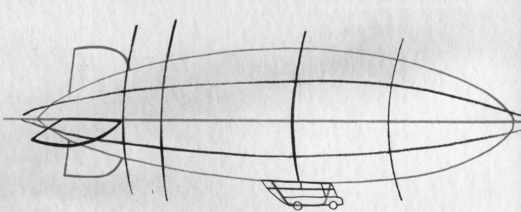

Use rectangle shapes for windows and circles for wheels.

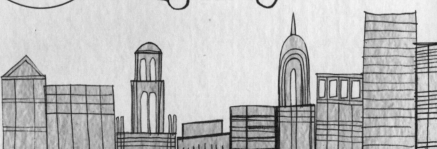

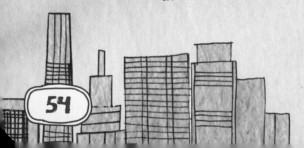

4

CHOOSE A PATTERN THEME, LIKE
TRIANGLES AND DIAMONDS, AND
ADD IT TO THE BLIMP AROUND
YOUR GUIDELINES.

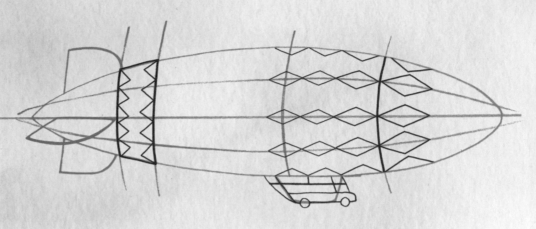

5

GO OVER YOUR LINE WORK WITH A BLACK PEN. THEN COLOR THE BLIMP USING WATERCOLOR PAINT.

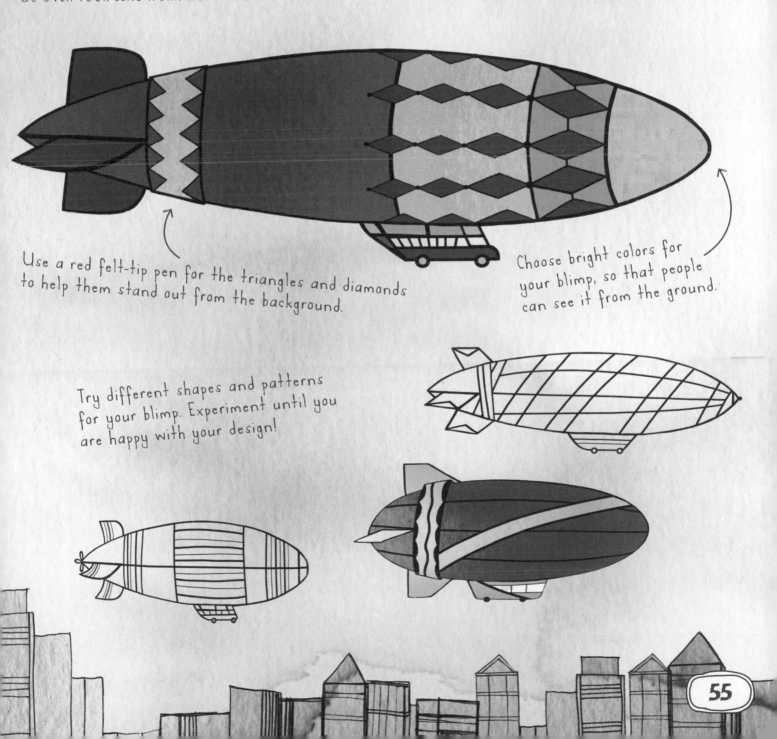

Use a red felt-tip pen for the triangles and diamonds
to help them stand out from the background.

Choose bright colors for
your blimp, so that people
can see it from the ground.

Try different shapes and patterns
for your blimp. Experiment until you
are happy with your design!

SYDNEY OPERA HOUSE

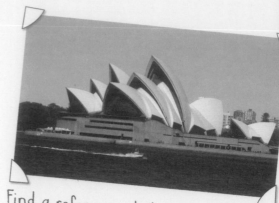

Find a reference photo of this famous Australian building before you start.

1

BREAK DOWN THE OPERA HOUSE INTO SIMPLE STAGES. FIRST, SKETCH OVERLAPPING TRIANGULAR SHAPES FOR THE SAILS OF THE BUILDING.

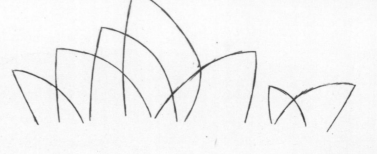

2

ADD A RECTANGULAR SHAPE BENEATH THE SAILS FOR THE BASE OF THE BUILDING AND A HORIZONTAL LINE FOR THE GROUND.

Add some people at the bottom of the building to give a sense of its huge scale.

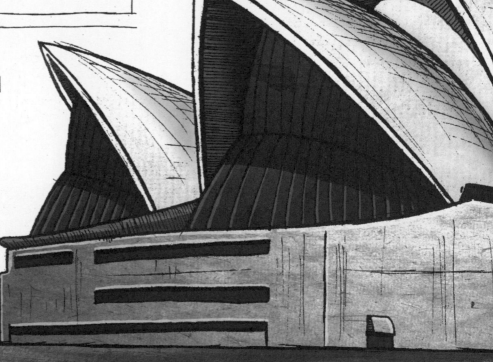

3

DRAW LINES INSIDE THE SAILS, AS SHOWN. DARKEN THESE LINES SO THE SHAPE OF THE BUILDING IS CLEAR.

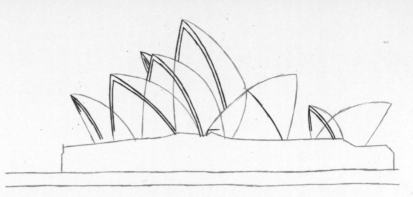

4

START FILLING IN THE DETAIL. DRAW MORE TRIANGULAR SHAPES INSIDE THE SAILS, AND ADD RECTANGULAR WINDOWS AND DOORS AT THE BASE OF THE BUILDING.

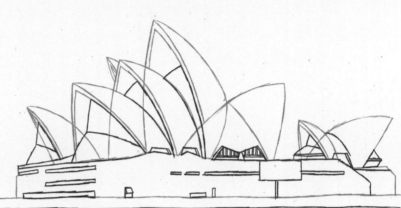

Use light and medium blues on the white sails for shading. Darken the areas inside the sails and on the windows to suggest the direction of light.

5

USE PEN OR INK TO GO AROUND THE OUTLINE OF THE BUILDING. ADD SOME HATCHING TO THE SAILS. THEN ADD COLOR! INCLUDE A HINT OF WATER FOR THE SETTING.

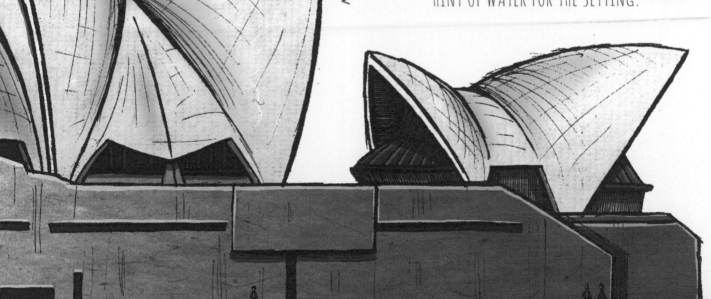

GYMNAST

1
DRAW A SIMPLE LINE OF ACTION FOR THE BASIC POSE AND GUIDES FOR THE BARS. GYMNASTS HAVE SUPPLE, BENDY BODIES!

2
ADD CONSTRUCTION SHAPES FOR THE DIFFERENT BODY PARTS, USING CIRCLES, OVALS, AND STICK LINES, TO SET YOUR PROPORTIONS.

3
DRAW THE OUTLINE OF THE BODY AROUND YOUR GUIDES. SKETCH SIMPLE SHAPES FOR THE ARMS, HANDS, LEGS, AND FEET.

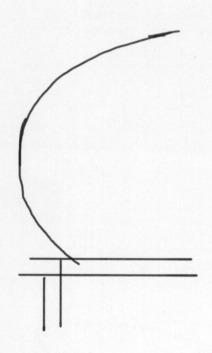

4
REFINE YOUR PENCIL LINES TO DEFINE THE BODY SHAPE. ADD MUSCLE TONE, BODY CONTOURS, AND THE SHAPE OF THE HEAD.

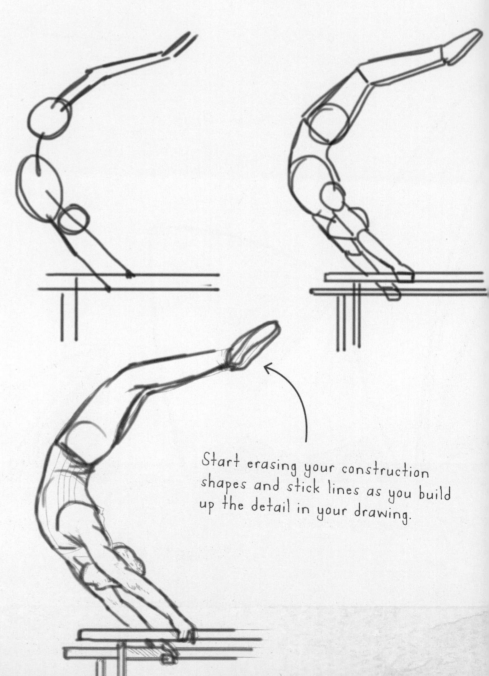

Start erasing your construction shapes and stick lines as you build up the detail in your drawing.

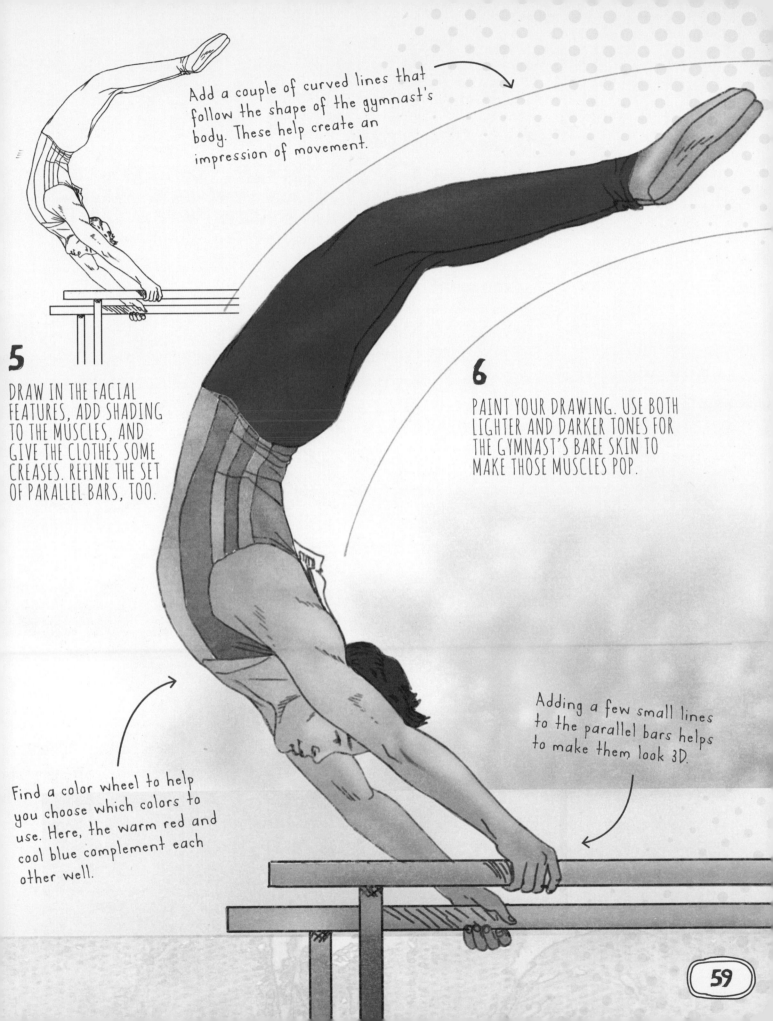

Add a couple of curved lines that follow the shape of the gymnast's body. These help create an impression of movement.

5

DRAW IN THE FACIAL FEATURES, ADD SHADING TO THE MUSCLES, AND GIVE THE CLOTHES SOME CREASES. REFINE THE SET OF PARALLEL BARS, TOO.

6

PAINT YOUR DRAWING. USE BOTH LIGHTER AND DARKER TONES FOR THE GYMNAST'S BARE SKIN TO MAKE THOSE MUSCLES POP.

Find a color wheel to help you choose which colors to use. Here, the warm red and cool blue complement each other well.

Adding a few small lines to the parallel bars helps to make them look 3D.

MUSTACHES

HAVE FUN DRAWING SIMPLE BUT EFFECTIVE MUSTACHES. ADD THEM TO YOUR DRAWINGS OF PEOPLE, OR CREATE YOUR OWN MUST-HAVE MUSTACHE FASHION ON T-SHIRTS OR BAGS WITH SOLID BLACK STYLIZED SHAPES.

1

DRAW A VERY WIDE "M" SHAPE FOR THE BASIC OUTLINE OF A MUSTACHE, LIKE THIS.

2

SKETCH SOFT, CURVED LINES FLOWING OUT FROM THE MIDDLE OF YOUR TASH, FOLLOWING ITS SHAPE. VARY THE PRESSURE OF YOUR PENCIL FOR INDIVIDUAL STRANDS.

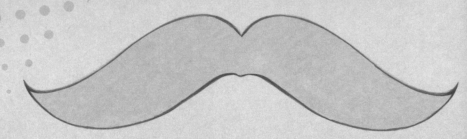

3

NOW PAINT YOUR MUSTACHE! USE LIGHT SHADING IN THE CENTER, GRADUALLY GOING DARKER TOWARD THE ENDS. ADD SHADING BETWEEN THE LINES.

NOW TRY DIFFERENT STYLES:

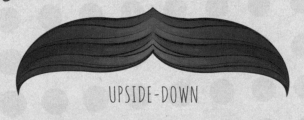

UPSIDE-DOWN

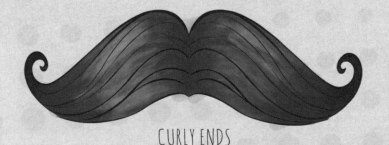

CURLY ENDS

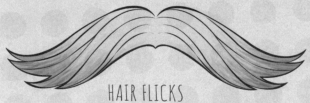

HAIR FLICKS

MINI TASH

NOW TRY THESE FUNNY STYLES, USING A BLACK MARKER OR PEN.

Bold "m" shape with long, curved sides and frayed ends.

Wide "m" shape, with a narrow middle and upward curving sides.

Thick and chunky "m" shape, with swirly, twirly ends.

Thick, semicircular "m" shape with downward, pointy ends.

Small, wavy "m" shape, like an upside-down tulip.

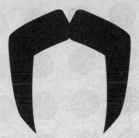

Angular "m" shape, like an inverted horseshoe.

Tall and chunky "m" shape with spindly curls at the ends.

Squashed "m" shape with thick, curly ends.

Thick and curvy "m" shape with soft, curly ends.

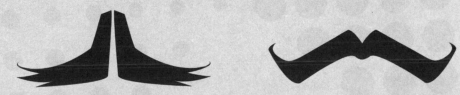

Split-down-the-middle "m" shape, with spiky ends.

Wide, angular "m" shape with pointy, tapered ends.

Wide, straight-edged "m" shape, with curved, pointy ends.

WIZARD

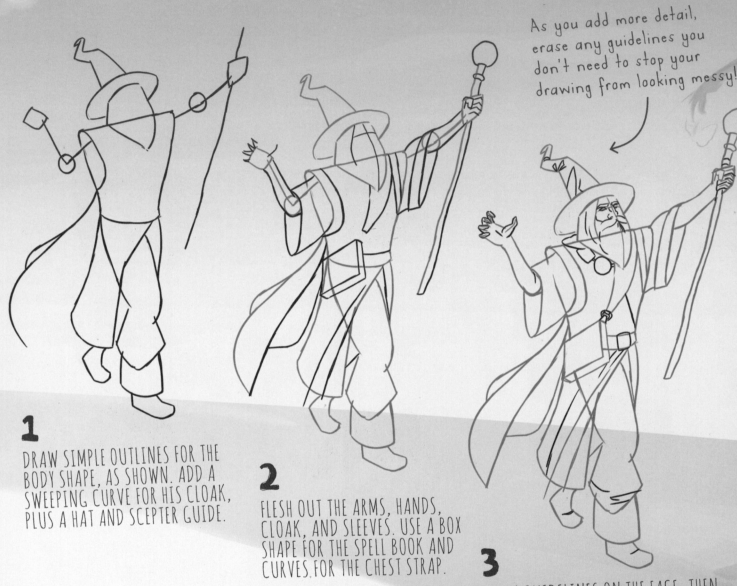

As you add more detail, erase any guidelines you don't need to stop your drawing from looking messy!

1
DRAW SIMPLE OUTLINES FOR THE BODY SHAPE, AS SHOWN. ADD A SWEEPING CURVE FOR HIS CLOAK, PLUS A HAT AND SCEPTER GUIDE.

2
FLESH OUT THE ARMS, HANDS, CLOAK, AND SLEEVES. USE A BOX SHAPE FOR THE SPELL BOOK AND CURVES FOR THE CHEST STRAP.

3
DRAW GUIDELINES ON THE FACE, THEN SKETCH THE WIZARD'S FEATURES. ADD FINGER DETAILS AND CREASES TO THE HAT AND PANTS. DRAW SQUARES AND CIRCLES FOR THE JEWELRY.

If you're not sure how to draw something in detail, it's a good idea to sketch simple guidelines and rough shapes first to help you!

4

CONCENTRATE ON THE FINE DETAILS, DRAWING SQUARES AND ZIGZAG PATTERNS ON THE WIZARD'S CLOTHES. ADD MORE LINES TO THE BOOK, AND DRAW AN EXTRA OVAL SHAPE UNDER THE HAT BRIM.

Paint lots of swirling, colorful flamelike shapes to create magic!

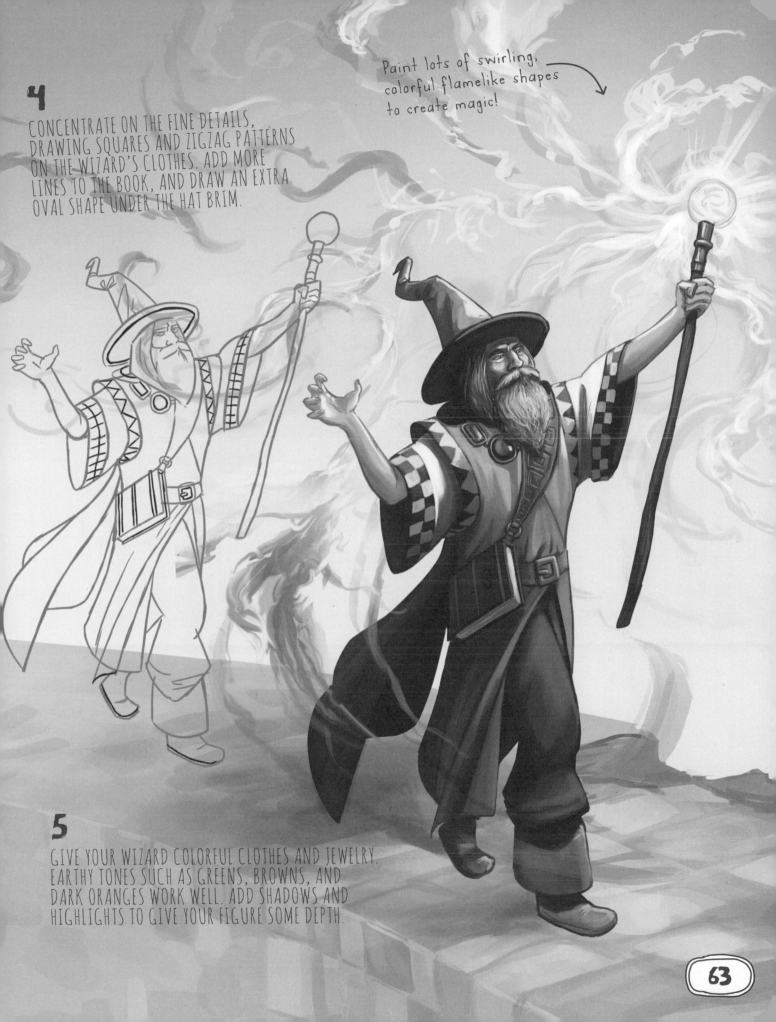

5

GIVE YOUR WIZARD COLORFUL CLOTHES AND JEWELRY. EARTHY TONES SUCH AS GREENS, BROWNS, AND DARK ORANGES WORK WELL. ADD SHADOWS AND HIGHLIGHTS TO GIVE YOUR FIGURE SOME DEPTH.

BULLDOG IN A BOW TIE

1 DRAW CIRCLES FOR THE DOG'S HEAD, BODY, AND OUTSIDE LEG, A SEMICIRCLE FOR THE INSIDE LEG, AND LINES FOR THE LEGS AND FEET.

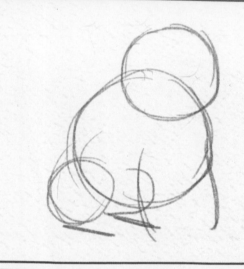

2 SKETCH AN OUTLINE AROUND THE SHAPES TO CONNECT THEM TOGETHER. DRAW A CROSS ON THE FACE AS A GUIDE FOR THE FEATURES, AND ADD TRIANGULAR SHAPES FOR THE EARS AND TAIL.

Look at pictures of bulldogs online or in books for reference as you draw.

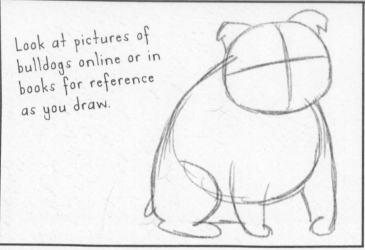

3 SKETCH CIRCLES FOR THE EYES, AN OVAL FOR THE NOSE, A WIDE "W" SHAPE FOR THE MOUTH, AND CURVED LINES FOR THE TONGUE AND CHIN. DRAW A RECTANGLE AND TRIANGULAR SHAPES FOR THE BOW TIE, AS SHOWN.

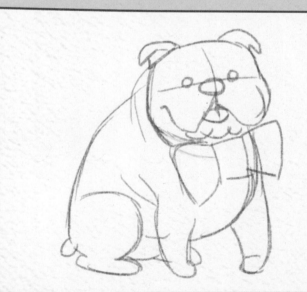

4 USE A STRONGER OUTLINE TO GO AROUND THE BULLDOG SHAPE, ADDING IN MORE DETAIL SUCH AS CURVED LINES FOR WRINKLES AND PAWS. ERASE ANY LINES YOU NO LONGER NEED.

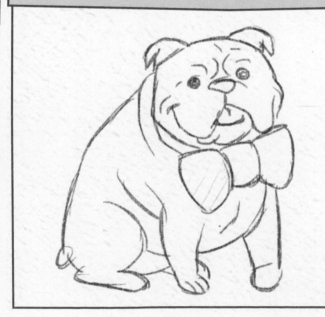

5 PRESS HARDER ON THE PENCIL TO START SHADING IN SOME OF THE DETAIL AROUND ONE EYE, THE NOSE, MOUTH, AND PAWS. DRAW DIAGONAL LINES ON THE BOW TIE, AND ADD CURVED LINES FOR CREASES.

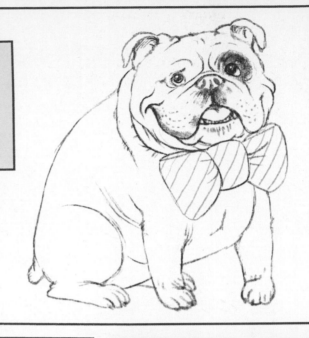

6 COLOR THE DOG IN DIFFERENT TONES OF BROWN, WHITE, AND GRAY. ADD SHORT, SHARP PENCIL STROKES TO SUGGEST FUR. LEAVE GLINTS IN THIS FUNNY DOG'S EYES!

Use smooth pencil strokes to color the bow tie. Add highlighted areas to suggest a silky shine and realistic folds.

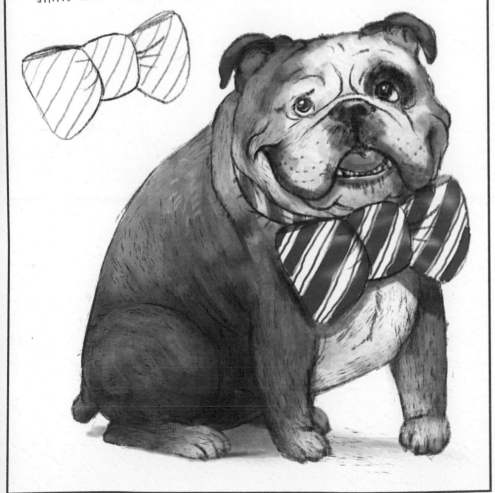

BOW TIES!

Try different patterns on your bow tie. Experiment with various shapes and colors. Tie-tastic!

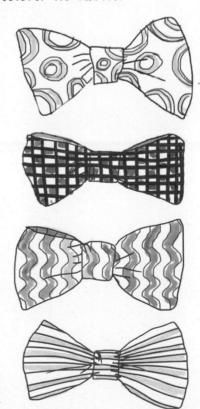

PAISLEY PATTERN

1

FIRST, DRAW ONE PIECE: SKETCH A CIRCLE WITH A BEAK SHAPE ON TOP TO FORM AN ANGLED TEARDROP.

2

DRAW ANOTHER TEARDROP INSIDE IT, FOLLOWING THE SAME SHAPE AS THE ONE ON THE OUTSIDE.

3

SKETCH A BRANCH AND LEAF PATTERN DESIGN INSIDE THE SMALLER TEARDROP.

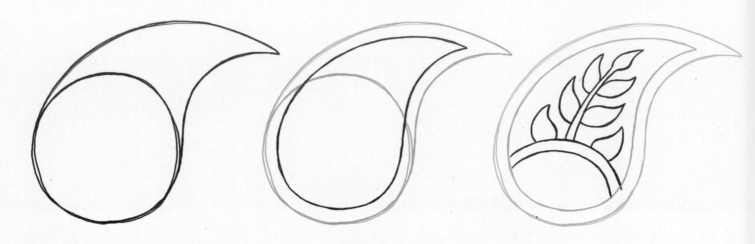

4

ADD MORE DETAIL, SUCH AS A WAVY OUTLINE, SHORT FINE LINES ON THE LEAVES, SMALL DOTS, AND OVERLAPPING CIRCLES, AS SHOWN.

5

SKETCH SEMICIRCLES IN THE BORDER BETWEEN THE TEARDROPS AND A WAVY SHAPE OVER THE TOP OF THE INNER TEARDROP.

6

DRAW OVER THE OUTLINES WITH A FINE PEN, AND ERASE THE PENCIL LINES. NOW HAVE FUN COLORING YOUR DESIGN!

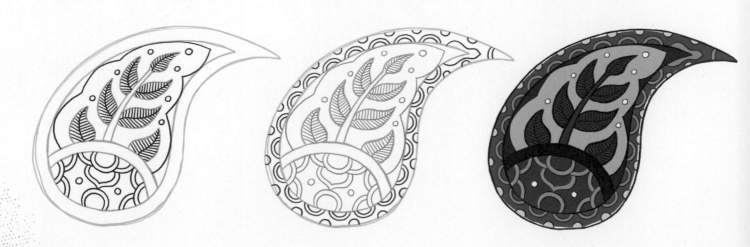

CREATE MORE TEARDROP SHAPES, LIKE THE ONES BELOW, EXPERIMENTING WITH DIFFERENT DESIGNS INSIDE. THEN PUT THEM TOGETHER TO MAKE THE PAISLEY PATTERN!

Paisley is a pretty, swirly Indian pattern often used on shawls, scarves, or ties. It's very trendy!

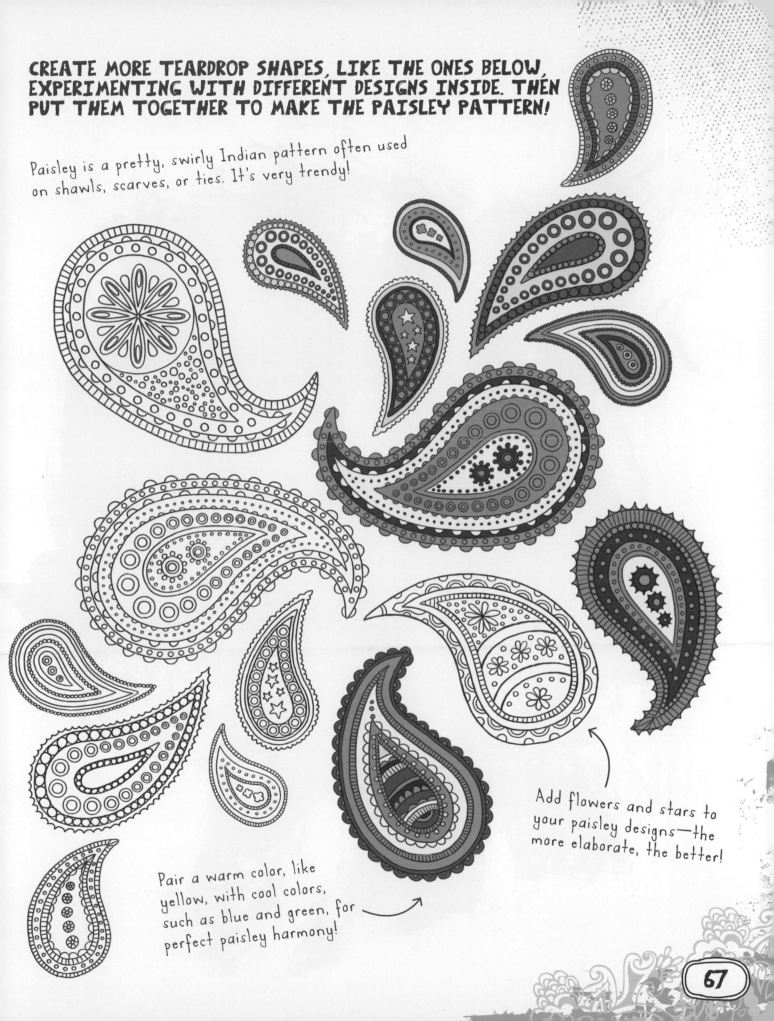

Add flowers and stars to your paisley designs—the more elaborate, the better!

Pair a warm color, like yellow, with cool colors, such as blue and green, for perfect paisley harmony!

WEIGHTLIFTER

1
USING A LIGHT PENCIL, SKETCH A STICK MAN TO SET YOUR BASIC WEIGHTLIFTING POSE. MAKE THE KNEES SLIGHTLY BENT.

2
DRAW THE WEIGHTLIFTER'S OUTLINE AROUND YOUR GUIDE. MAKE HIS MUSCULAR LEGS AND BICEPS EXTRA CHUNKY.

3
SKETCH CURVED LINES TO DEFINE THE MUSCLE TONE. OUTLINE THE CLOTHING, ROUGH FACIAL FEATURES, AND THE BARBELLS.

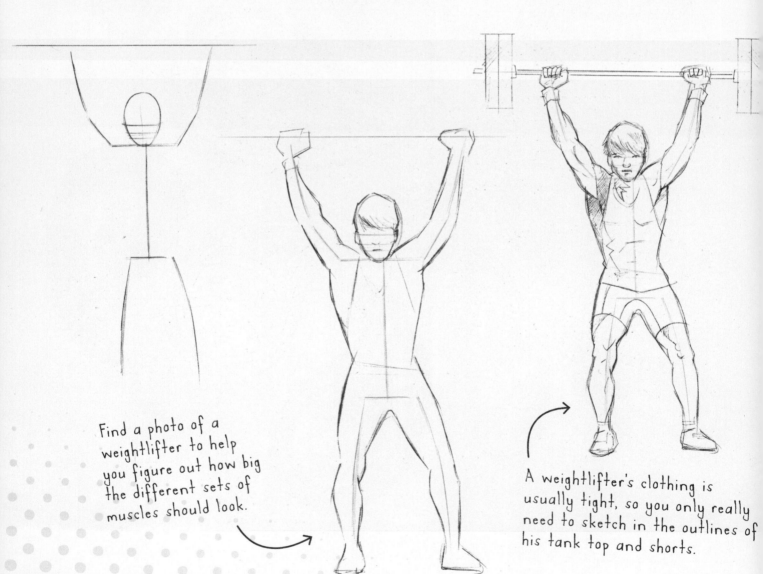

Find a photo of a weightlifter to help you figure out how big the different sets of muscles should look.

A weightlifter's clothing is usually tight, so you only really need to sketch in the outlines of his tank top and shorts.

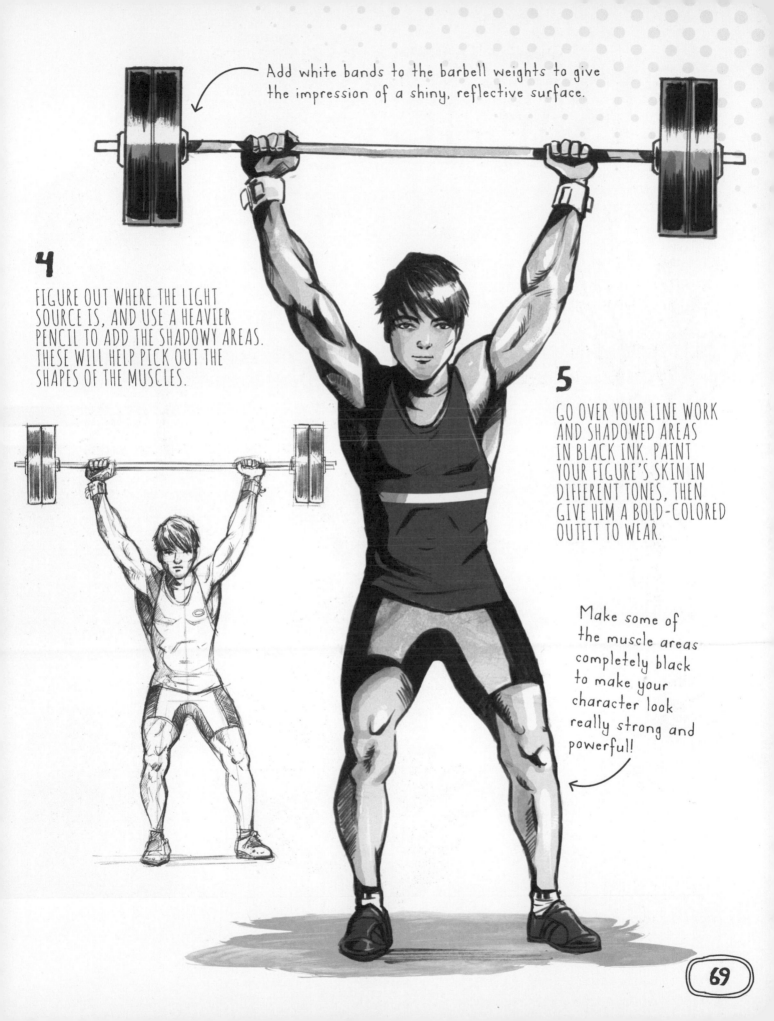

Add white bands to the barbell weights to give the impression of a shiny, reflective surface.

4

FIGURE OUT WHERE THE LIGHT SOURCE IS, AND USE A HEAVIER PENCIL TO ADD THE SHADOWY AREAS. THESE WILL HELP PICK OUT THE SHAPES OF THE MUSCLES.

5

GO OVER YOUR LINE WORK AND SHADOWED AREAS IN BLACK INK. PAINT YOUR FIGURE'S SKIN IN DIFFERENT TONES, THEN GIVE HIM A BOLD-COLORED OUTFIT TO WEAR.

Make some of the muscle areas completely black to make your character look really strong and powerful!

TREES

BASIC TREE
Draw a rough, bushy outline, then add a few branches, varying the thickness of each one. Draw simple leaf shapes in the gaps.

Use black ink to draw a bare tree that looks like it's been scorched!

PINE TREE
Sketch the trunk first, then add branches on both sides, each one angled slightly upward. Next, add lots of needles using short, thin lines.

For a natural look, give your tree drawings quirks and irregularities. For example, some branches or twigs could look bare, apart from a couple of leaves!

Notice how some pine branches can divide up into more smaller branches.

CHERRY TREE IN BLOSSOM

Draw a short tree trunk breaking into branches. Use ink for the blossom shapes, then add a blob of pink paint to each one.

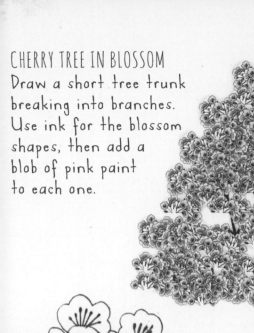

Practice drawing the blossom in detail. You may want to simplify it a bit, depending on the size of your drawing.

HOLLY TREE

Draw a rough triangle for the basic tree shape, then add clusters of round berries, each surrounded by a group of leaves.

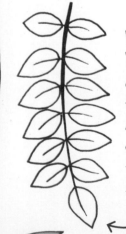

When you draw holly close up, use small, curved lines to sketch each pointed leaf shape.

LEAVES

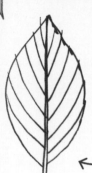

Draw the central vein, then add the pointed oval shape. Fill the space with smaller veins.

For this leaf, draw the main vein and smaller veins, then sketch the wobbly leaf outline.

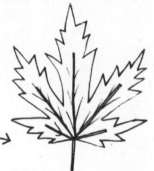

Start with five finger lines, then add the jagged shape of the leaf around them.

Draw a curved line, thicker at one end than the other. Add horizontal curves and then sketch small leaves.

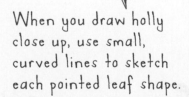

BIG BEN

4

DRAW THE INTRICATE CLOCK FACE AND ADD MORE SURFACE DETAIL ON EITHER SIDE. USE A DARK PENCIL TO ADD SHADING TO THE INDENTED SHAPES ON THE TOWER'S SURFACE.

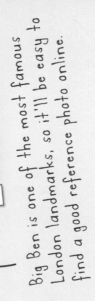

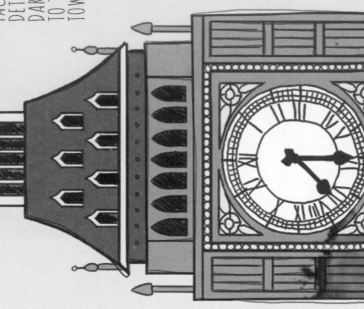

Big Ben is one of the most famous London landmarks, so it'll be easy to find a good reference photo online.

1

DRAW THE BASIC OUTLINE OF BIG BEN USING SQUARES, RECTANGLES, AND TRIANGULAR SHAPES. DIVIDE THE TOWER BENEATH THE CLOCK INTO FOUR EQUAL-SIZED SECTIONS.

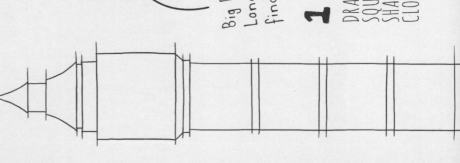

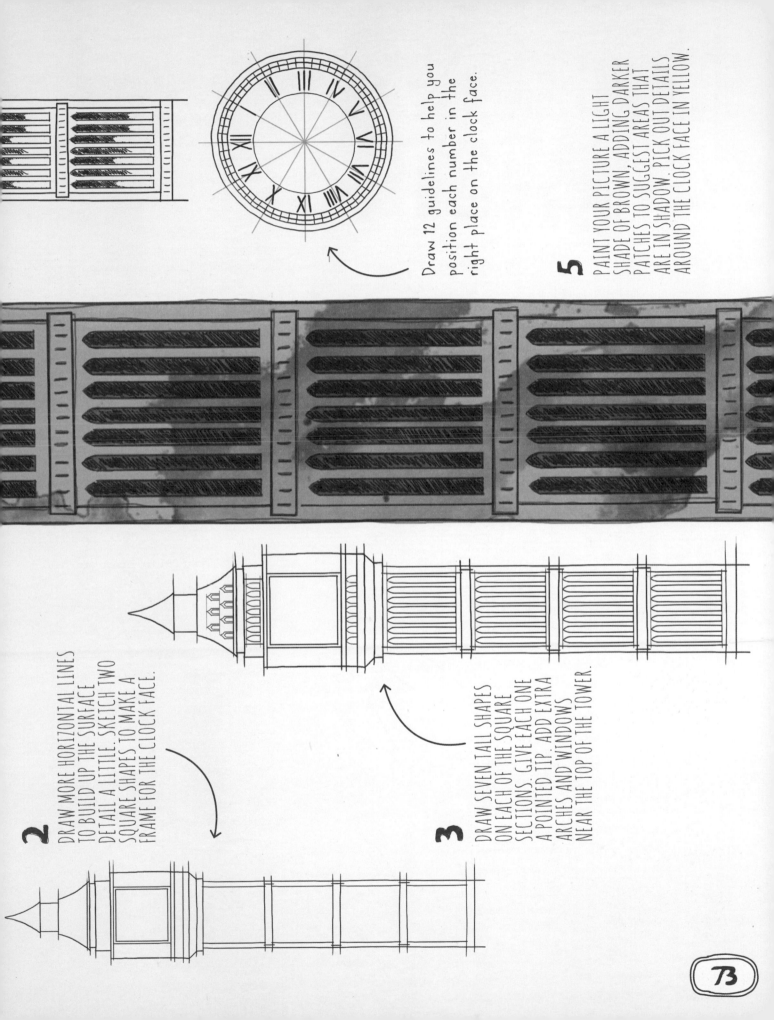

Draw 12 guidelines to help you position each number in the right place on the clock face.

5
PAINT YOUR PICTURE A LIGHT SHADE OF BROWN, ADDING DARKER PATCHES TO SUGGEST AREAS THAT ARE IN SHADOW. PICK OUT DETAILS AROUND THE CLOCK FACE IN YELLOW.

2
DRAW MORE HORIZONTAL LINES TO BUILD UP THE SURFACE DETAIL A LITTLE. SKETCH TWO SQUARE SHAPES TO MAKE A FRAME FOR THE CLOCK FACE.

3
DRAW SEVEN TALL SHAPES ON EACH OF THE SQUARE SECTIONS. GIVE EACH ONE A POINTED TIP. ADD EXTRA ARCHES AND WINDOWS NEAR THE TOP OF THE TOWER.

73

LOCH NESS MONSTER

NO ONE KNOWS IF THIS FAMOUS CREATURE FROM SCOTLAND REALLY EXISTS. BUT YOU CAN CREATE A VERY REAL DRAWING OF IT!

1

SKETCH A ROUGH OVAL SHAPE FOR THE MONSTER'S BODY AND A LONG, ROUNDED CYLINDER SHAPE FOR THE NECK, AS SHOWN.

2

DRAW SQUASHED OVAL SHAPES FOR THE HEAD, TAIL, AND ONE OF THE BACK FINS. DRAW TWO SMALL OVALS UNDER THE BODY.

Sketch the tail and large fin at an angle for a swimming creature.

3

ADD A CIRCULAR EYE, A CURVED LINE FOR THE MOUTH, AND A WING-SHAPED FIN ON THE BODY. START DRAWING AN OUTLINE AROUND THE SHAPES TO LINK THEM ALL TOGETHER.

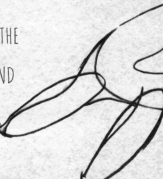

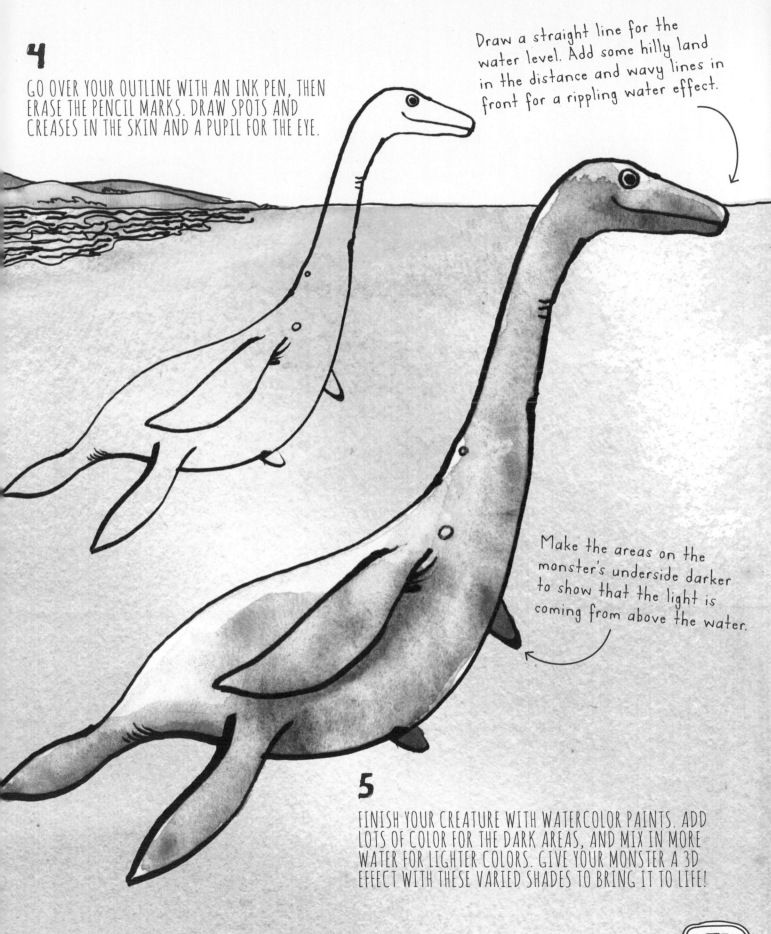

4

GO OVER YOUR OUTLINE WITH AN INK PEN, THEN ERASE THE PENCIL MARKS. DRAW SPOTS AND CREASES IN THE SKIN AND A PUPIL FOR THE EYE.

Draw a straight line for the water level. Add some hilly land in the distance and wavy lines in front for a rippling water effect.

Make the areas on the monster's underside darker to show that the light is coming from above the water.

5

FINISH YOUR CREATURE WITH WATERCOLOR PAINTS. ADD LOTS OF COLOR FOR THE DARK AREAS, AND MIX IN MORE WATER FOR LIGHTER COLORS. GIVE YOUR MONSTER A 3D EFFECT WITH THESE VARIED SHADES TO BRING IT TO LIFE!

MAGNIFYING GLASS

WHEN YOU DRAW AS IF THROUGH A MAGNIFYING GLASS, YOU CAN ADD FANTASTIC-LOOKING DETAILS YOU MIGHT NOT OTHERWISE SEE!

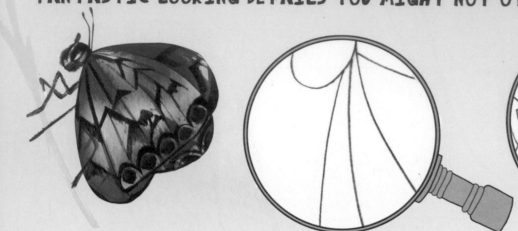 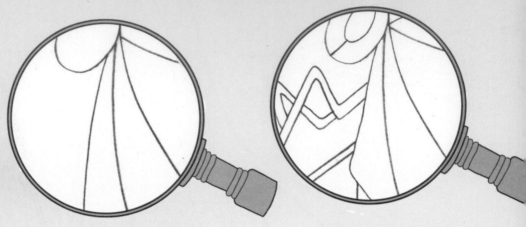

1 BEFORE YOU START DRAWING, FIND A PHOTO OF YOUR IMAGE ONLINE OR CHOOSE ONE FROM A BOOK. THIS WILL HELP YOU GET THE TINY DETAILS RIGHT.

2 USING A PENCIL, DRAW A BIG CIRCLE FOR THE MAGNIFYING GLASS, THEN BUILD UP THE HANDLE SHAPE WITH DIFFERENT-SIZED RECTANGLES. SKETCH SIMPLE SHAPES TO FORM A BUTTERFLY'S BODY.

3 START ADDING MORE DETAIL TO THE DIFFERENT BODY PARTS. DRAW EXTRA LINES ON THE WINGS AND A FEW MORE CURVES ON THE HEAD SECTION.

4 CONCENTRATE ON THE FINE DETAILS USING A SHARP PENCIL. DRAW TINY HAIRS ON THE BUTTERFLY'S HEAD AND LEGS, THEN ADD PATTERNS OF SHADING TO ITS WINGS.

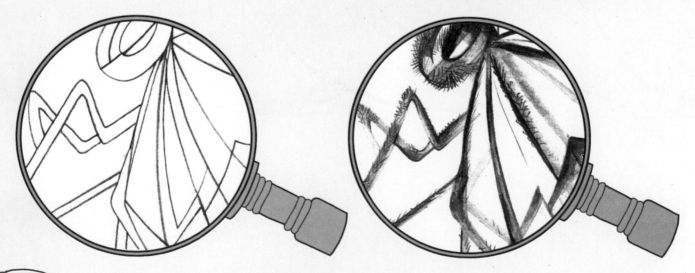

5

USE AN INK PEN TO GO OVER THE PENCIL LINES AND SHADED AREAS. COLOR YOUR BUTTERFLY USING INKS IN DIFFERENT TONES AND LEAVE TO DRY. FINALLY, USE COLORED PENCILS TO ADD SOME SUBTLE SHADED TEXTURE ON TOP.

Think about how the parts enlarged through the magnifying glass will look different to the smaller version outside the glass.

To create reflections on the glass, add bands of watery white paint over the top of your butterfly.

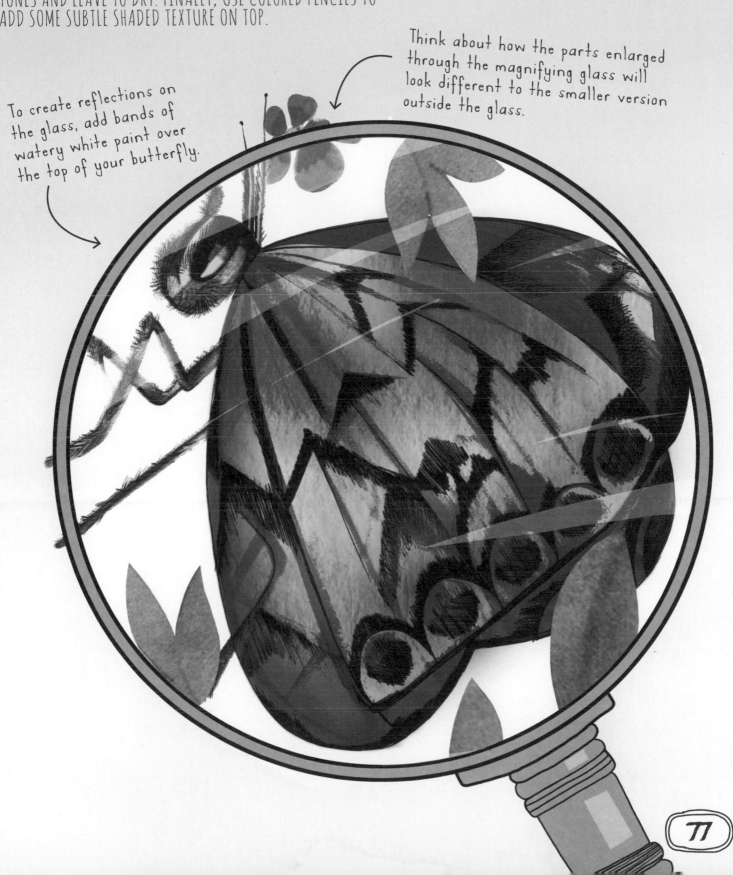

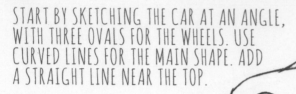

1

START BY SKETCHING THE CAR AT AN ANGLE, WITH THREE OVALS FOR THE WHEELS. USE CURVED LINES FOR THE MAIN SHAPE. ADD A STRAIGHT LINE NEAR THE TOP.

2

USE VERTICAL LINES FOR THE WINDSHIELD AND WINDOWS. THEN ADD WAVY LINES TO CREATE THE CAR'S BASIC BODY CURVES.

3

DRAW THE TIRES, RIMS, HEADLIGHTS, SIDE MIRRORS, AND BUMPER USING A MIXTURE OF LINES, RECTANGLES, TRIANGLES, AND CIRCLES, AS SHOWN.

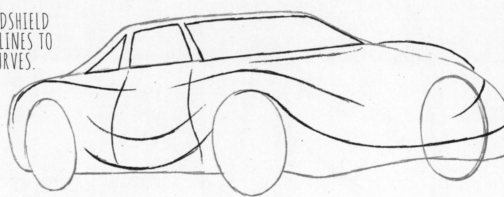

4

GO OVER YOUR DRAWING WITH A SOFT LEADED PENCIL. LIGHTLY SHADE THE BODY TO HIGHLIGHT THE CURVES. ADD DARK SHADING ON THE WHEELS.

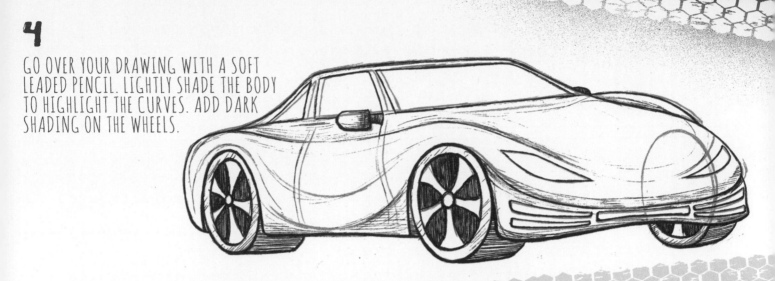

5

FINISH WITH A BRIGHT COLOR FOR THE BODY. REMEMBER TO GRADUALLY BUILD UP YOUR SHADING FOR A REALISTIC EFFECT, GOING WITH THE CONTOURS OF THE CAR FOR A SLEEK LOOK.

Add lots of white to the windshield for a really bright reflection.

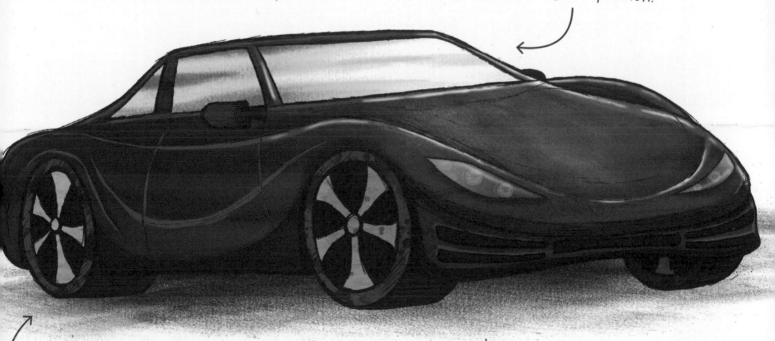

Add shiny highlights on the car, using small amounts of white color. Apply sparingly to keep your drawing looking realistic.

CAT IN SUNGLASSES

LEARN TO DRAW A PICTURE OF A CAT, THEN GIVE IT SOME PERSONALITY WITH A PAIR OF COOL-LOOKING SHADES. PURR-FECT!

1 SKETCH THREE CIRCLE GUIDES FOR THE CAT'S BODY. ADD EARS AND A TAIL. USE A RULER TO ADD A HORIZONTAL LINE IN THE BACKGROUND.

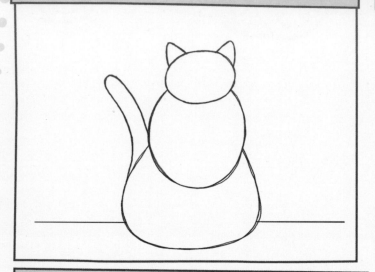

2 DRAW TWO CIRCLES TO PLACE THE CAT'S BACK PAWS. DRAW TWO STRAIGHT LEGS AT THE FRONT TO SHOW THE CAT SITTING UP.

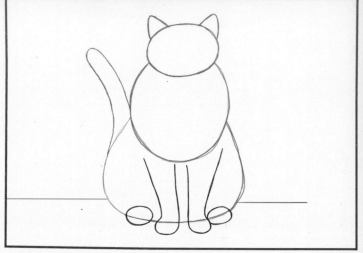

3 ADD TWO DOTS FOR THE CAT'S EYES, A SMALL TRIANGLE FOR HER NOSE, AND AN UPSIDE-DOWN "Y" FOR THE MOUTH.

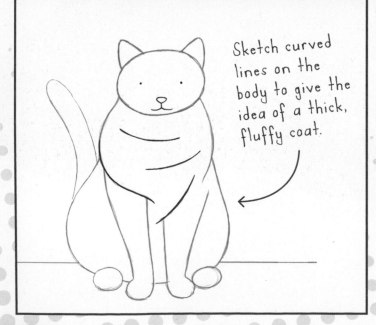

Sketch curved lines on the body to give the idea of a thick, fluffy coat.

4 APPLY SHORT, WIGGLY LINES OVER YOUR PENCIL MARKS TO SUGGEST FUR. THEN ADD A POINTY CURVE BENEATH THE CAT'S MOUTH FOR A CHIN.

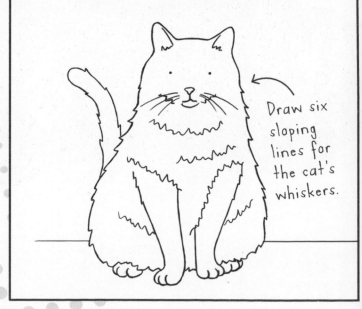

Draw six sloping lines for the cat's whiskers.

5 ACCESSORIZE! DRAW AN OVERSIZED PAIR OF SUNGLASSES AROUND THE FACE. ADD A GLASS WITH A SLICE OF ORANGE AND A STRAW. GO OVER YOUR LINES WITH AN INK PEN, AND START COLORING IN.

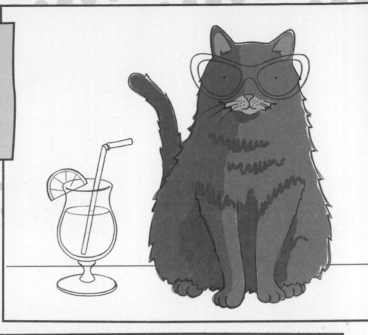

6 USE THE HORIZONTAL LINE AS A GUIDE TO CREATE A WALL FOR THE CAT TO PERCH ON. WHEN COLORING YOUR PICTURE, START WITH PALER COLORS, THEN BUILD UP DARKER TONES FOR DEPTH AND A PURR-FECT 3D FEEL.

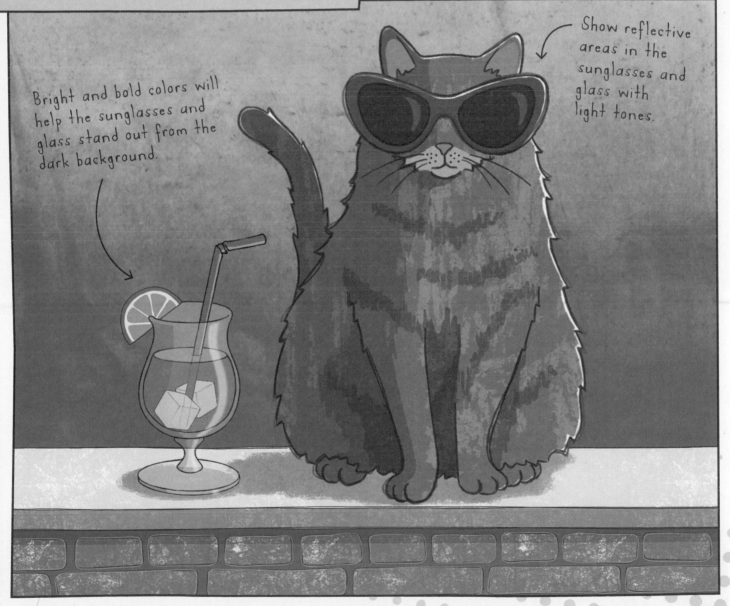

Bright and bold colors will help the sunglasses and glass stand out from the dark background.

Show reflective areas in the sunglasses and glass with light tones.

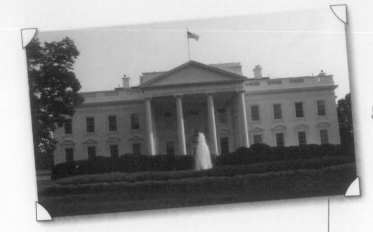

Find a photo of the White House for inspiration before you start drawing.

1

USE A RULER TO DRAW A HORIZONTAL RECTANGULAR SHAPE, LIKE THIS. DRAW A GUIDELINE DOWN THE CENTER.

2

SKETCH A RECTANGLE AROUND THE GUIDELINE AND A TRIANGLE AT THE TOP. ADD A HORIZONTAL LINE UNDER THE TOP OF YOUR LARGE RECTANGLE.

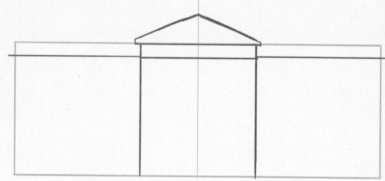

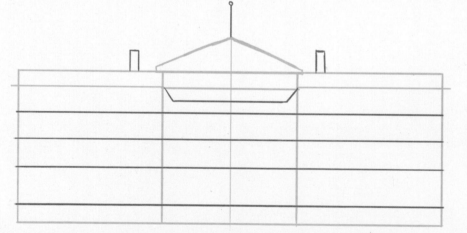

3

DRAW AN UPSIDE-DOWN TRAPEZOID SHAPE BENEATH THE TRIANGLE. ADD FOUR MORE HORIZONTAL LINES FOR WINDOW GUIDES. THE TOP TWO LINES SHOULD BE CLOSER TOGETHER SINCE THESE WINDOWS ARE SHORTER. ADD TWO SMALL RECTANGULAR CHIMNEYS AND A CIRCLE AT THE TOP OF THE FLAGPOLE.

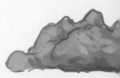

4

DRAW RECTANGLES, TRIANGLES, CYLINDERS, CIRCLES, AND OVALS FOR THE WINDOWS, DOOR, ROOF, COLUMNS, AND HANGING LIGHT, AS SHOWN. ERASE ANY GUIDELINES.

Use wavy lines to create the effect of bushes and a flag.

Sketch oval-shaped posts for the balustrade.

5

ADD DETAILS TO THE WINDOWS, ROOF, FOUNTAIN, AND BUSHES USING CRISSCROSS LINES, SEMICIRCLES, TRIANGLES, OVALS, AND CURVED LINES, LIKE THIS.

6 NOW COLOR YOUR PICTURE, USING LONG, SWEEPING STROKES FOR THE BUILDING AND SHORT, DABBING STROKES FOR THE RED FLOWERS AND GREEN BUSHES.

Follow the flag's wavy outline when you paint for a rippling effect.

Paint bluey-gray shades on the building and windows to show reflections from the sky.

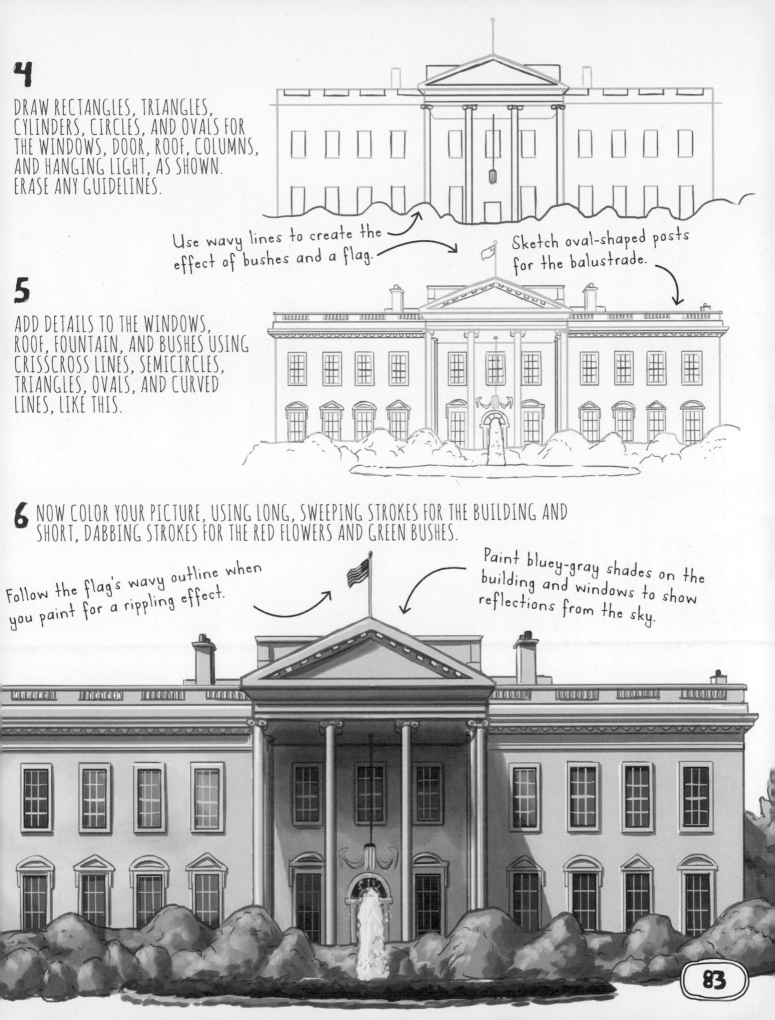

TREE BARK

These tree pictures were created using "mixed media," which means you can combine different materials to get the right texture or effect. Pen, pencil, ink, and gouache (a thick kind of paint) all work well together.

Create this bark by using a pencil to shade long, vertical strips. Then use an ink pen to add some crosshatch areas on top.

Using different shades of green, dab the end of your paintbrush onto the paper to get this leafy effect.

Use a soft pencil and flow the pencil marks in different directions to produce a natural-looking texture.

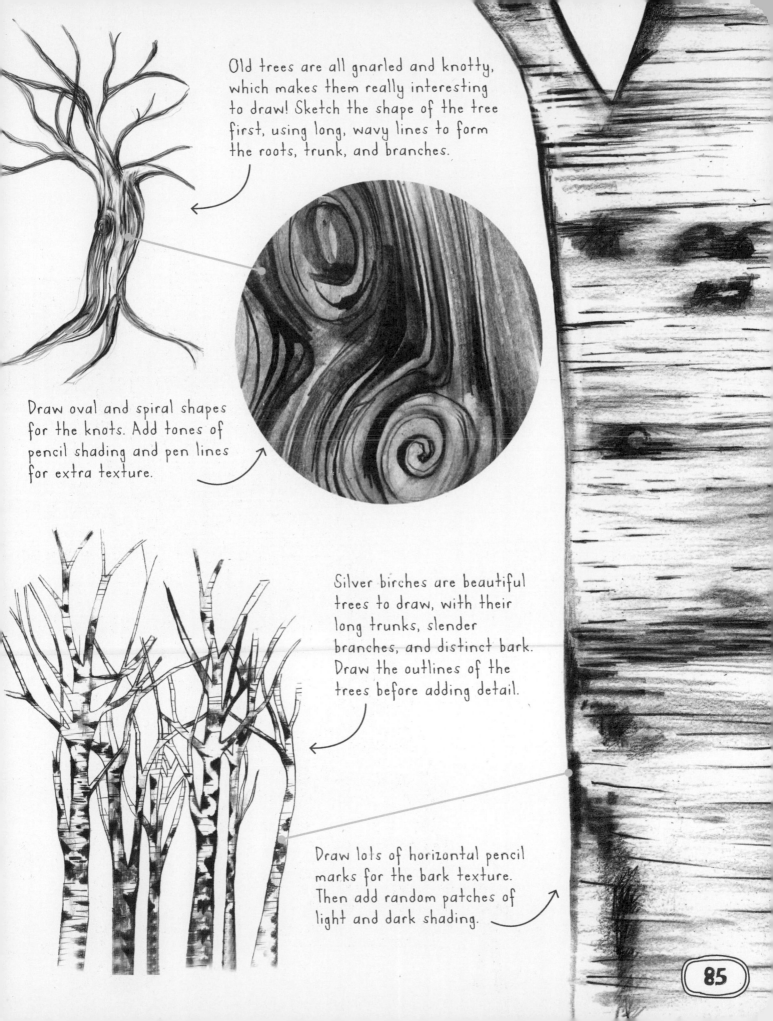

Old trees are all gnarled and knotty, which makes them really interesting to draw! Sketch the shape of the tree first, using long, wavy lines to form the roots, trunk, and branches.

Draw oval and spiral shapes for the knots. Add tones of pencil shading and pen lines for extra texture.

Silver birches are beautiful trees to draw, with their long trunks, slender branches, and distinct bark. Draw the outlines of the trees before adding detail.

Draw lots of horizontal pencil marks for the bark texture. Then add random patches of light and dark shading.

3D MAZE

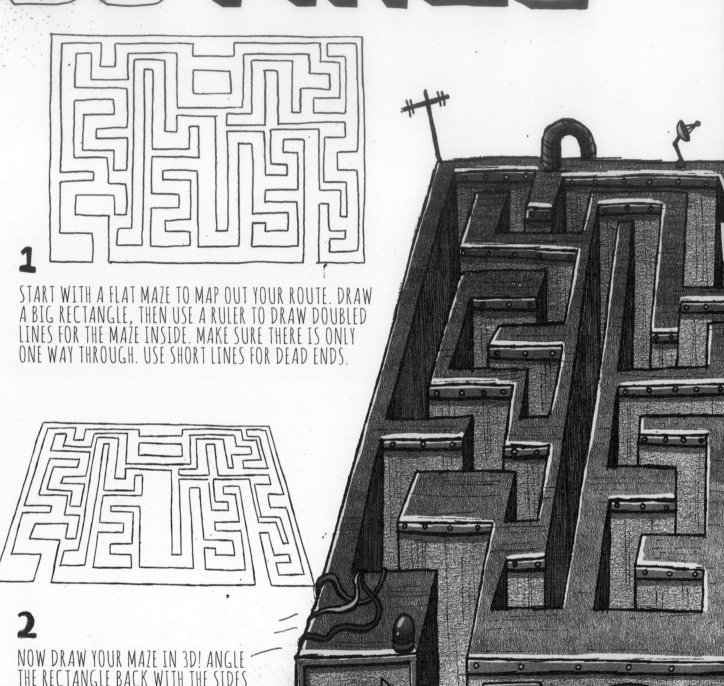

1

START WITH A FLAT MAZE TO MAP OUT YOUR ROUTE. DRAW A BIG RECTANGLE, THEN USE A RULER TO DRAW DOUBLED LINES FOR THE MAZE INSIDE. MAKE SURE THERE IS ONLY ONE WAY THROUGH. USE SHORT LINES FOR DEAD ENDS.

2

NOW DRAW YOUR MAZE IN 3D! ANGLE THE RECTANGLE BACK WITH THE SIDES SLANTING INWARD. THEN DRAW THE LINES INSIDE IT, COPYING THE ROUTE YOU SET IN YOUR FLAT MAZE.

IN

3 USE TRACING PAPER TO COPY AND PRINT YOUR MAZE OVER THE ORIGINAL, BUT MOVE IT SLIGHTLY LOWER DOWN, AS SHOWN.

This isn't any ordinary maze! Add extra details like pipes, aerials, and steam for personality. Don't forget the person about to get lost in there!

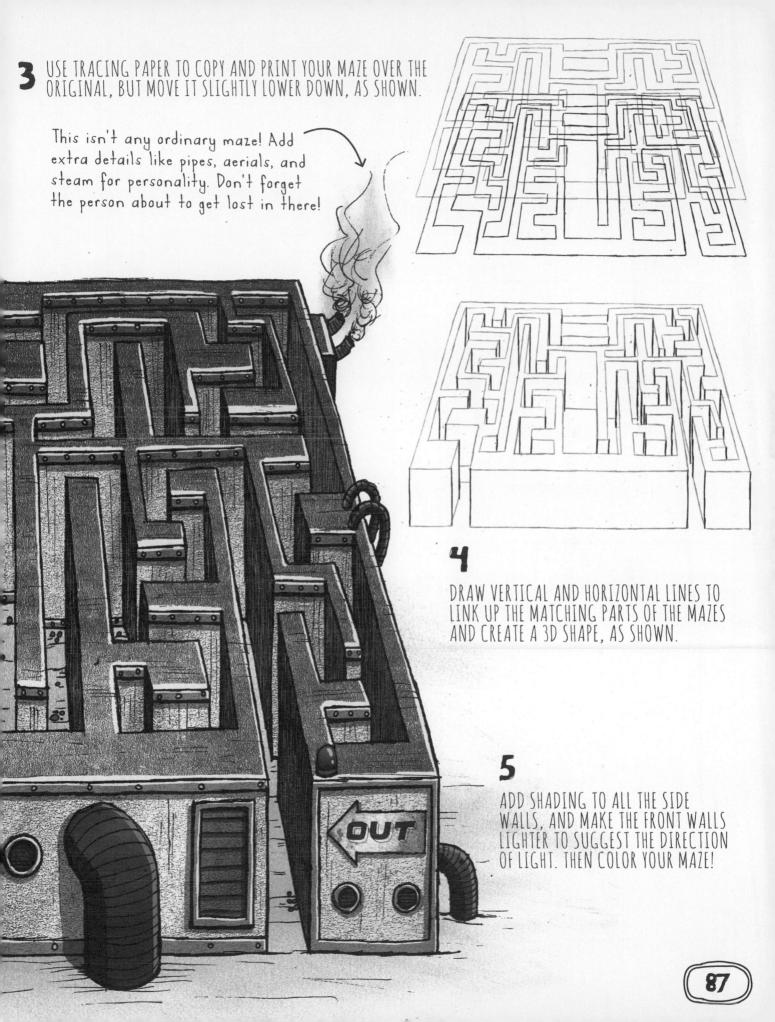

4

DRAW VERTICAL AND HORIZONTAL LINES TO LINK UP THE MATCHING PARTS OF THE MAZES AND CREATE A 3D SHAPE, AS SHOWN.

5

ADD SHADING TO ALL THE SIDE WALLS, AND MAKE THE FRONT WALLS LIGHTER TO SUGGEST THE DIRECTION OF LIGHT. THEN COLOR YOUR MAZE!

OUT

SUNRISE

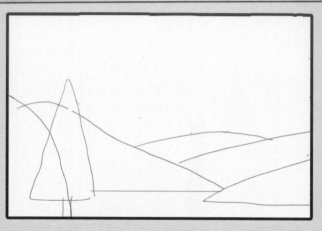

1 SKETCH A ROUGH LANDSCAPE USING SIMPLE CURVES. DRAW TRIANGULAR SHAPES FOR TREES.

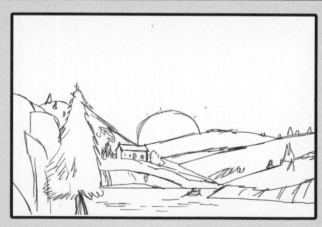

2 KEEPING YOUR LINEWORK LOOSE, SKETCH A RISING SUN IN THE DISTANCE. ADD OTHER DETAILS, SUCH AS A HOUSE AND ROWBOAT. SKETCH IN MORE LANDSCAPE FEATURES AS WELL.

Use lighter shades for the middle area of your picture. This will help draw your eye to the most interesting parts—the sun, house, and rowboat.

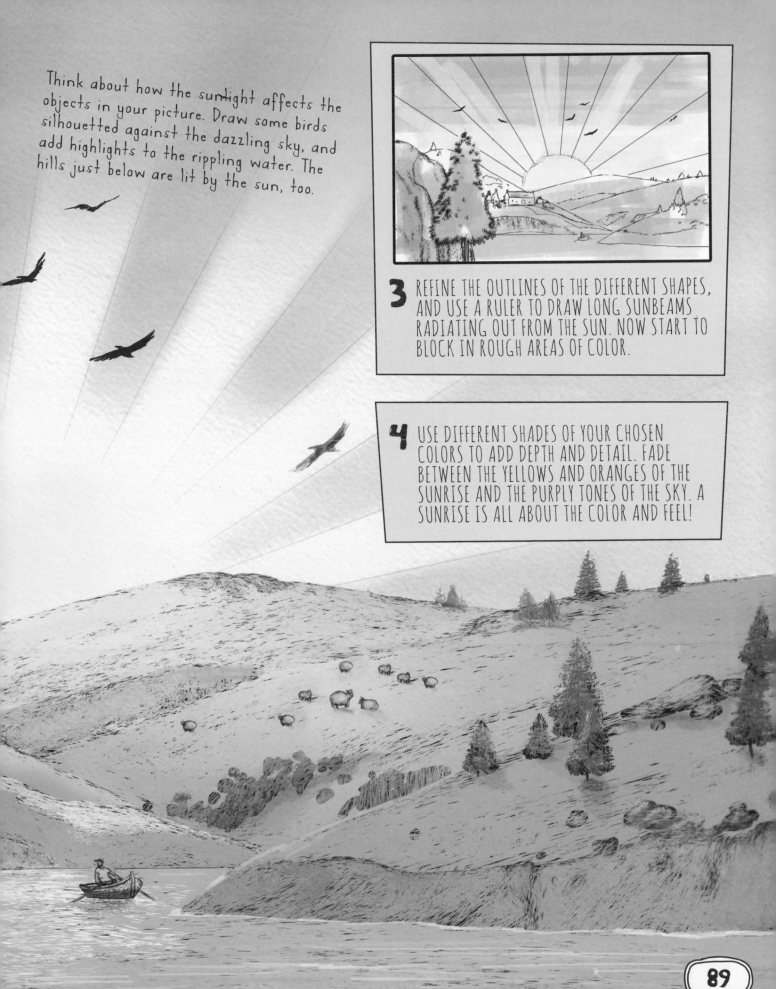

Think about how the sunlight affects the objects in your picture. Draw some birds silhouetted against the dazzling sky, and add highlights to the rippling water. The hills just below are lit by the sun, too.

3 REFINE THE OUTLINES OF THE DIFFERENT SHAPES, AND USE A RULER TO DRAW LONG SUNBEAMS RADIATING OUT FROM THE SUN. NOW START TO BLOCK IN ROUGH AREAS OF COLOR.

4 USE DIFFERENT SHADES OF YOUR CHOSEN COLORS TO ADD DEPTH AND DETAIL. FADE BETWEEN THE YELLOWS AND ORANGES OF THE SUNRISE AND THE PURPLY TONES OF THE SKY. A SUNRISE IS ALL ABOUT THE COLOR AND FEEL!

SHOES

DRAW DIFFERENT STYLES OF FOOTWEAR, THEN CREATE YOUR OWN PATTERNED FASHIONS!

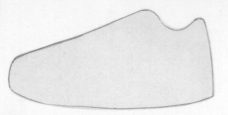

1

USE CURVED LINES TO DRAW THE SIMPLE SHAPE OF A SNEAKER.

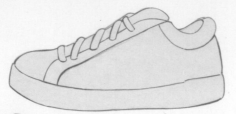

2

ADD IN THE RUBBER SOLE, THE TONGUE, SHOELACES, AND EDGING, AS SHOWN.

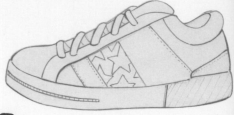

3

DRAW LINES TO SUGGEST DIFFERENT FABRICS ON THE SIDES AND AROUND THE BACK. SKETCH DASHED LINES FOR STITCHING, AND ADD A PATTERN.

ONCE YOU'VE MASTERED THE BASIC SHOE, TRY THESE TECHNIQUES ...

OXFORD SHOE

Vary the shape of your shoe and include Oxford-type stitching using circles and zigzags.

Draw shapes on your shoe to suggest multiple fabrics.

Create laces from short and long lines, and ovals.

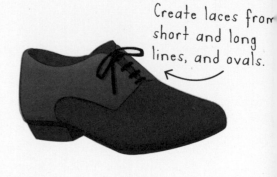

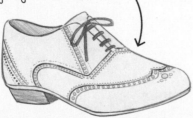

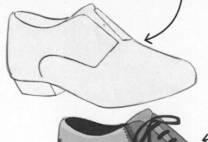

This zigzag pattern uses small, teethlike lines to frame the fabric.

PLATFORM

Exaggerate the shoe's arch, heel, and sole to create a high-heeled platform shoe.

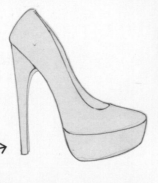

This zigzag pattern uses bold, contrasting colors for the overall pattern of the shoe.

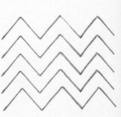

TRY BUILDING UP SIMPLE SHAPES TO CREATE COOL SHOE PATTERNS.

THE CHECKERED LOAFER

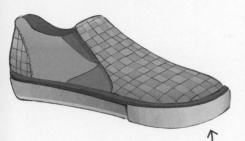

Horizontal and vertical lines create an eye-catching, two-tone checkered pattern.

Contrasting and complementary colors help make patterns, such as stars, spots, and zigzags, pop.

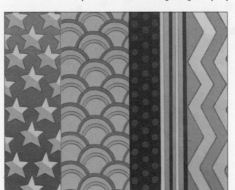

THE STARRY HIGH-TOP SNEAKER

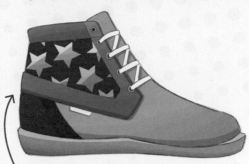

Isolate your pattern to just one part of the shoe for a pattern pop!

THE BALLET PUMP

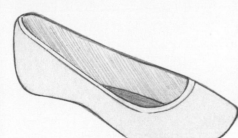

Sketch a long oval shape, then draw curved lines around it to create a ballet shoe.

Repeat semicircles for a rainbow pattern.

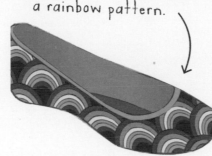

Break up a spotted pattern with a chunky rectangular band.

THE KITTEN HEEL

Draw a simple shoe shape and add a small heel.

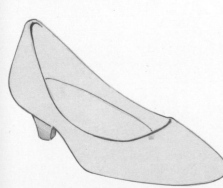

Use curved shapes, spiraling outward from the center, for a rose pattern.

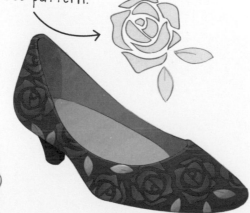

Curvy rectangles make this simple shoe buckle for a higher-heeled shoe.

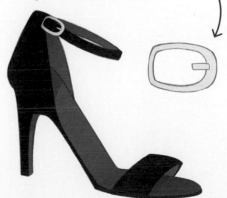

ROBOT

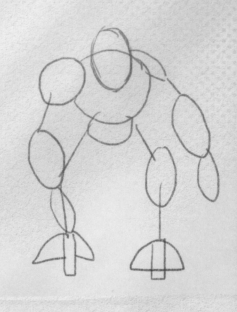

1 DRAW STICK LINES FOR THE GENERAL SHAPE AND LIMBS. MAKE THE ARMS LONG TO GIVE A SENSE OF THE ROBOT LEANING FORWARD.

2 USE SIMPLE OVALS TO FLESH OUT THE SHAPES OF THE HEAD, CHEST, AND HIP AREA. ADD SIMPLE LINES FOR THE HANDS.

3 DRAW MORE OVALS FOR THE SHOULDERS, ARMS, AND LEGS. USE SEMICIRCLES AND RECTANGLES TO SKETCH FEET.

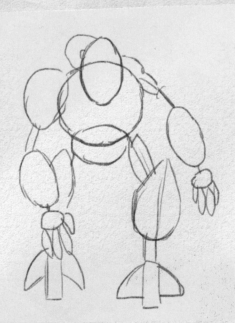
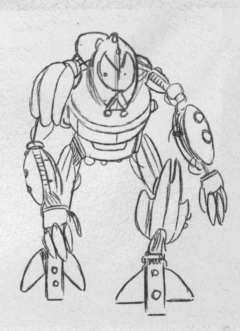
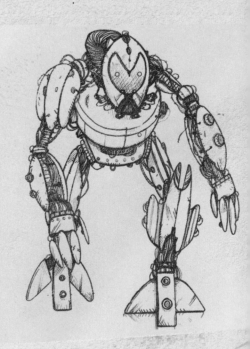

4 FLESH OUT YOUR STICK FIGURE EVEN MORE. CONNECT THE OVALS WITH THICKER LINES, ADD TUBING BEHIND THE HEAD, AND DRAW FINGERS ON EACH HAND.

5 START ADDING LINES AND CURVES TO THE BODY PARTS TO MAKE THEM LOOK MORE 3D. DRAW IN THE ROBOT'S FACIAL FEATURES, AND ADD MORE SURFACE DETAIL.

6 CONCENTRATE ON THE FINER DETAILS, ADDING THINGS LIKE WIRES AND RIVETS. DRAW LOTS OF TINY LINES TO GIVE CERTAIN AREAS A TUBELIKE TEXTURE.

7 PAINT YOUR ROBOT IN DIFFERENT SHADES OF GRAY. USE A SINGLE BASE COLOR TO START WITH, THEN ADD LIGHTER GRAYS FOR THE HIGHLIGHTED AREAS, WITH DARKER TONES FOR THE AREAS THAT ARE IN SHADE.

Pick out some of the smaller details in bright colors. These will help add interest to your drawing.

Painting bands of lighter and darker grays will help give the robot's body a more metallic and reflective texture.

Use a watery gray wash for the robot's reflections. These help connect the robot to its background.

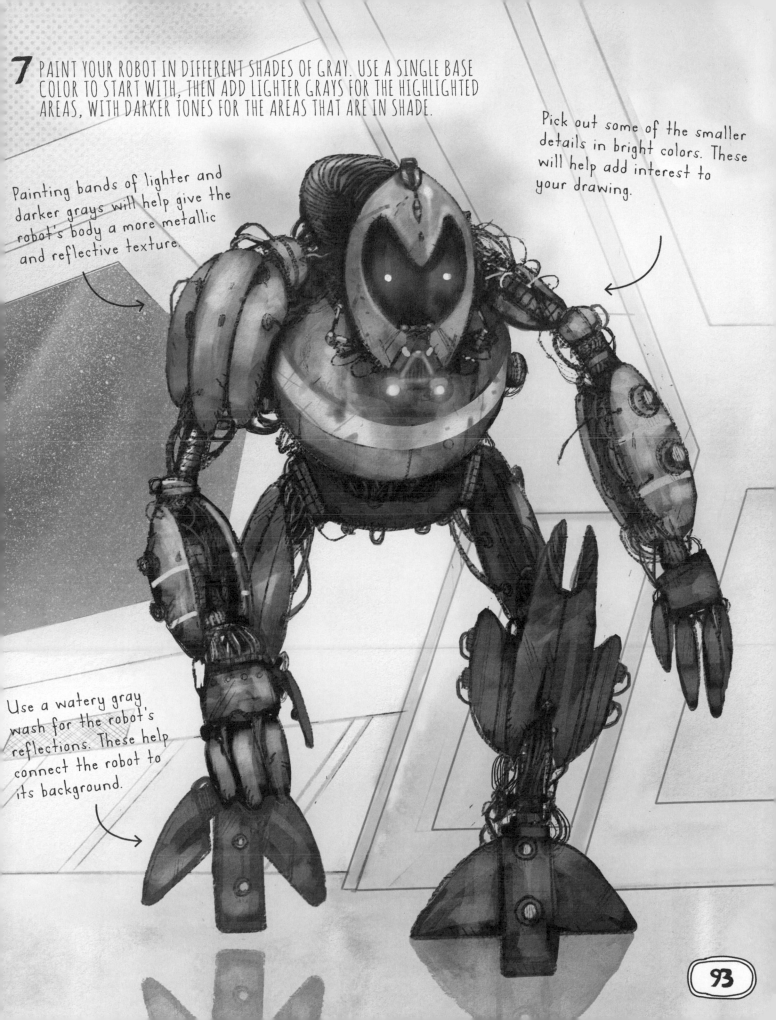

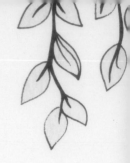
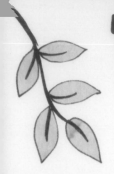

VINTAGE BICYCLE

1 BREAK THE BICYCLE INTO SIMPLE SHAPES. DRAW TWO CIRCLES FOR THE WHEELS, THEN USE A RULER TO CONNECT THEM. DRAW TWO ANGLED LINES FOR THE FRAME AND A SHORT LINE FOR THE SEAT.

2 USE RECTANGLES, STRAIGHT LINES, AND CURVED LINES TO ADD MORE DETAIL TO THE FRAMEWORK AND TO CREATE HANDLEBARS AND A SHOPPING BASKET, AS SHOWN.

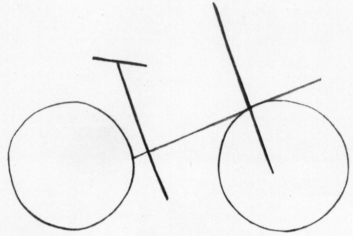

3 SKETCH A RECTANGLE FOR THE SEAT AND A SPIRAL FOR ITS SPRING. DRAW MORE CIRCLES FOR THE WHEELS, CHAIN WHEEL, AND HUB. ADD A CYLINDER-SHAPED CHAIN AND A TRIANGULAR HEADLIGHT.

4 FOR THE SPOKES, DRAW LINES RADIATING OUT FROM THE WHEEL HUB AND CHAIN. THEN START TO GO OVER YOUR LINES WITH A WATER-RESISTANT INK PEN. ERASE ANY PENCIL MARKS.

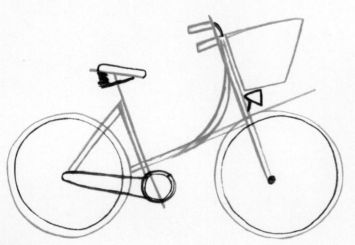
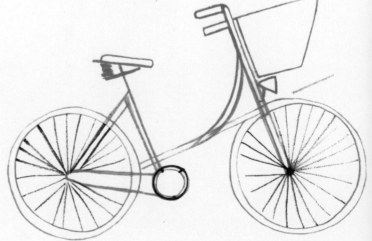

5 USING THE PEN, DRAW LINES ON THE HANDLEBARS AND THE BASKET TO CREATE TEXTURE. FILL IN THE WHEELS TO MAKE TIRES. ADD A CIRCLE AND LINES ON THE CHAIN WHEEL. DRAW CURVED LINES AROUND THE WHEELS FOR THE MUDGUARDS.

The texture on the basket and handlebars contrasts with the smooth appearance of the frames and spokes.

6 DRAW HANDBRAKES AND PEDALS, AND A LONG, CURVED LINE FOR THE BRAKE CABLE. ADD COLOR USING WATERCOLOR INK OR PAINTS.

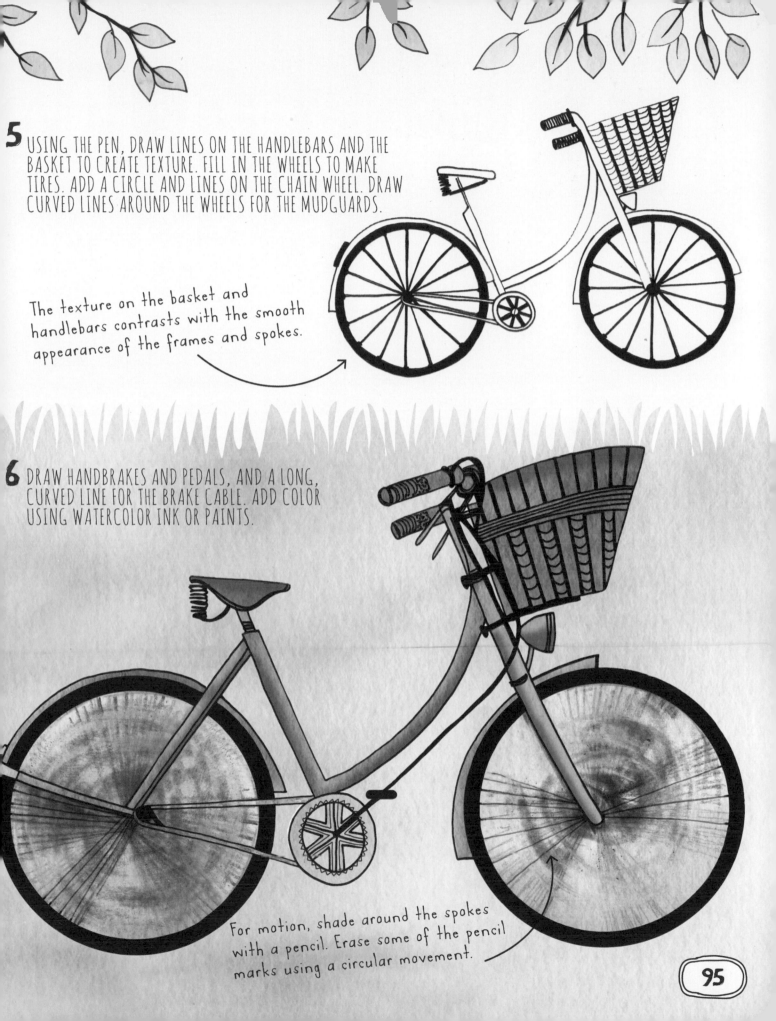

For motion, shade around the spokes with a pencil. Erase some of the pencil marks using a circular movement.

TENNIS PLAYER

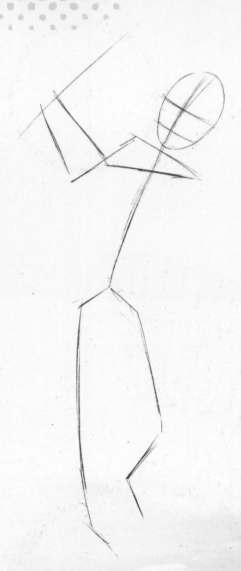

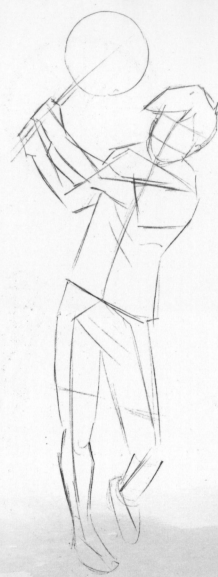

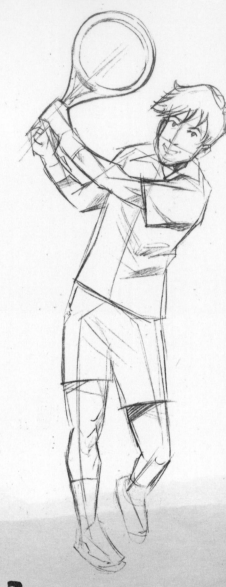

1

LIGHTLY SKETCH A STICK FIGURE IN AN ACTION POSE WITH THE LEFT ARM ACROSS THE CHEST, HOLDING ONTO A STICK. THE RIGHT LEG SHOULD BE STRAIGHT AND THE LEFT ONE BENT.

2

SKETCH THE LOOSE OUTLINE OF THE PLAYER AROUND THE GUIDES. THE RIGHT SHOULDER IS SLIGHTLY HIGHER, SO THE CLOTHES SHOULD APPEAR SLIGHTLY TWISTED.

3

START WORKING ON THE DETAIL. ADD THE FACIAL FEATURES, AND GIVE THE RACKET SOME SHAPE. USE LIGHT SHADING TO SHOW THE FOLDS IN THE CLOTHES.

Think about which direction the light is coming from to help you figure out where the shadowed areas should be.

Add small, colorful details for interest, such as a simple three-tone design on the racket frame.

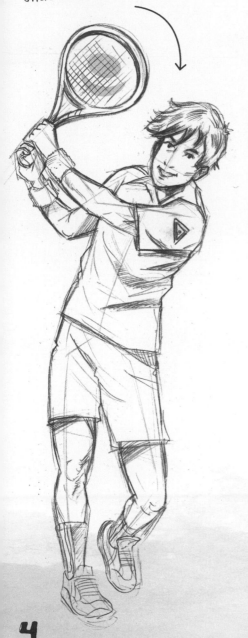

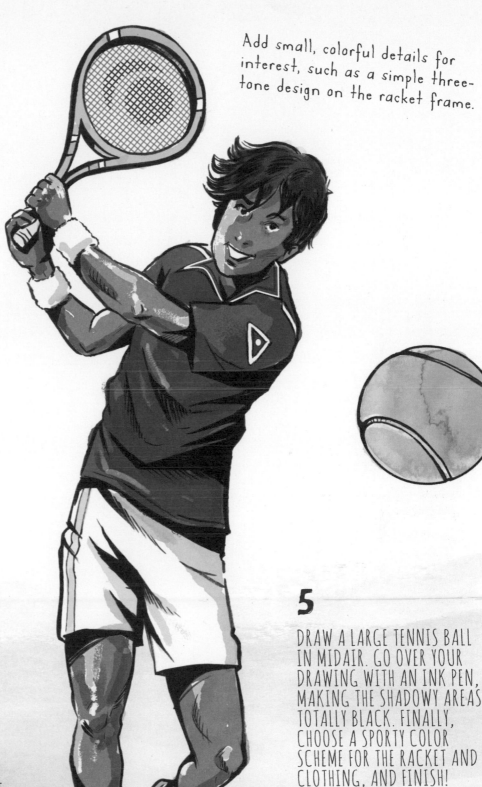

4

USING A 4B PENCIL, ADD DEFINED AREAS OF SHADOW AND MUSCLE TONE. USE CRISSCROSSING LINES FOR THE RACKET STRINGS, AND ADD DETAIL TO THE HANDS, HAIR, AND SHOES.

5

DRAW A LARGE TENNIS BALL IN MIDAIR. GO OVER YOUR DRAWING WITH AN INK PEN, MAKING THE SHADOWY AREAS TOTALLY BLACK. FINALLY, CHOOSE A SPORTY COLOR SCHEME FOR THE RACKET AND CLOTHING, AND FINISH!

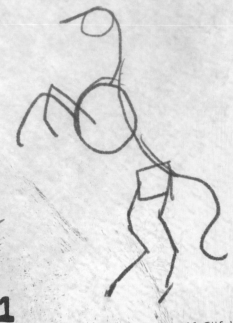

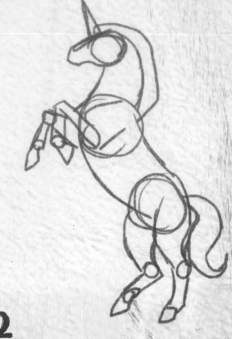

1

DRAW A STICK FIGURE SHOWING THE UNICORN IN AN ACTION POSE. WORK ON GETTING THE PROPORTIONS RIGHT. ADD A LONG, WAVY LINE FROM THE HEAD DOWN TO THE TIP OF THE TAIL.

2

FLESH OUT THE UNICORN'S HEAD, BODY, AND LIMBS. DRAW SMALL CIRCLES FOR THE LEG AND ANKLE JOINTS. USE WAVY LINES FOR THE MANE AND TAIL. ADD A SMALL TRIANGLE FOR A HORN.

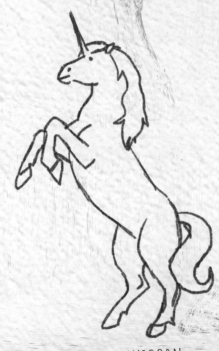

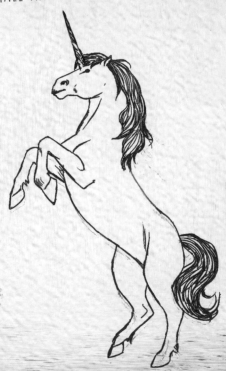

3

REFINE THE OUTLINE OF THE UNICORN. ERASE THE GUIDELINES. ADD FACIAL FEATURES AND DEFINE THE MANE.

4

GO OVER YOUR DRAWING WITH AN INK PEN, ADDING EXTRA LINES FOR DEFINITION. ADD LOTS OF WAVY LINES TO THE MANE AND TAIL FOR A HAIR TEXTURE. ADD A LITTLE SHADING TO THE HORN, TOO.

UNICORN

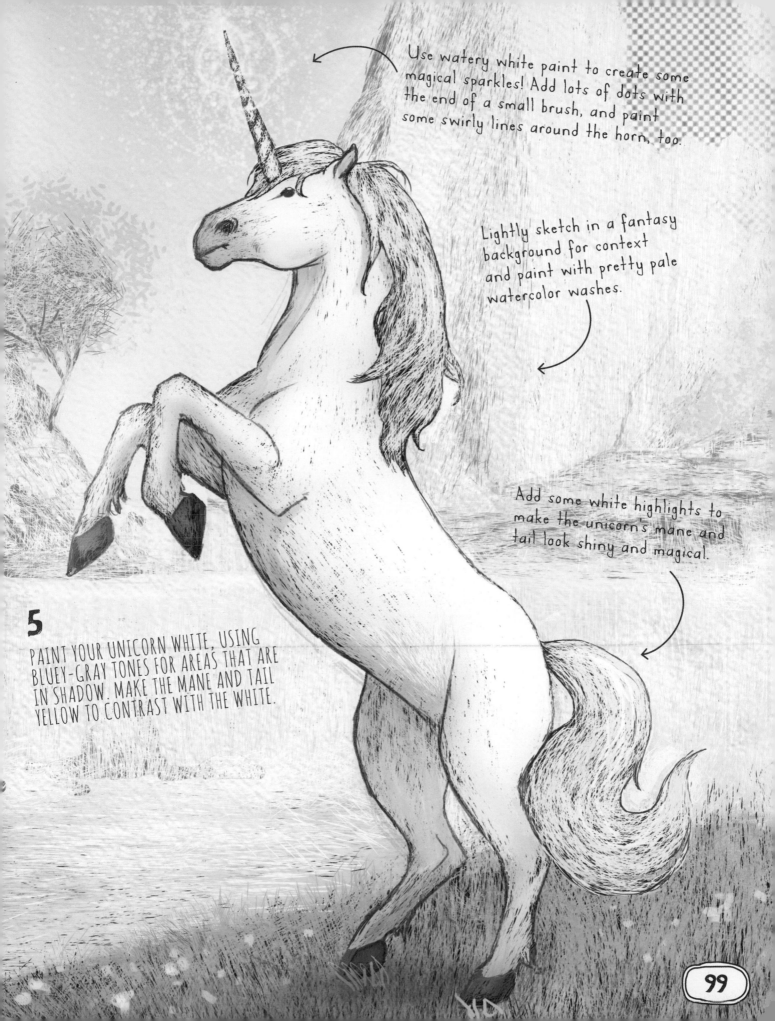

Use watery white paint to create some magical sparkles! Add lots of dots with the end of a small brush, and paint some swirly lines around the horn, too.

Lightly sketch in a fantasy background for context and paint with pretty pale watercolor washes.

Add some white highlights to make the unicorn's mane and tail look shiny and magical.

5
PAINT YOUR UNICORN WHITE, USING BLUEY-GRAY TONES FOR AREAS THAT ARE IN SHADOW. MAKE THE MANE AND TAIL YELLOW TO CONTRAST WITH THE WHITE.

AVATAR

AN AVATAR IS A COMPUTER-GENERATED VERSION OF YOU! DRAW YOUR OWN DIGITAL ALTER EGO, MIXING AND MATCHING THESE BODY PARTS.

1 CHOOSE THE FACE SHAPE AND SKIN TONE THAT BEST REPRESENTS YOU. LOOK IN A MIRROR IF YOU'RE NOT SURE!

OVAL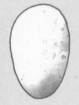

SQUARE

ROUND

OBLONG

HEART

SKIN TONES: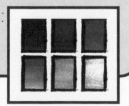

2 NOW ADD YOUR HAIRSTYLE. USE LONG, SHORT, OR WAVY PENCIL FLICKS AND VARIED COLOR TONES.

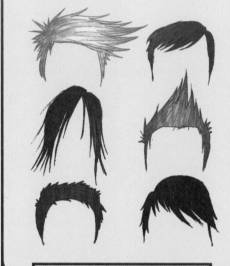

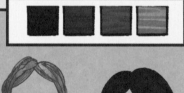

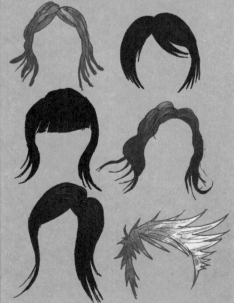

3 EYES AREN'T ALWAYS CIRCULAR. TRY DIFFERENT SHAPES FOR DIFFERENT EXPRESSIONS. SLEEPY, PRETTY, OR STARTLED, PERHAPS?

  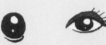

IS YOUR AVATAR BRAINY, COOL, BOTH OR NEITHER? IF YOU WANT, DRAW GLASSES OR SHADES TO SUIT YOUR CHARACTER'S PERSONALITY.

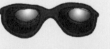
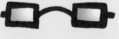

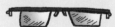

4 FOR A BIG NOSE, DRAW LONG LINES AND WIDER CURVES. USE SHORTER, SOFTER LINES FOR A DAINTIER NOSE.

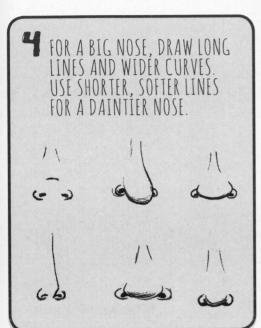

5 YOUR MOUTH COULD BE CHATTY, SHOUTY, SWEET, SHY, TOOTHY, OR JUST PLAIN SILLY. IT'S UP TO YOU!

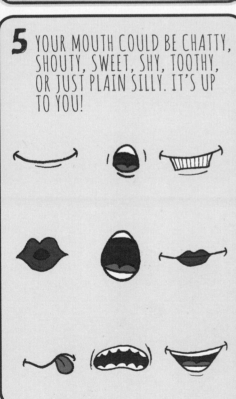

6 SKETCH YOUR BODY SHAPE AND CLOTHES. WILL YOUR AVATAR HAVE A SHORT AND WIDE SUITED BODY, OR A TALL AND THIN DRESSSED-TO-IMPRESS SHAPE? THINK OF A FAVORITE OUTFIT YOU COULD USE TO REPRESENT YOU.

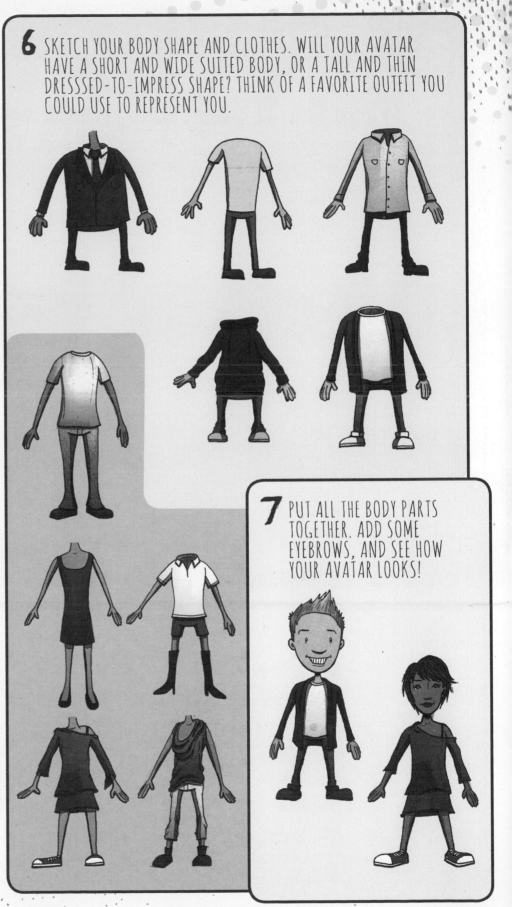

7 PUT ALL THE BODY PARTS TOGETHER. ADD SOME EYEBROWS, AND SEE HOW YOUR AVATAR LOOKS!

GLASSES

FIND OUT HOW TO DRAW DIFFERENT TYPES OF GLASSES. THEN CREATE YOUR OWN FUN STYLES!

1 FOR BASIC FRAMES, DRAW TWO LENS SHAPES. SKETCH A LINE AROUND EACH ONE FOR THE FRAMES, AND ADD A BRIDGE WHERE THE GLASSES SIT ON THE NOSE. SHOW THE ARMS THROUGH THE LENSES.

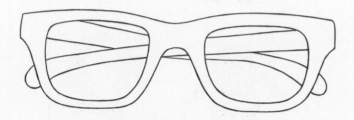

2 COLOR THE FRAMES, THEN USE A WHITE PENCIL FOR LIGHT DIAGONAL SHADING ON THE LENSES. ADD REFLECTIONS ON EACH ONE, FOLLOWING THE CURVE OF THE FRAMES FOR A 3D EFFECT.

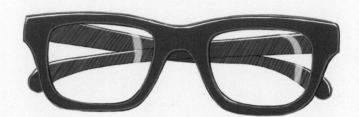

PUT THEM ON!

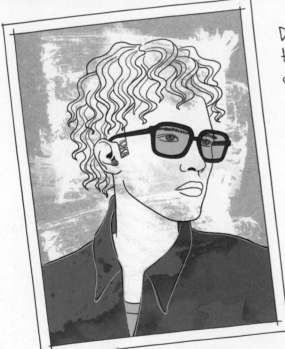

Draw a character, then add in the glasses at an angle to match the face. Lightly shade the lenses, so that the character's eyes and face are partially visible beneath.

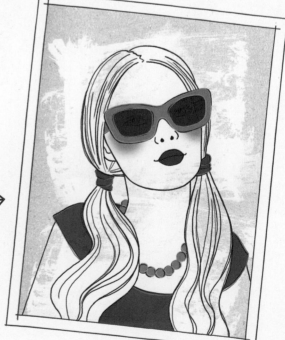

Color the frames in similar shades to the clothes and accessories worn by your character. Superstylish! Use dark lenses for sunglasses.

NOW EXPERIMENT WITH MORE COLORS, PATTERNS, AND SHAPES ...

BLOCK COLOR

DRAW SIMPLE LENS SHAPES, THEN FRAME THEM IN BRIGHT AND BOLD COLORS FOR STATEMENT STYLE.

HALF-MOON

ROUND

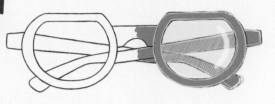

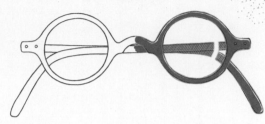

PERFECT PATTERNS

CREATE A GINGHAM PRINT WITH CRISSCROSSING LINES, OR TRY A WACKY ANIMAL PRINT MADE WITH SPOTS AND NATURAL COLORS.

MOVIE STAR

POP STAR

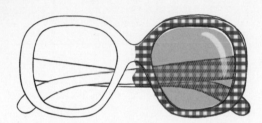

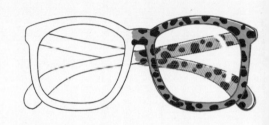

FUN SHAPES

SKETCH YOUR OWN FUN-SHAPED FRAMES. THEN USE CONTRASTING OR COMPLEMENTARY COLORS ON THE LENSES FOR STYLIN' SHADES.

HEART

STARRY

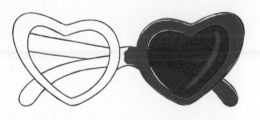

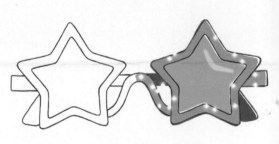

FASHION SHADES

FOR A TRENDY PAIR OF SUNGLASSES, COLOR THE LENSES IN A DARK SHADE. KEEP THE ARMS JUST VISIBLE BENEATH.

AVIATOR

DESIGNER

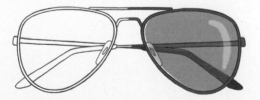

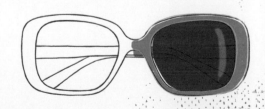

WINDMILL

1 START WITH A BASIC CONE WITH A ROUNDED-OFF TIP. USE A PENCIL AT THIS STAGE.

2 DRAW FOUR TRIANGULAR SHAPES TO MAKE THE SAILS. TRY TO DRAW THEM AS IF YOU'RE LOOKING AT THE WINDMILL FROM THE SIDE. THEN SKETCH THE UPPER SECTION OF THE BUILDING.

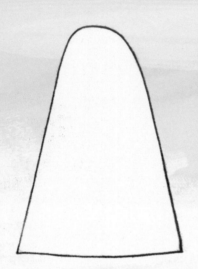

Drawing the sails from a side-on perspective will help add movement to your drawing. The ones that are farthest away from us need to look a little smaller.

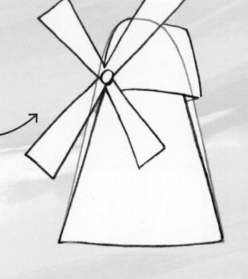

3 ADD STRAIGHT LINES TO THE SIDES OF THE WINDMILL AND TO THE SAILS.

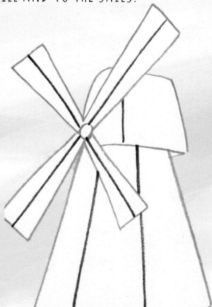

4 DRAW A BASE WITH CURVED SIDES AND RAILINGS TO ANCHOR THE BUILDING TO THE GROUND.

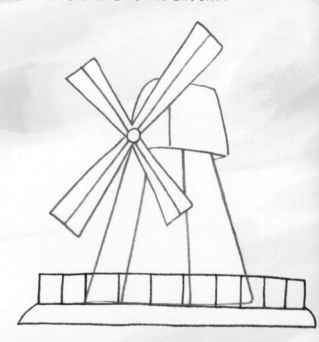

5 DRAW WINDOWS ON THE SIDES OF THE WINDMILL. ADD A COUPLE FROM A SIDE-ON PERSPECTIVE TO MAKE THE DRAWING LOOK 3D. ADD A RECTANGLE FOR THE FRONT DOOR.

Don't worry if your sails look a little uneven. This will make your windmill look man-made! Paint them in brown tones to suggest that they're made of wood.

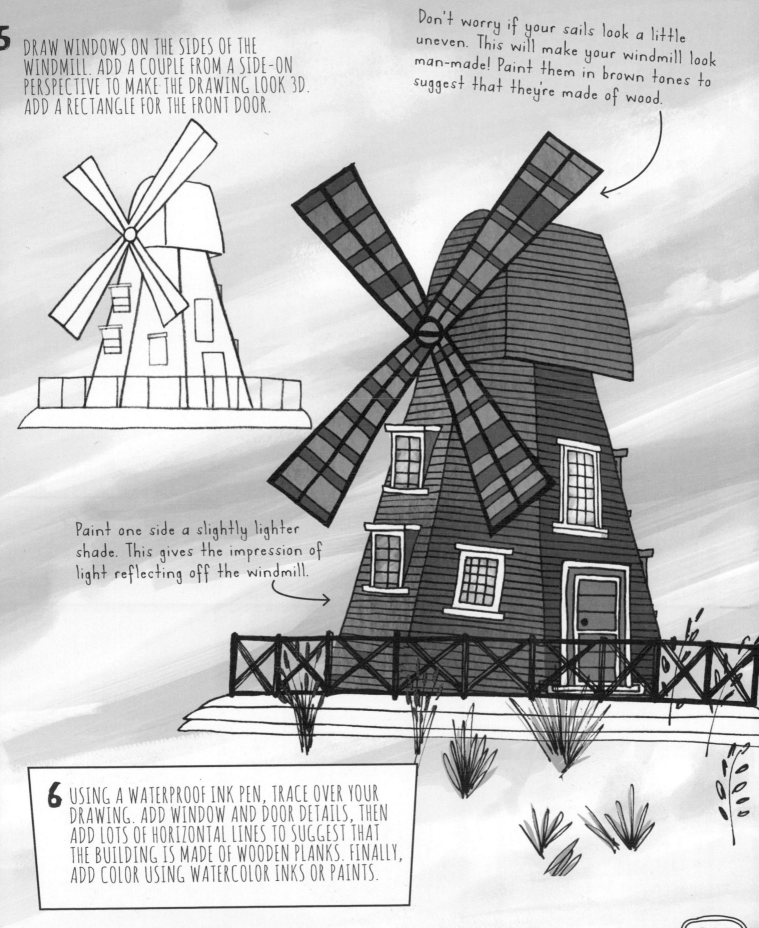

Paint one side a slightly lighter shade. This gives the impression of light reflecting off the windmill.

6 USING A WATERPROOF INK PEN, TRACE OVER YOUR DRAWING. ADD WINDOW AND DOOR DETAILS, THEN ADD LOTS OF HORIZONTAL LINES TO SUGGEST THAT THE BUILDING IS MADE OF WOODEN PLANKS. FINALLY, ADD COLOR USING WATERCOLOR INKS OR PAINTS.

EXPRESSIONS

JUST VARY FACIAL FEATURES TO CONVEY DIFFERENT EXPRESSIONS.

HAPPY

Draw the mouth with upturned corners. Make each eyelid cover the iris just a little. The happier someone is, the more their eyes narrow. Add a glint to each eye.

SAD

Sketch the mouth turned down a little. Draw the eyebrows at an angle, and make the eyes small, as if partially closed.

ANGRY

Draw the eyes wide open with the whites showing. Add pointed eyebrows above. Draw an open mouth with lots of teeth showing!

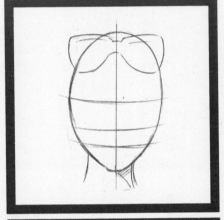
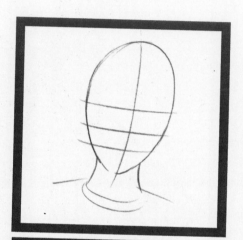
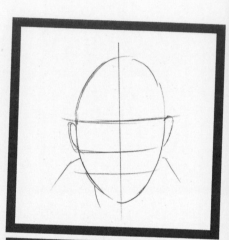

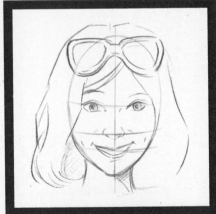
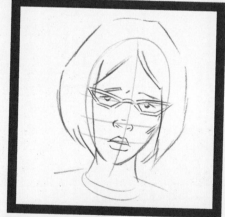
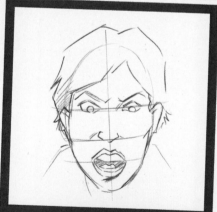

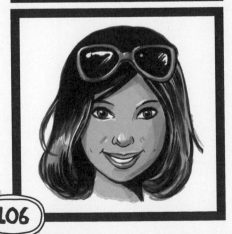
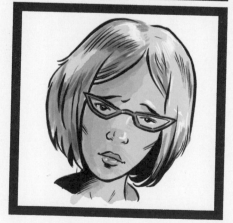
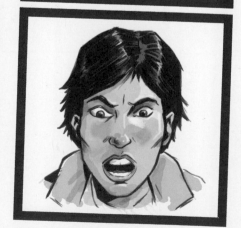

CONFUSED

Confused and worried expressions look quite similar. Draw a furrow between the eyebrows, and make the bottom lip droop a bit. The top teeth can be biting the lower lip, too.

SURPRISED

Draw big oval shapes for the eyes, showing both the irises and whites of the eyes. Raise up the eyebrows and round the mouth. Imagine someone saying "OOH"!

LAUGHING

Sketch arched eyebrows. Use curved lines for shut eyes. Draw an open mouth showing the top row of teeth. Tilt the head back a little for a hearty laugh.

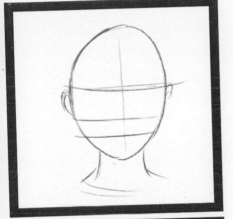

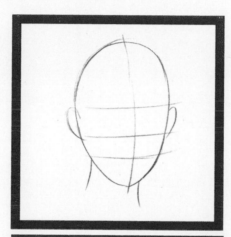

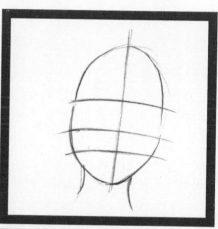

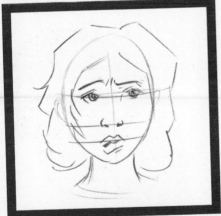

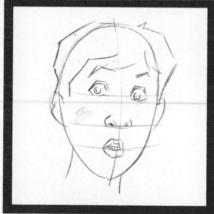

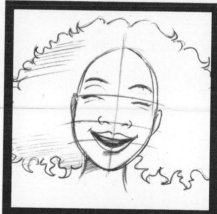

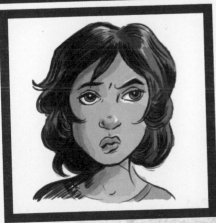

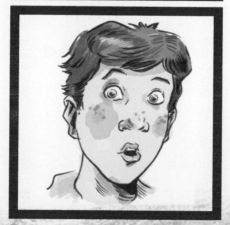

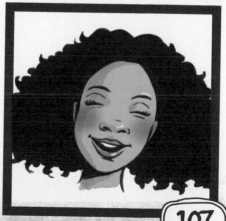

ANIMALS IN CLOTHES

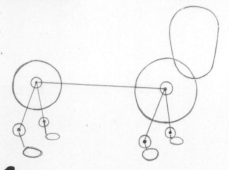

1

TO DRAW A DOG, SKETCH OVALS FOR THE HEAD AND FEET, CIRCLES FOR THE CHEST, REAR, AND JOINTS, AND LINES FOR THE BACK AND LEGS, AS SHOWN.

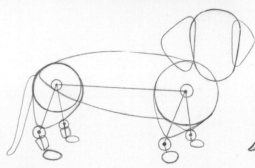

2

START OUTLINING THE DOG'S BODY SHAPE, GOING AROUND THE GUIDELINES, AS SHOWN. THEN SKETCH THE EARS AND TAIL.

3

CONNECT THE SHAPES USING A STRONGER OUTLINE TO BRING OUT THE REAL CONTOUR OF THE DOG'S BODY.

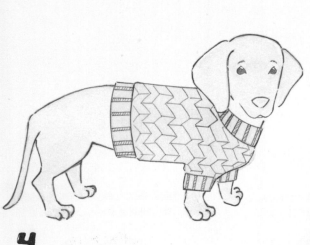

4

ERASE THE GUIDELINES, THEN DRAW THE DOG'S FACIAL FEATURES, TOES, AND CLAWS. ADD A ZIGZAG PATTERNED SWEATER.

Adding more water to your paints will give a diluted, washlike effect.

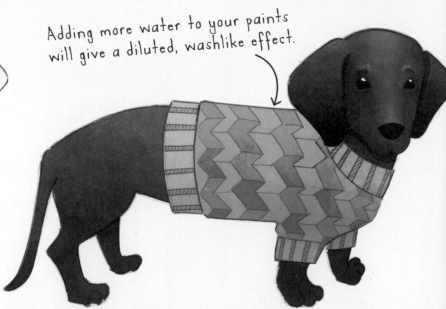

5

USE WATERCOLOR PAINTS TO COLOR THE DOG AND SWEATER. CHOOSE BRIGHT COLORS FOR THE SWEATER TO MAKE IT STAND OUT FROM THE DOG'S DARK FUR. ADD SOME LIGHT AND DARK SHADING FOR DEPTH AND TEXTURE.

GO CRAZY DRAWING OTHER ANIMALS IN FUNNY CLOTHES AND ACCESSORIES!

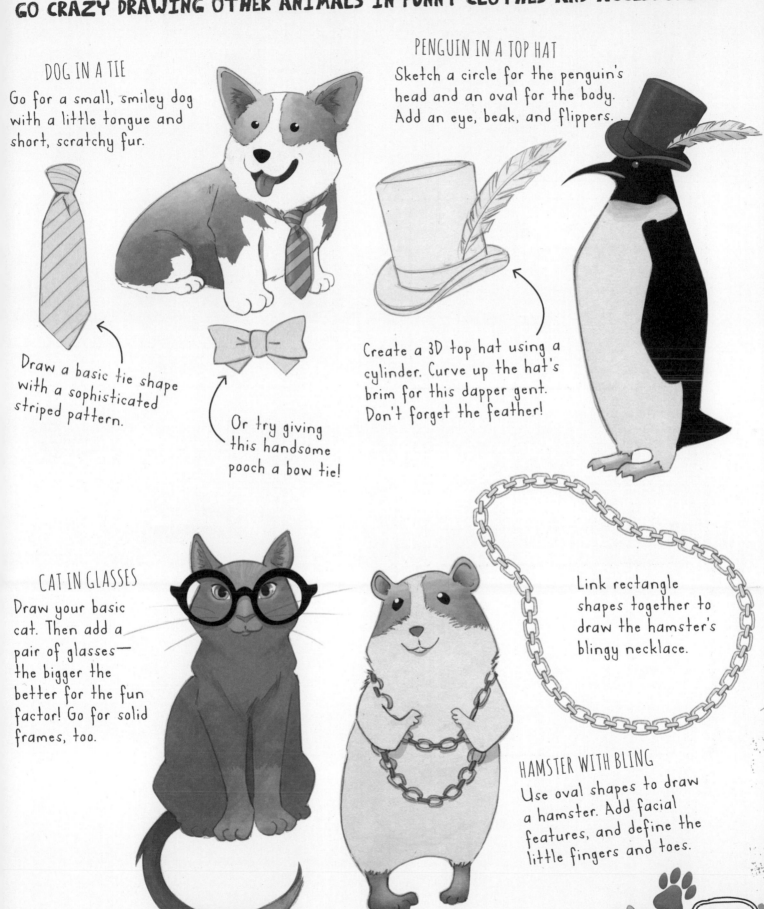

DOG IN A TIE

Go for a small, smiley dog with a little tongue and short, scratchy fur.

Draw a basic tie shape with a sophisticated striped pattern.

Or try giving this handsome pooch a bow tie!

PENGUIN IN A TOP HAT

Sketch a circle for the penguin's head and an oval for the body. Add an eye, beak, and flippers.

Create a 3D top hat using a cylinder. Curve up the hat's brim for this dapper gent. Don't forget the feather!

CAT IN GLASSES

Draw your basic cat. Then add a pair of glasses— the bigger the better for the fun factor! Go for solid frames, too.

Link rectangle shapes together to draw the hamster's blingy necklace.

HAMSTER WITH BLING

Use oval shapes to draw a hamster. Add facial features, and define the little fingers and toes.

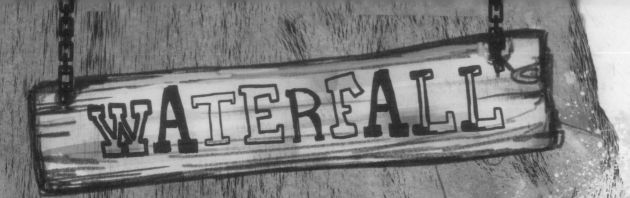

WATERFALL

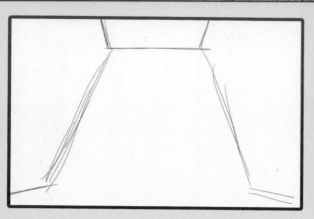

1 USE STRAIGHT LINES TO DRAW THE BASIC SHAPE OF THE WATERFALL AND SURROUNDING CLIFF FACES. THE WATERFALL LOOKS NARROWER AT THE TOP BECAUSE IT IS FARTHER AWAY FROM US.

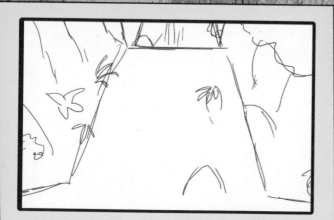

2 ADD FOLIAGE TO THE SIDES OF THE CLIFFS BY DRAWING GROUPS OF LEAF SHAPES. SKETCH A LARGE ROCK AT THE BASE OF THE WATERFALL WITH A ROUGH CURVE.

To create the effect of water spray, rub your finger along the end of your paintbrush and flick dots of white paint onto the paper.

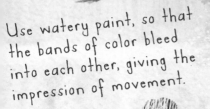

Use watery paint, so that the bands of color bleed into each other, giving the impression of movement.

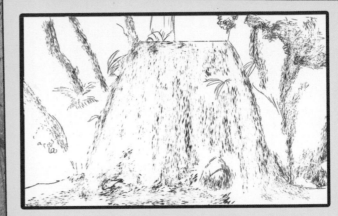

3 USING A PEN OR PENCIL, ADD SOME SURFACE DETAIL TO THE GUSHING WATER AND CLIFF FACES. KEEPING YOUR STROKES SHORT, SKETCH LOTS OF SHORT LINES.

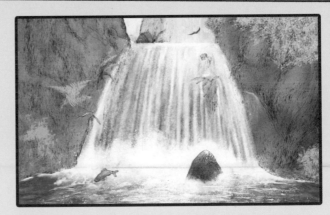

4 TO COLOR THE WATERFALL, USE A DEEP BLUE AS A BASE TONE, THEN PAINT VERTICAL BANDS OF PALER BLUES ON TOP, ALONG WITH STREAKS OF WHITE.

5 USE DIFFERENT SHADES OF BLUE FOR THE POOL AT THE BOTTOM OF THE WATERFALL. ADD HIGHLIGHTS TO THE SURFACE OF THE WATER BY PAINTING LOTS OF THIN, HORIZONTAL LINES.

HELICOPTER

1

START WITH SIMPLE SHAPES. DRAW THREE ROUNDED RECTANGLES FOR THE CABIN, A LONG TUBE WITH A TRIANGLE AT THE END FOR THE TAIL, AND AN OVAL ON TOP FOR THE ROTOR BLADES.

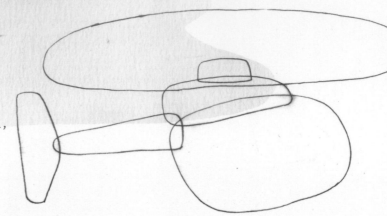

2

ADD MORE SIMPLE SHAPES TO THE TAIL AND ROTORS, AS SHOWN. DRAW ROUNDED WINDOWS AND SKETCH THE LANDING SKIDS.

3

REFINE YOUR OUTLINES, AND ERASE THE CONSTRUCTION SHAPES. ADD SMALLER DETAILS, SUCH AS AN OVAL FOR THE TAIL ROTOR AND SMALL CIRCLES FOR THE LIGHTS.

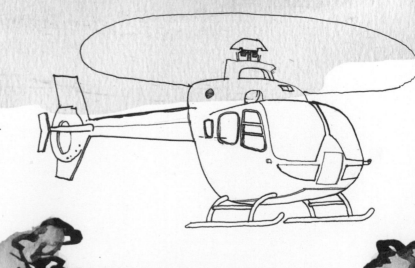

4

TRACE OVER YOUR DRAWING IN BLACK INK. USE WAVY LINES TO CREATE THE IMPRESSION OF FAST, SPINNING BLADES. ADD REFLECTIONS TO THE WINDOWS USING MORE WAVY LINES.

Enhance the sense of movement by coloring the wavy rotor lines in a bluey-gray shade.

5

PAINT THE HELICOPTER IN A BRIGHT COLOR. USE A BLUE WASH FOR THE WINDOWS, AS IF THEY'RE REFLECTING THE SKY. PICK OUT THE WAVY REFLECTIONS IN A LIGHTER TONE.

Draw lots of gentle curves to create a simple landscape below. Color with patches of yellow and green watercolors.

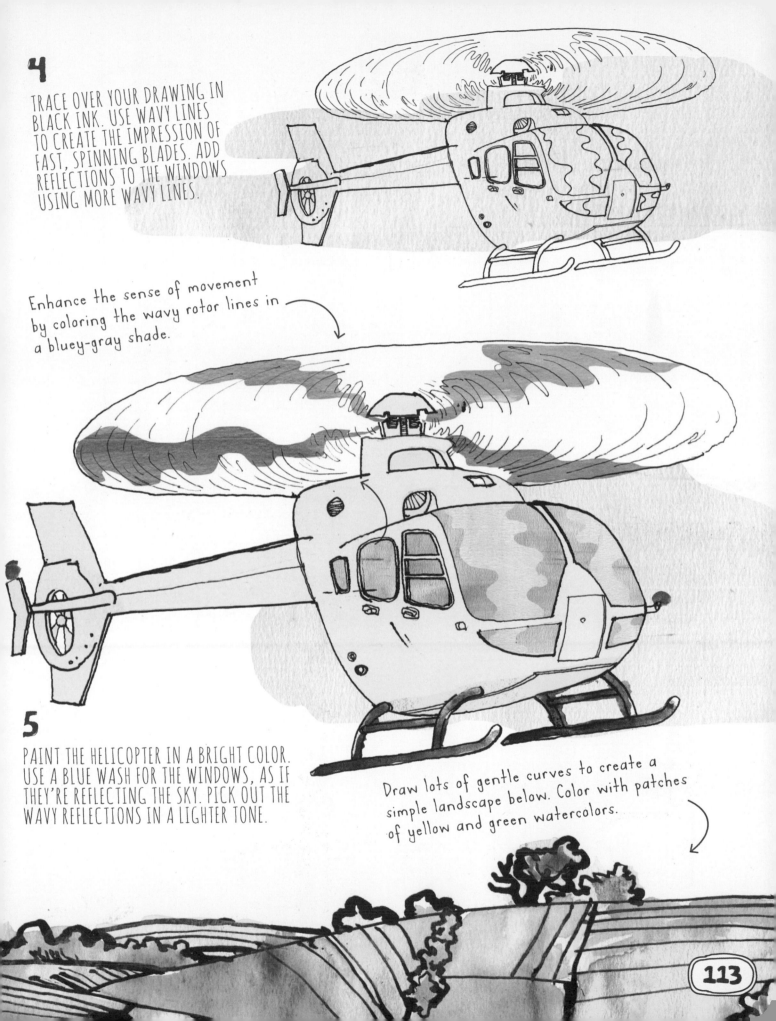

KEYS

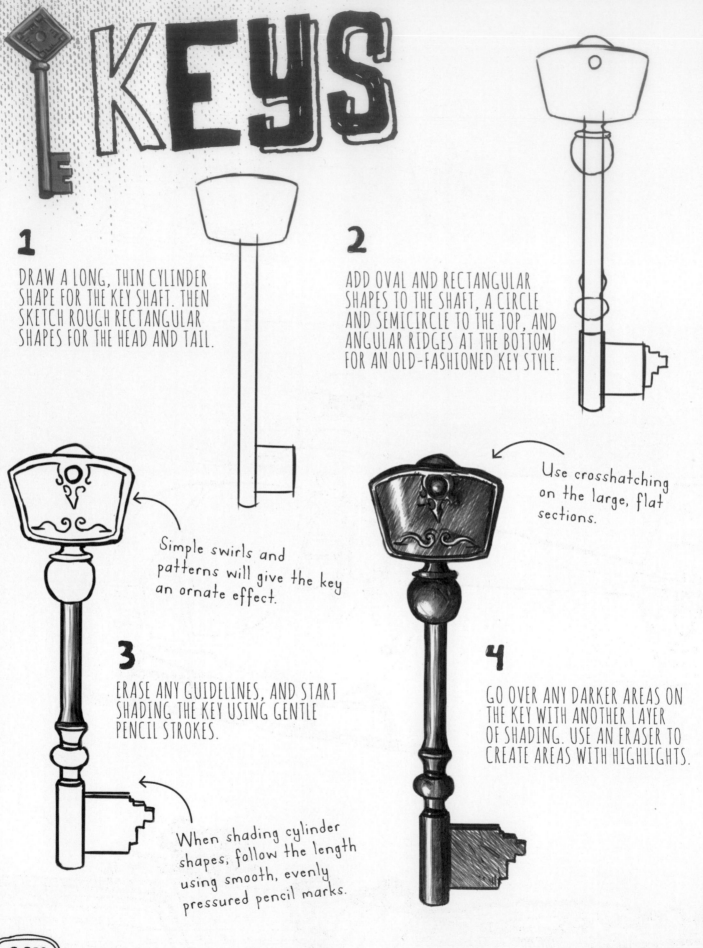

1
DRAW A LONG, THIN CYLINDER SHAPE FOR THE KEY SHAFT. THEN SKETCH ROUGH RECTANGULAR SHAPES FOR THE HEAD AND TAIL.

2
ADD OVAL AND RECTANGULAR SHAPES TO THE SHAFT, A CIRCLE AND SEMICIRCLE TO THE TOP, AND ANGULAR RIDGES AT THE BOTTOM FOR AN OLD-FASHIONED KEY STYLE.

Use crosshatching on the large, flat sections.

Simple swirls and patterns will give the key an ornate effect.

3
ERASE ANY GUIDELINES, AND START SHADING THE KEY USING GENTLE PENCIL STROKES.

When shading cylinder shapes, follow the length using smooth, evenly pressured pencil marks.

4
GO OVER ANY DARKER AREAS ON THE KEY WITH ANOTHER LAYER OF SHADING. USE AN ERASER TO CREATE AREAS WITH HIGHLIGHTS.

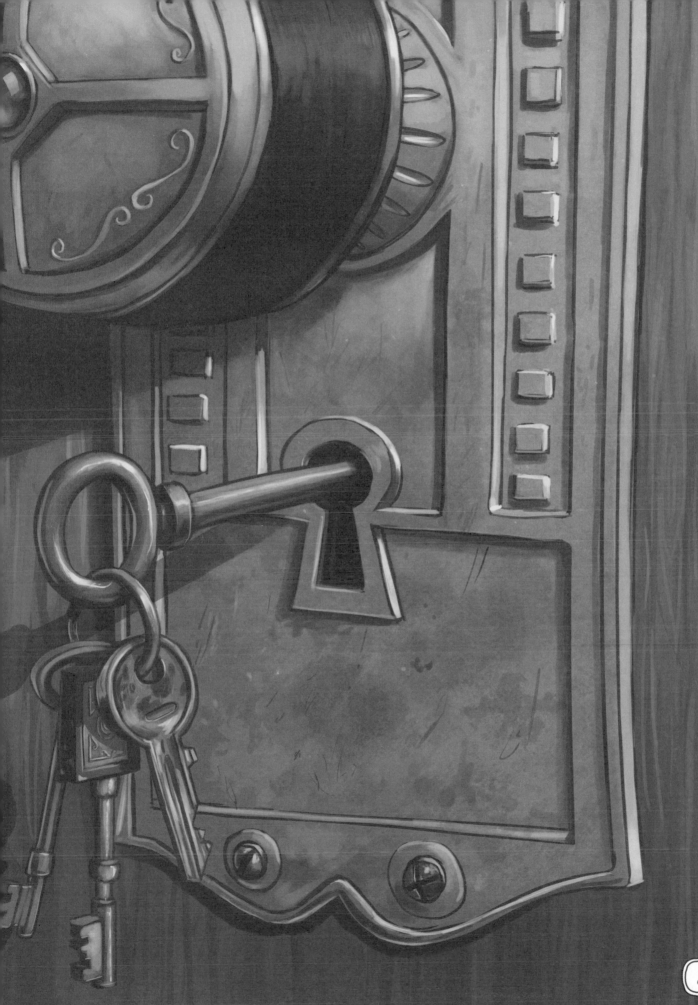

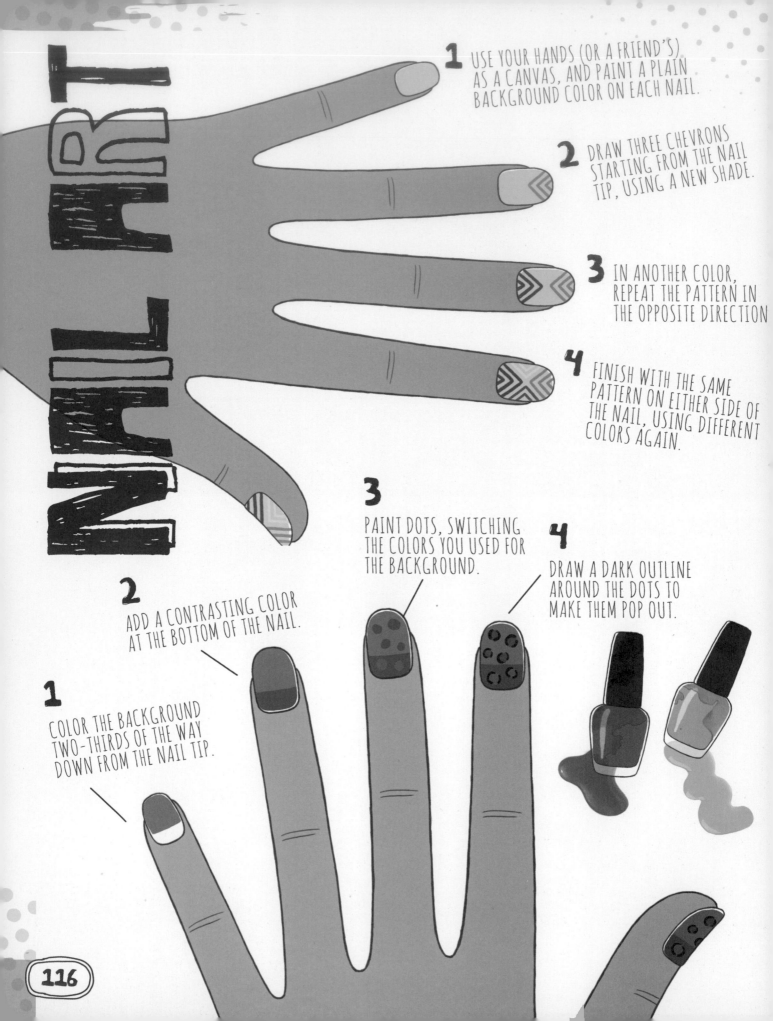

NAIL ART

1 USE YOUR HANDS (OR A FRIEND'S) AS A CANVAS, AND PAINT A PLAIN BACKGROUND COLOR ON EACH NAIL.

2 DRAW THREE CHEVRONS STARTING FROM THE NAIL TIP, USING A NEW SHADE.

3 IN ANOTHER COLOR, REPEAT THE PATTERN IN THE OPPOSITE DIRECTION

4 FINISH WITH THE SAME PATTERN ON EITHER SIDE OF THE NAIL, USING DIFFERENT COLORS AGAIN.

3 PAINT DOTS, SWITCHING THE COLORS YOU USED FOR THE BACKGROUND.

4 DRAW A DARK OUTLINE AROUND THE DOTS TO MAKE THEM POP OUT.

2 ADD A CONTRASTING COLOR AT THE BOTTOM OF THE NAIL.

1 COLOR THE BACKGROUND TWO-THIRDS OF THE WAY DOWN FROM THE NAIL TIP.

1 COLOR THE NAIL IN A LIGHT SHADE.

2 PAINT TWO THIN TRIANGLES ON EITHER SIDE OF THE NAIL IN BLACK, AS SHOWN.

3 PAINT A TINY BOW TIE NEAR THE CUTICLE.

4 ADD TWO BLACK DOTS FOR BUTTONS DOWN THE CENTER OF THE NAIL TO FINISH A TUXEDO PATTERN.

CREATE MORE NAIL PATTERNS USING SIMPLE SHAPES ...

HEARTS AND SPOTS
Decorate a simple heart shape with tiny spots in and around the heart.

ZIGZAGS
Experiment with thick and thin zigzags for a lively-looking pattern.

STARS
Try painting glitzy stars in a variety of sizes and colors.

DOTS
Overlapping dots in different colors and shades create a pretty confetti-like appearance.

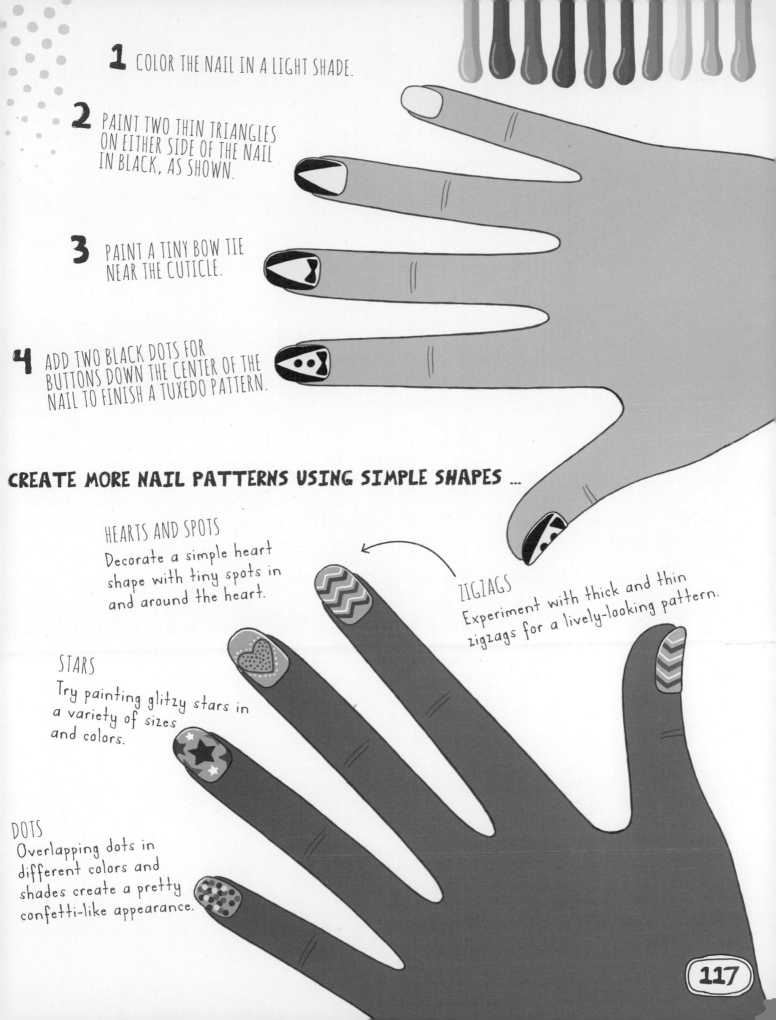

BIPLANE

1 DRAW A LONG, BREADLIKE SHAPE, WITH A CURVE AT THE BOTTOM. TAPER OFF THE ENDS, THEN ADD TWO ROUNDED LINES IN THE CENTER AND ANOTHER AT THE FRONT, LIKE THIS.

2 SKETCH AN OVAL SHAPE FOR THE VERTICAL TAIL AT THE BACK OF THE PLANE. ADD ROUNDED RECTANGLES FOR THE WINGS AND HORIZONTAL TAIL. DRAW A CIRCLE FOR THE PROPELLER AT THE FRONT AND MORE LINES ON THE BODY.

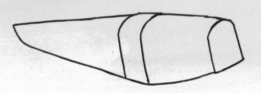

3 FOR THE WING SUPPORTS AND PROPELLER BLADES, DRAW LONG RECTANGLE SHAPES. SKETCH OVAL-SHAPED WHEELS, THEN ADD THE ENGINE COMPONENTS, USING OVALS AND RECTANGLES, ONTO THE BIPLANE'S BODY.

4 FILL IN MORE DETAIL USING STRAIGHT LINES, CIRCLES, AND RECTANGLES, AS SHOWN. CREATE A PILOT USING AN OVAL FOR THE HEAD AND CURVED LINES FOR THE SHOULDERS.

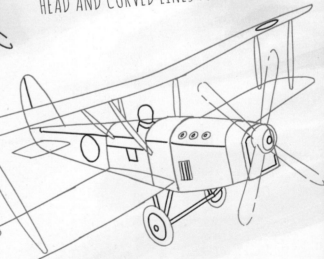

5

ADD STRAIGHT LINES ON THE WINGS AND TAIL. SKETCH CURVED LINES BEHIND THE PILOT FOR THE COCKPIT AND AROUND THE PROPELLER TO SUGGEST MOTION. GIVE YOUR PILOT SOME GOGGLES, A HELMET, AND A FLOWING SCARF.

Create bull's-eye markings using circles and ovals.

To make the wings look more 3D, add a thin, dark shadow along the bottom.

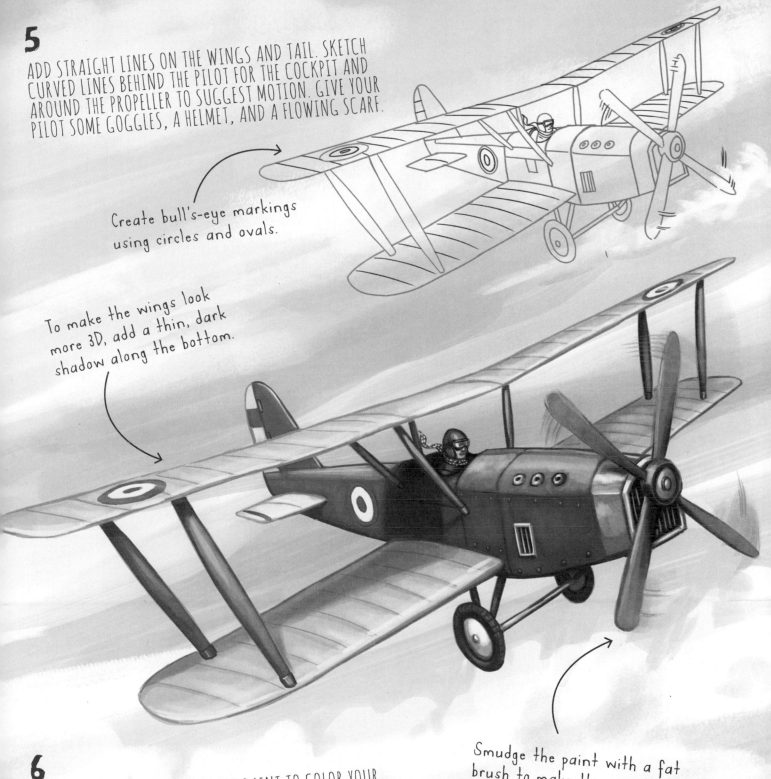

6

USE OPAQUE (THICK) OR ACRYLIC PAINT TO COLOR YOUR DRAWING. ADD LIGHT AND DARK SHADING ON THE AIRCRAFT AND PILOT. FINISH WITH A SPOTTED SCARF FOR THE PILOT AND A STRIPY PATTERN ON THE HORIZONTAL AND VERTICAL TAILS FOR CHARACTER.

Smudge the paint with a fat brush to make the propeller look like it's spinning fast.

SPRING

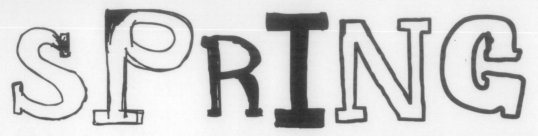

CREATE A SUNNY SPRINGTIME PARK SCENE, FULL OF LOOSE PENCIL AND PAINT STROKES FOR A LIGHT FEEL.

Draw a stick figure, then flesh it out. If you're stuck for ideas, leaf through fashion magazines for inspiration!

For tree blossom, sketch groups of five leaves. When you paint the leaves, use rough splotches of color. To get the texture of tree bark, use a pencil to make short, sketchy strokes.

Use lots of short, delicate pencil marks to create a feathery texture on birds.

Use both light and heavy shading to give your sketch character and depth. Draw random, wiggly lines on the skirt for a cool, light print.

Draw daffodils with six petals. From the side, the middle part looks trumpet shaped.

Draw some blossoms on the ground, as if they have just fallen from the trees. Try drawing the flowers at different angles and add some random leaves as well.

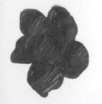

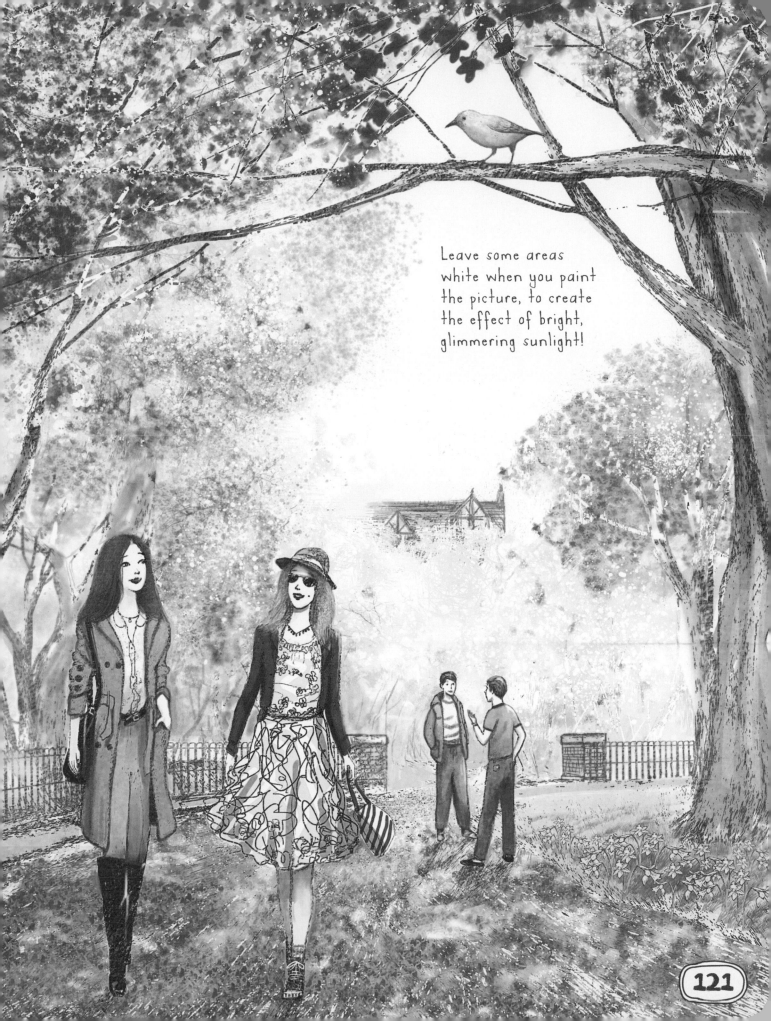

Leave some areas white when you paint the picture, to create the effect of bright, glimmering sunlight!

SUMMER

NOTHING SAYS SUMMER MORE THAN SANDY BEACHES, BRIGHT GREEN LEAVES, AND CLEAR, SUNNY SKIES!

Sketch the sun shape with a light pencil, using a ruler to draw the shapes of the sunbeams. If you place the sun high in the sky, the shadows it casts will look short and it will feel like supersunny noon.

Paint the leaves on the trees in light shades of green. Use a pale yellow around the edges of the treetops to show the sun's highlights.

Sketch a figure wearing a light summer outfit. Add movement where you can—you could draw hair blowing in the breeze, a flowing skirt, or a puppy pulling on its leash!

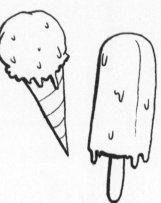

Give some of your figures tasty ice-cream cone or ba Draw your outlines with "U" shapes at the bottom to give the impression they're melting in the heat

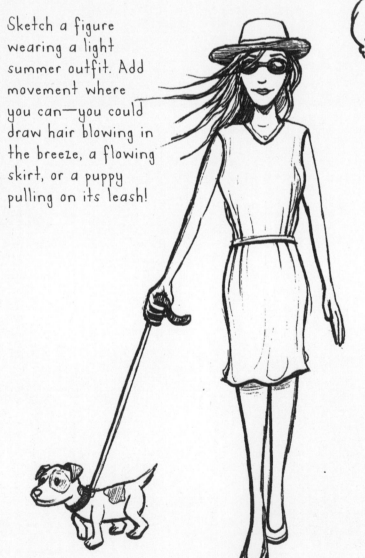

To draw someone on a bike, it's easiest to sketch the bike frame and wheels first. Then add someone riding it.

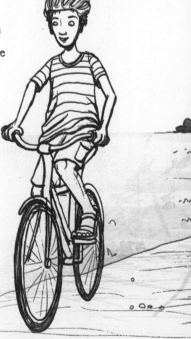

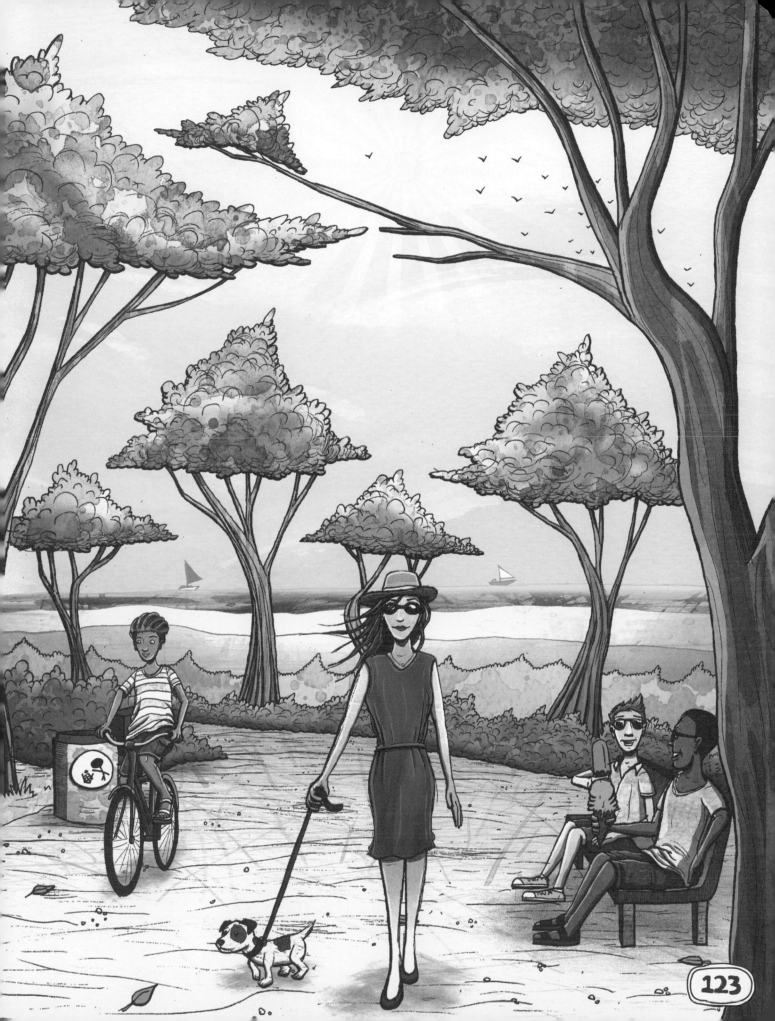

FALL

USE LOTS OF BROWNS, YELLOWS, AND ORANGES TO CREATE THE FEEL OF A FALL SCENE.

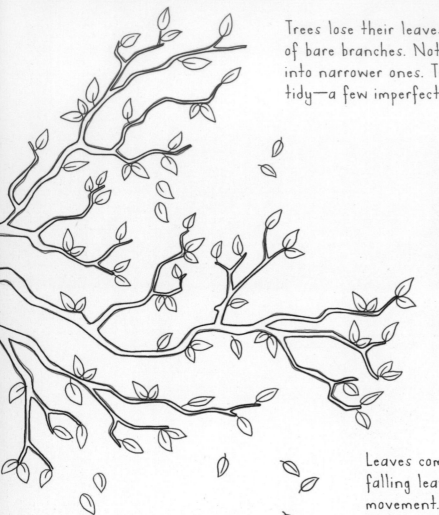

Trees lose their leaves in the fall, so sketch them with lots of bare branches. Notice how the branches themselves split into narrower ones. Try not to make your tree too neat and tidy—a few imperfections make it look more natural!

In your picture, scatter a few fallen acorns on the ground. The upper part of an acorn is dome-shaped, with a rounded section underneath. Create texture with lots of tiny curves.

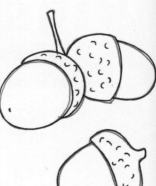

Leaves come in all kinds of shapes and sizes! Add falling leaves to your picture to create a sense of movement. Color the treetops with areas of orange and brown, then add lots of blobs in earthy tones to represent the hundreds of leaves.

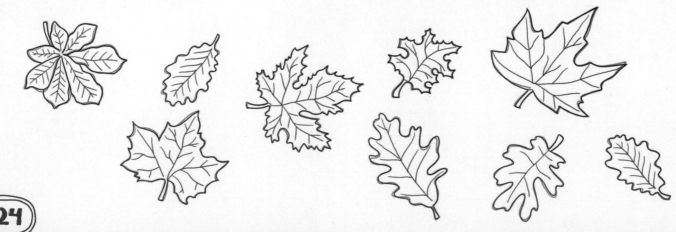

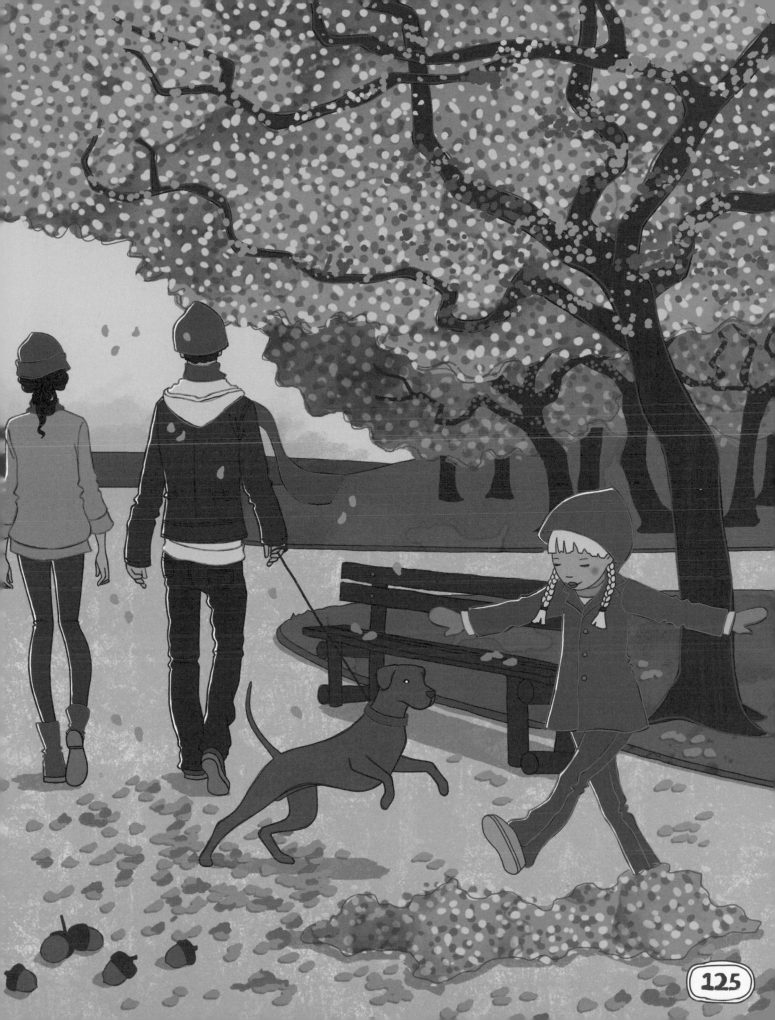

WINTER

IT'S EASY TO SET A WINTER SCENE—LANDSCAPES SUDDENLY LOOK
DIFFERENT WHEN THEY'RE COVERED IN SNOW AND ICICLES!

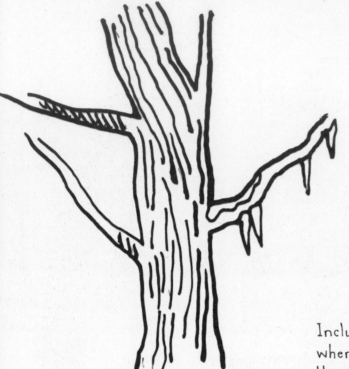

Sketch the basic shape of
a snowman by drawing
three different-sized
circles on top of each
other. Create character
by adding tiny details.

Draw trees using long, wavy
lines for the bare branches.
Add vertical wavy lines for
bark. For hanging icicles,
draw sharp "V" shapes.

Include action poses
when you can in scenes.
Here, sketch someone
with his weight on his
back foot and his arm
up, ready to throw a
snowball!

Use a few simple wavy lines here and
there to give the impression of mounds
of snow. Add watery blue washes near
the figures to create subtle shadows. Give
yellow glows around lights to stand out
against the wintery blue sky.

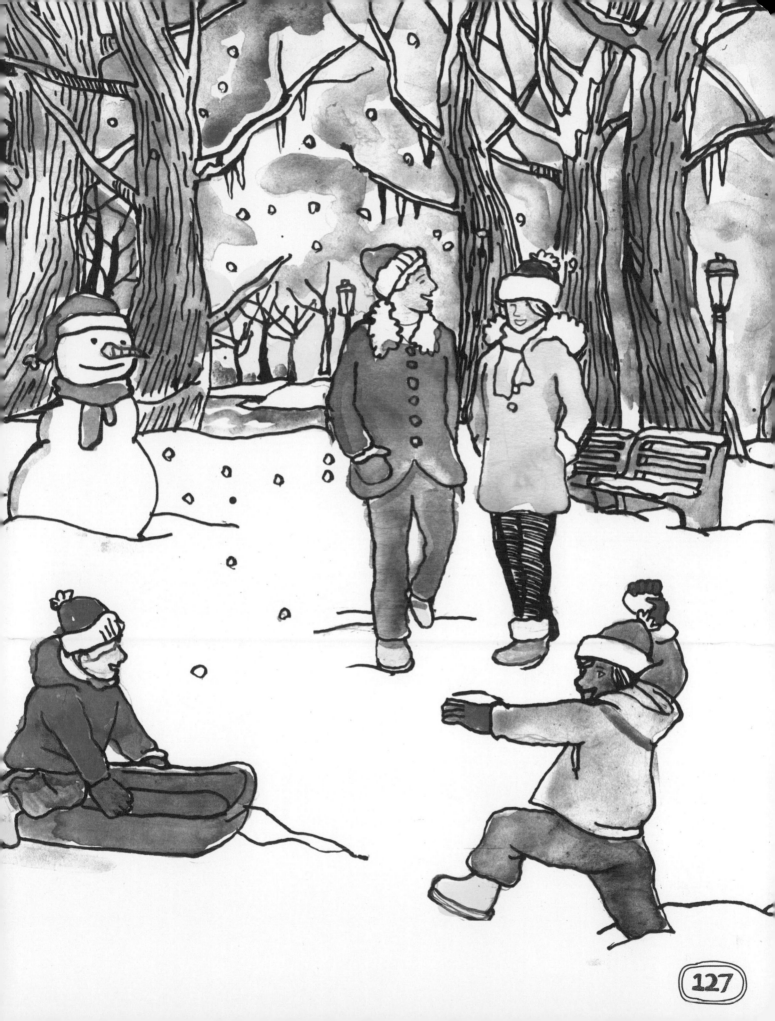

CHAISE LONGUE

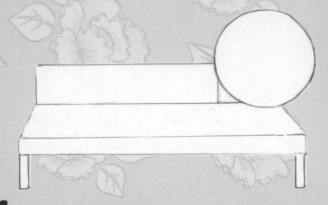

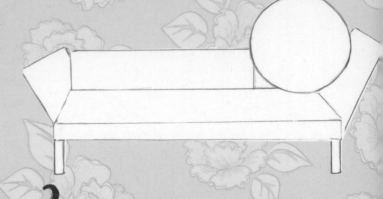

1

DRAW A CIRCLE FOR THE UPPER BACK OF THE CHAISE AND RECTANGLES FOR THE SEAT, LOWER BACK, AND LEGS.

2

ADD TWO ROUGH GUIDES FOR ARMRESTS ON EITHER END OF THE SEAT, AS SHOWN.

Keep the line work soft and fluid to give the chair a luxurious appearance.

Use curved, swirly lines on the legs and framework to suggest carved wood, and straight lines for stitching and creases.

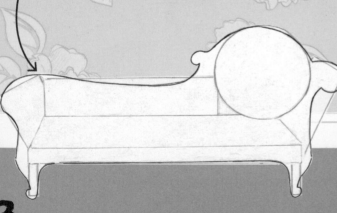

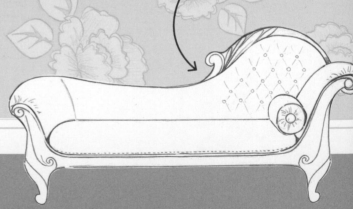

3

CONNECT THE SHAPES WITH A SMOOTH, STRONGER OUTLINE, ADDING CURVES AROUND THE EDGES AND TWO ROUNDED FEET.

4

ERASE THE GUIDELINES, AND START ADDING IN MORE DETAIL, SUCH AS THE CUSHION AND DECORATIVE ELEMENTS.

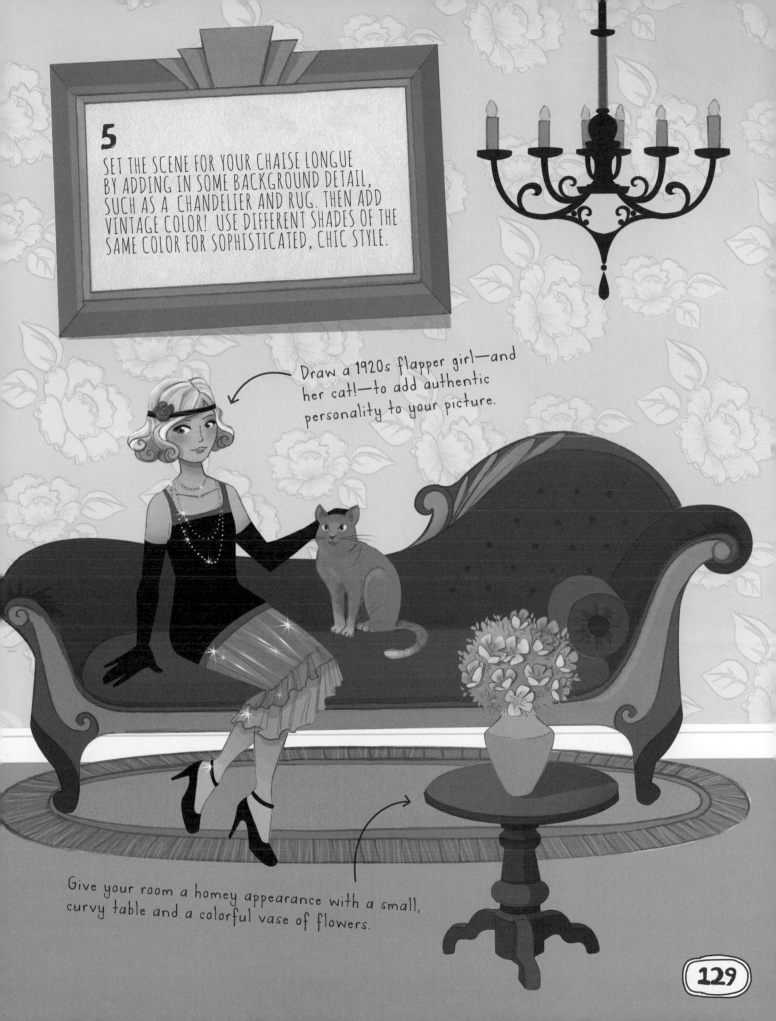

5
SET THE SCENE FOR YOUR CHAISE LONGUE BY ADDING IN SOME BACKGROUND DETAIL, SUCH AS A CHANDELIER AND RUG. THEN ADD VINTAGE COLOR! USE DIFFERENT SHADES OF THE SAME COLOR FOR SOPHISTICATED, CHIC STYLE.

Draw a 1920s flapper girl—and her cat!—to add authentic personality to your picture.

Give your room a homey appearance with a small, curvy table and a colorful vase of flowers.

ALIENS

TRY DRAWING DIFFERENT TYPES OF BODY PARTS TO CREATE ALL KINDS OF BIZARRE ALIEN BEINGS. JUST USE YOUR IMAGINATION!

BODY

1

GET SOME IDEAS BY LOOKING AT THE BODY SHAPES OF HUMANS AND UNUSUAL ANIMALS. EVEN PLANTS CAN GIVE YOU INSPIRATION!

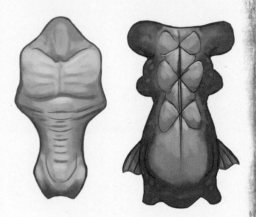

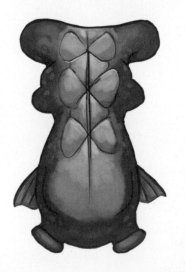

LEGS

2

DESIGN THE LEGS. A LARGE ALIEN MIGHT HAVE SHORTER, FATTER LEGS, WHILE A MORE ATHLETIC CREATURE COULD HAVE LONG, SPINDLY ONES.

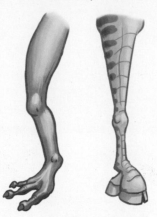

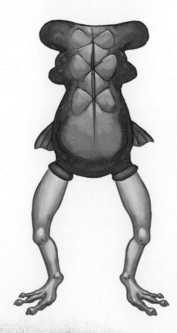

ARMS

3

IT'S EASY TO DRAW ODD-LOOKING LIMBS. FOR EXAMPLE, YOU COULD DRAW A CRAB'S CLAW ATTACHED TO A FROG'S ARM. IT'S UP TO YOU!

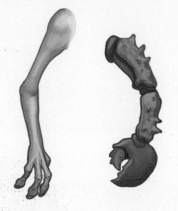

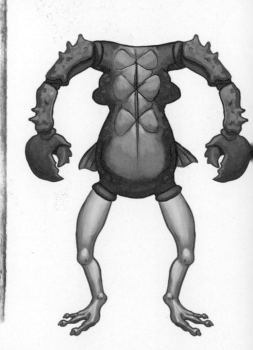

HEADS

4

THE SHAPE OF YOUR ALIEN'S HEAD AFFECTS HOW AGGRESSIVE OR SMART IT LOOKS. A BIG SKULL SUGGESTS A BIG BRAIN. A BIG JAW SUGGESTS FIERCENESS!

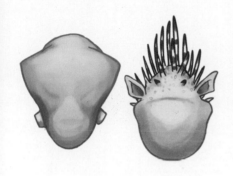

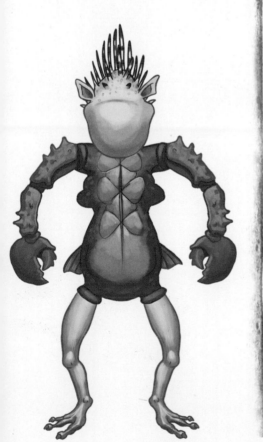

MOUTHS

5

MOUTH SHAPES ALSO AFFECT YOUR CREATURE'S PERCEPTION. BIG LIPS AND FUNNY TEETH LOOK HARMLESS AND SILLY, WHEREAS HUGE, SPIKY FANGS LOOK REALLY SCARY!

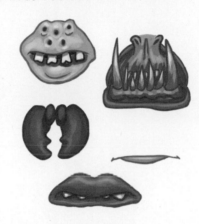

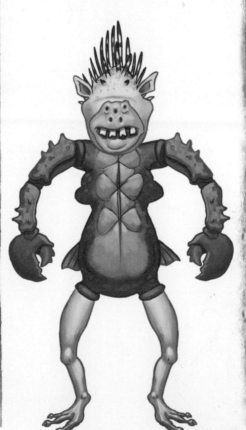

EYES

6

GIVE YOUR ALIEN AS MANY EYES AS YOU LIKE. BIG EYES WILL MAKE IT LOOK CUTER AND MORE CHILDLIKE. SMALLER OR NARROWED EYES WILL MAKE IT LOOK MEAN AND ANGRY.

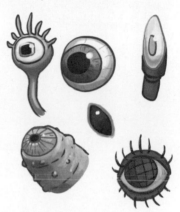

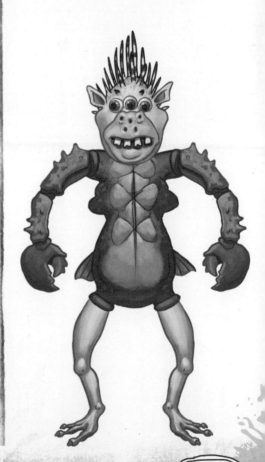

URBAN ART

COMBINE SIMPLE SHAPES AND EXCITING PAINT EFFECTS TO CREATE YOUR OWN URBAN ART.

STENCILS

Cut out a shape, lay it onto some paper, then flick ink or paint all over it. Remove the stencil to reveal the shape underneath!

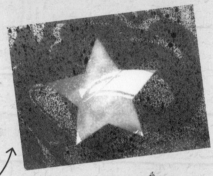

Experiment with different paint techniques, such as splashing or spraying within the stencil.

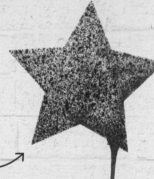

STIPPLING

Load a bristle brush with paint, and flick it onto some paper. Practice to figure out how much water to use—too much will make the splats too big.

Or, spread some paint thinly on a plate. Dip a sponge into it, then dab the sponge onto paper.

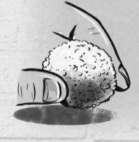

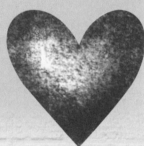

COLOR SHADING

Create a cool color gradient by bleeding one watercolor tone into another. Wet the paper first.

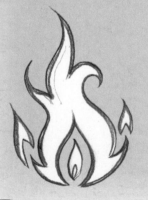

3D SHAPES

Make a star look 3D by sketching curves trailing away from it, gradually becoming closer together.

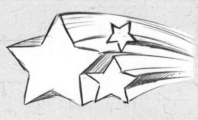

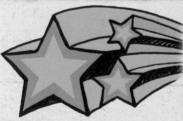

To add to the 3D effect, think about where the light source is, then add areas of shadow in solid black.

CREATING URBAN ART

Practice drawing simple shapes on their own. Use hearts, flames, wings—whatever you like! Give them thick outlines so they stand out.

3D HEART

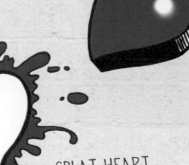

WING

TWISTED ROPE

SPLAT HEART

Then bring all your shapes together to create an amazing piece of artwork with lots of overlapping layers. Use different paint techniques to create a riot of color and a real sense of movement!

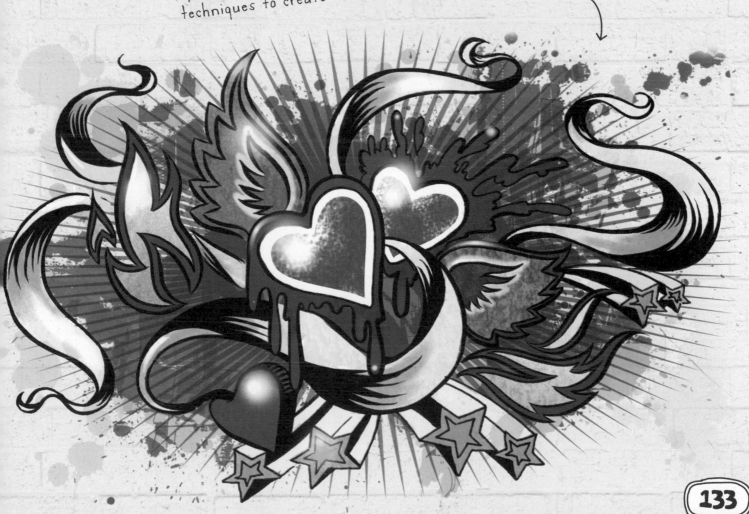

DOORS AND WINDOWS

YOU CAN USE ALL KINDS OF SHAPES AND PATTERNS TO DRAW ORNATE DOORS AND WINDOWS. HAVE FUN!

HOUSE FRONT DOORS

First, decide the basic shape of your door. Draw rectangles for the door itself, plus any panels or door posts. Then add details such as arches, handles, and ornamental decoration.

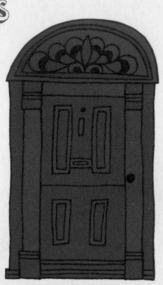
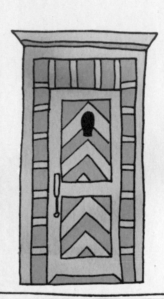
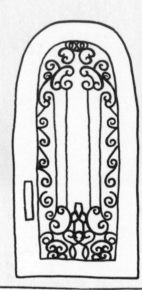

OTHER DOORS

Try drawing other types of doors. A castle entrance could have a simple arch shape, while a temple door could look more unusual. Some doors look very plain, while others can have beautiful markings.

CASTLE DOOR

TEMPLE DOOR

STABLE DOOR

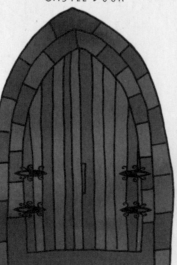
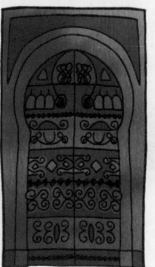
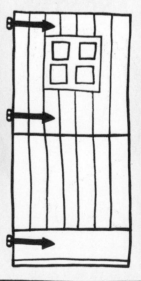

WINDOW SHAPES

Build up the shapes of windows using rectangles, squares, and curves. To make the glass look reflective, first paint it light gray, then wash away bands of color with a clean brush.

RECTANGULAR

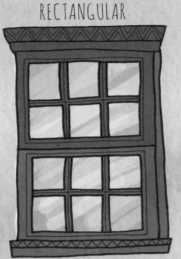

ROUNDED

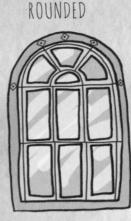

PATTERNED

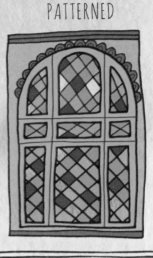

WINDOW FRAMES

Window frames can look more interesting than the actual windows! Use curls, swirls, and other patterns to give your windows beautifully decorated borders.

DECORATIVE WINDOW

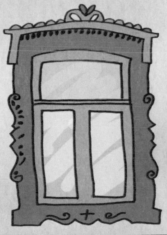

CHURCH WINDOW

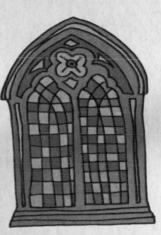

WROUGHT IRON

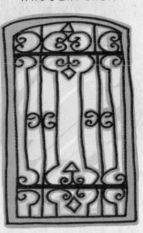

STAINED GLASS

Stained-glass windows have amazing multicolored patterns. Paint them using watercolors, as if the sunlight is shining through.

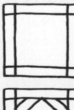

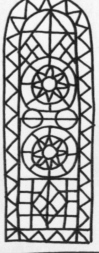
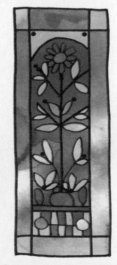
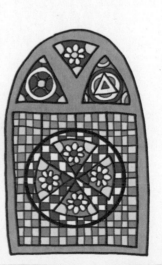

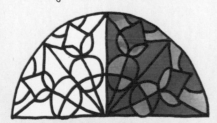

SKELETON

1

SKETCH AN OVAL FOR THE HEAD, CIRCLES FOR THE SHOULDERS, ELBOWS, AND KNEES, AND LINES FOR THE BASIC BODY FRAME.

2

ADD GUIDELINES, TRIANGLES, AND CIRCLES, READY TO POSITION THE EYES, NOSE, MOUTH, RIB CAGE, AND PELVIS, AS SHOWN.

3

USING THE SHAPES AND GUIDELINES, DRAW THE OUTLINE OF THE SKELETON. ADD CYLINDER SHAPES FOR THE HANDS AND FEET.

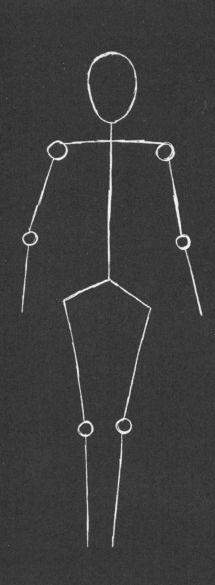
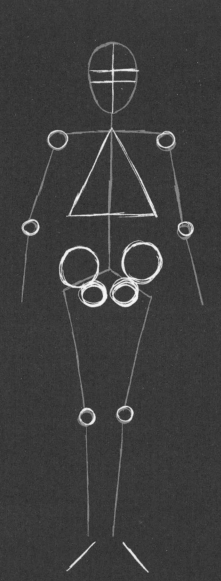
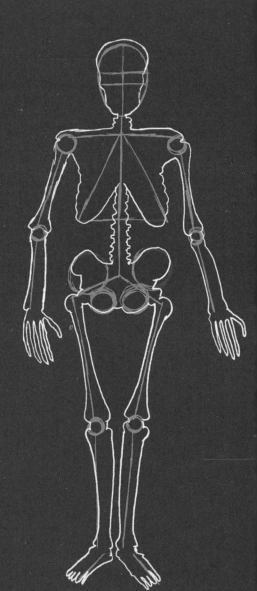

4

NOW SKETCH IN ALL THE BONE SHAPES, USING OVALS, RECTANGLES, TRIANGLES, AND CURVED LINES, LIKE THIS.

For the rib cage, draw the central bone first, then add the ribs one side at a time.

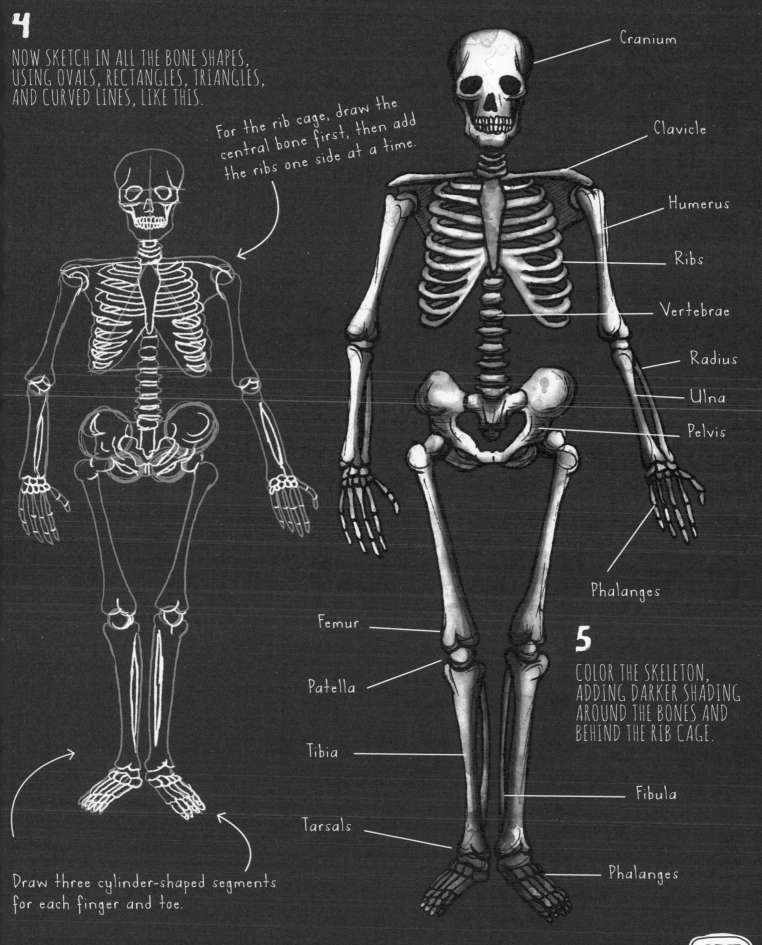

Cranium

Clavicle

Humerus

Ribs

Vertebrae

Radius

Ulna

Pelvis

Phalanges

Femur

Patella

Tibia

Tarsals

5

COLOR THE SKELETON, ADDING DARKER SHADING AROUND THE BONES AND BEHIND THE RIB CAGE.

Fibula

Phalanges

Draw three cylinder-shaped segments for each finger and toe.

CAMOUFLAGE PATTERNS

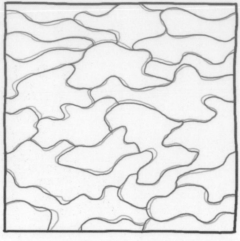

COMBAT STYLE

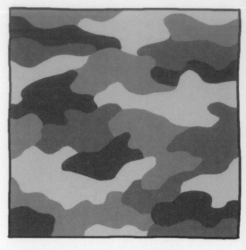

DRAW LOTS OF INTERLOCKING SHAPES AS SHOWN. COLOR WITH DIFFERENT SHADES OF GREEN AND BROWN.

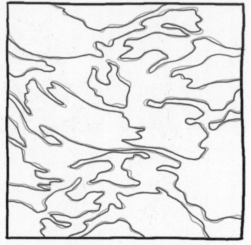

DESERT STYLE

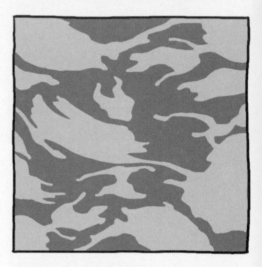

SKETCH MORE COMPLICATED SHAPES, BUT USE A SIMPLE TWO-TONE COLOR SCHEME, SUCH AS BEIGE AND KHAKI.

EXPERIMENT WITH DIFFERENT SHAPES AND COLORS TO CREATE THESE COOL CAMO DESIGNS!

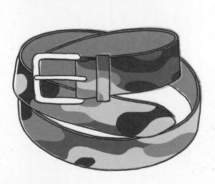

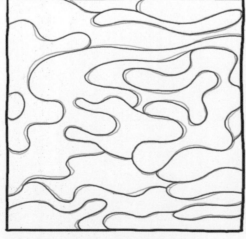

NAVY STYLE

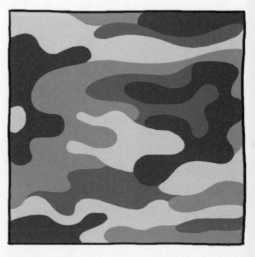

CREATE THE EFFECT OF RIPPLING WATER USING FOUR CONTRASTING BLUE TONES

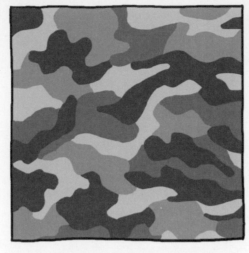

EXPERIMENT WITH DIFFERENT DESIGNS. THIS PATTERN USES A LOT OF SMALLER, LONGER, INTERLOCKING SHAPES.

CREATE A JUNGLE-STYLE CAMOUFLAGE BY COLORING YOUR PATTERN WITH FOUR DIFFERENT SHADES OF GREEN.

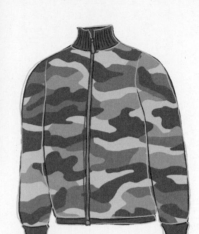

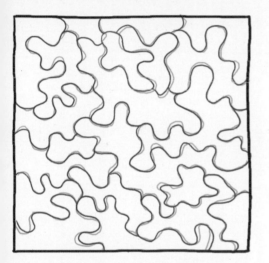

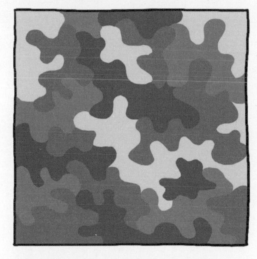

USE HOOPS AND LOOPS TO CREATE SHAPES THAT LOOK MORE ROUNDED— AND MORE FUN!

YOU DON'T ALWAYS HAVE TO USE EARTHY TONES. BRIGHT AND BOLD COLORS CAN WORK REALLY WELL, TOO.

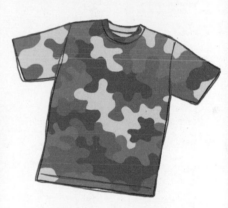

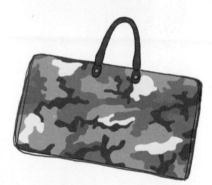

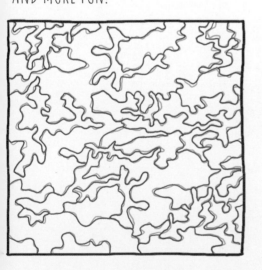

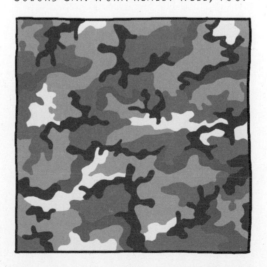

USE NATURE AS INSPIRATION. EVEN SEAWEED SHAPES WORK WELL!

USE VARYING NEUTRAL TONES WITH A SINGLE ACCENT COLOR FOR IMPACT.

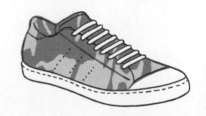

SPACE SHUTTLE

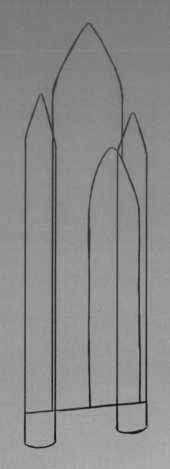

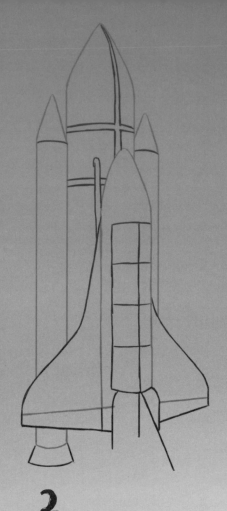

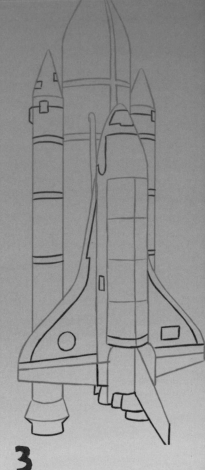

1

DRAW A TALL CYLINDER SHAPE WITH A POINTED TIP. ADD TWO SIMILAR, BUT THINNER, SHAPES ON EITHER SIDE, THEN A THIRD, SHORTER SIMILAR SHAPE IN FRONT.

2

DRAW THE OUTLINE OF THE SPACE SHUTTLE, AND ADD ITS CURVED DOORS. DRAW CURVES ON THE TWO BOOSTERS AND FUEL TANK TO MAKE THEM LOOK MORE 3D.

3

DRAW EXTRA CURVED BANDS ON THE ROCKET BOOSTERS, PLUS OTHER DETAILS AT THE TOP. ADD MORE LINES ON THE WINGS, FOLLOWING THE CURVED SHAPE OF EACH ONE.

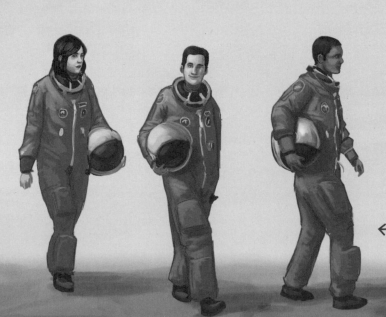

Don't forget to add astronauts in spacesuits, walking toward their shuttle and mission!

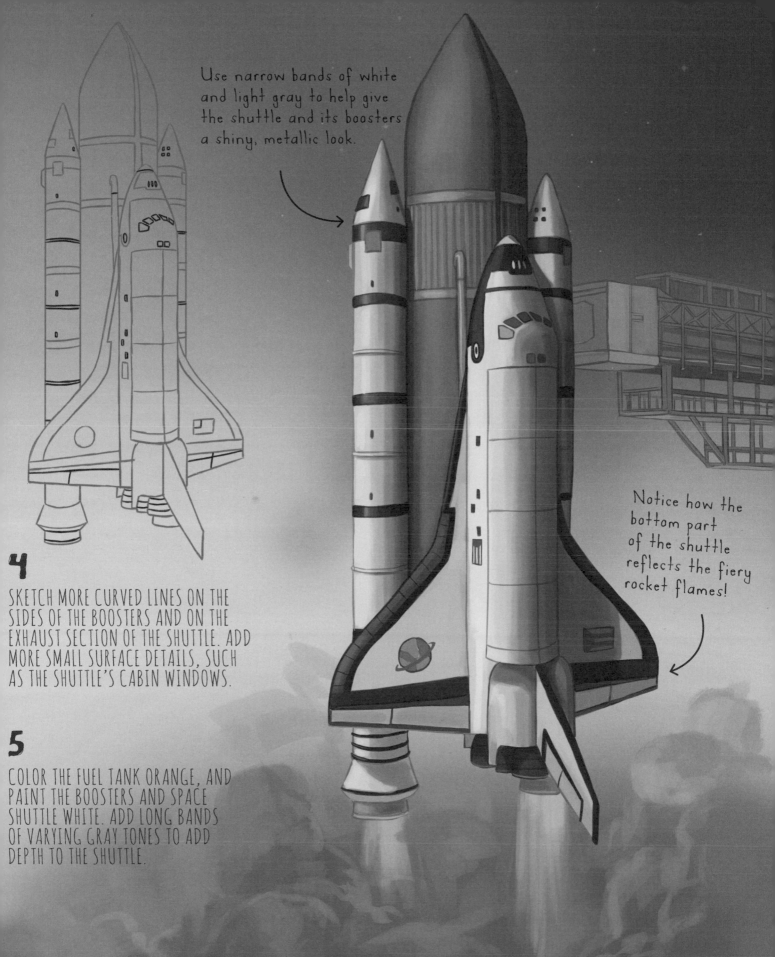

Use narrow bands of white and light gray to help give the shuttle and its boosters a shiny, metallic look.

4

SKETCH MORE CURVED LINES ON THE SIDES OF THE BOOSTERS AND ON THE EXHAUST SECTION OF THE SHUTTLE. ADD MORE SMALL SURFACE DETAILS, SUCH AS THE SHUTTLE'S CABIN WINDOWS.

5

COLOR THE FUEL TANK ORANGE, AND PAINT THE BOOSTERS AND SPACE SHUTTLE WHITE. ADD LONG BANDS OF VARYING GRAY TONES TO ADD DEPTH TO THE SHUTTLE.

Notice how the bottom part of the shuttle reflects the fiery rocket flames!

PINEAPPLE PRINT

LEARN TO DRAW A PINEAPPLE, THEN CREATE STYLISTIC VARIATIONS FOR COOL PATTERNS AND PRINTS.

1

FOR A BASIC PINEAPPLE, START BY SKETCHING AN OVAL SHAPE.

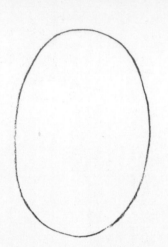

2

DRAW CRISSCROSSING LINES CURVING ACROSS THE OVAL. ADD POINTED LEAF SHAPES AT THE TOP.

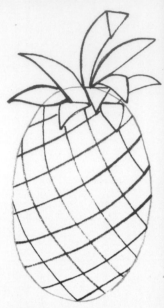

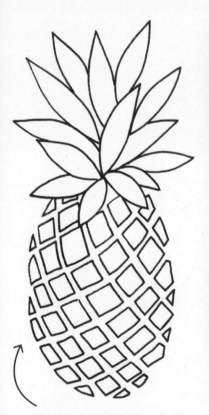

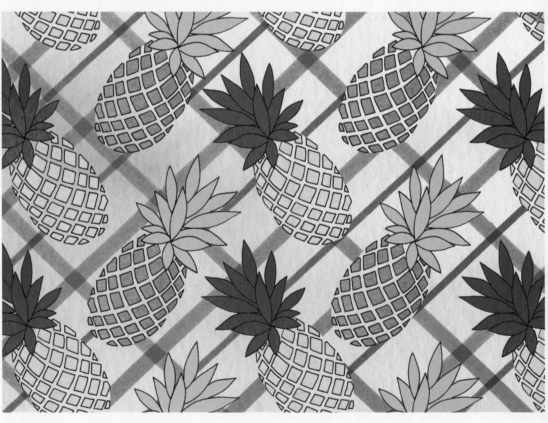

Try a simpler, stylistic variation of your pineapple. Copy this pineapple onto tracing paper. Turn over the tracing paper, and use the back of a spoon to rub and print the pineapple onto plain paper. Repeat the print across the plain paper at angles. Go over each pineapple with a pen, then color.

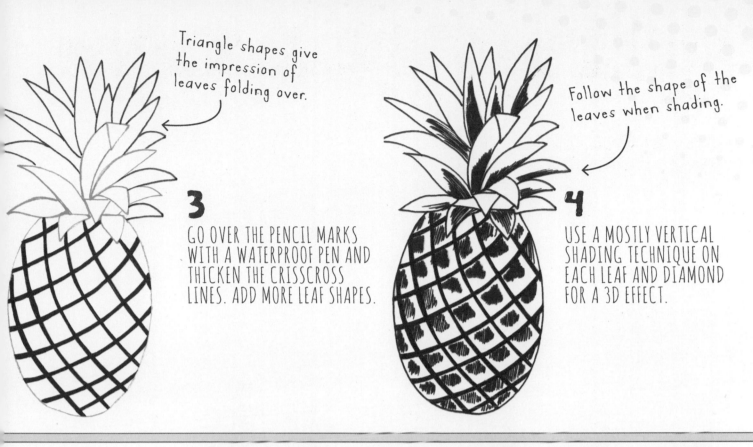

Triangle shapes give the impression of leaves folding over.

3

GO OVER THE PENCIL MARKS WITH A WATERPROOF PEN AND THICKEN THE CRISSCROSS LINES. ADD MORE LEAF SHAPES.

Follow the shape of the leaves when shading.

4

USE A MOSTLY VERTICAL SHADING TECHNIQUE ON EACH LEAF AND DIAMOND FOR A 3D EFFECT.

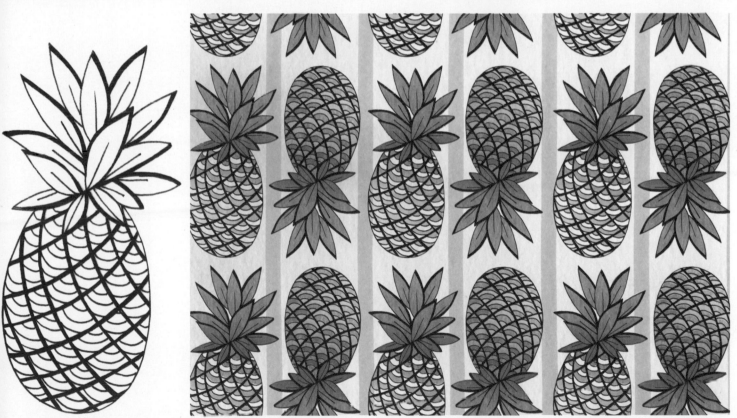

This time, create a more detailed drawing of a pineapple, using a mixture of thick, thin, straight, and wavy lines. Apply the same printing technique as on the opposite page. Rotate the pineapple print to make a pattern suitable for gift wrap or even clothing fabric! Try cool colors.

POINTILLISM

IN THIS DRAWING STYLE, PICTURES ARE MADE OUT OF LOTS OF LITTLE DOTS.

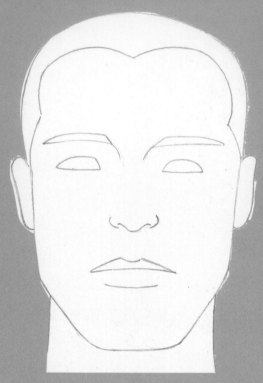

1

START WITH A PHOTO OF A FACE, THEN TRACE OVER IT WITH SOFT PENCIL LINES. ONLY DRAW THE SHAPES OF THE MAIN FACIAL FEATURES AT THIS STAGE.

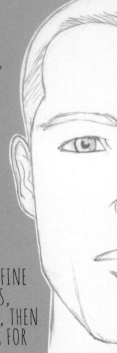

2

ADD SOME DETAILS. DEFINE THE SHAPES OF THE EARS, EYES, NOSE, AND CHIN, THEN ADD A LITTLE SHADING FOR THE HAIR.

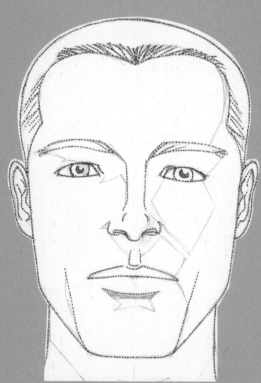

3

GO OVER THE DRAWING WITH AN INK PEN, MAKING LOTS OF SMALL DOTS. NEXT, LIGHTLY DRAW A PENCIL OUTLINE TO SEPARATE THE MAIN AREAS OF LIGHT AND DARK IN THE IMAGE.

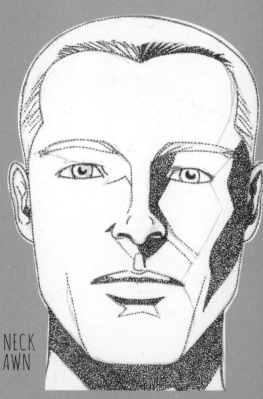

4

SHADE IN THE DARKEST AREAS OF THE FACE AND NECK USING LOTS OF DOTS DRAWN VERY CLOSE TOGETHER.

5

LEAVE THE LIGHTER AREAS OF THE FACE WHITE. TO ADD MORE SUBTLE SHADING, VARY THE QUANTITY OF DOTS YOU USE, AS WELL AS THE AMOUNT OF SPACING BETWEEN THEM.

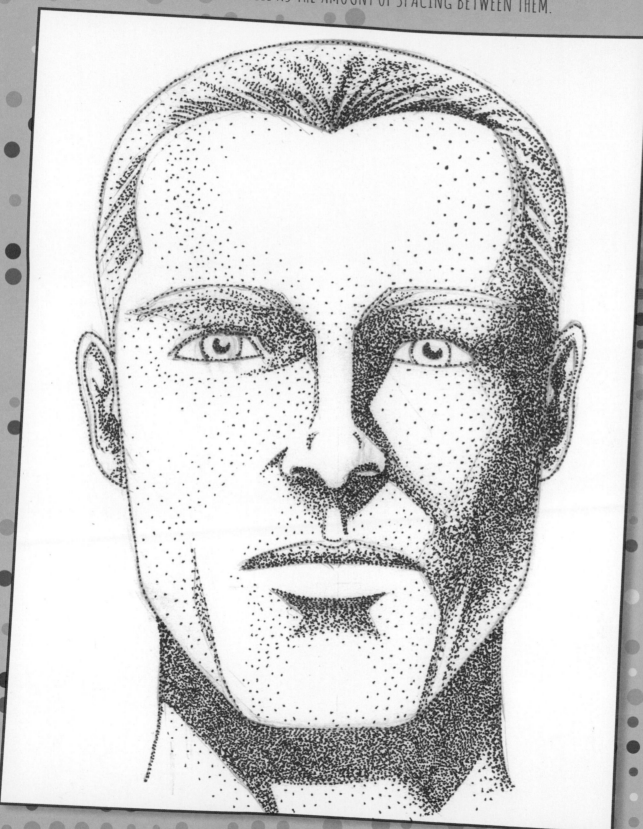

SAILBOAT

1 DRAW TWO BASIC TRIANGLES FOR THE SAILS, THEN A LONG, CURVED SHAPE WITH A HOOK FOR THE TOP OF THE BOAT, AS SHOWN.

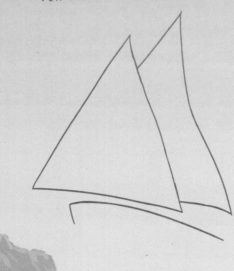

2 SKETCH THIN CYLINDER SHAPES AT THE TOP AND SIDES OF THE SAILS AND BOAT. DRAW A RECTANGULAR-SHAPED CABIN UNDER THE SAILS.

Add small overlapping shapes to start creating splashy waves.

3 ATTACH A LONG FLAGPOLE TO THE MAST, THEN DRAW ROPE RINGS ON THE MAST AND SPAR. ADD A SMALL CYLINDER AT THE FRONT OF THE BOAT, AND MAKE RAILINGS USING LONG AND SHORT LINES.

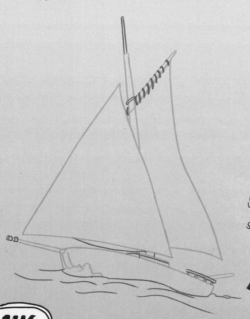

Smooth, curved lines suggest rolling waves.

4 DRAW A WAVY, FLAPPING FLAG, AND ADD ROPES TO JOIN THE SAILS TO THE BOAT. SKETCH SMALL CIRCLES AND RECTANGLES ON THE ROPES TO CREATE THE APPEARANCE OF RIGGING.

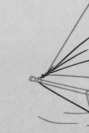

Add slightly curved lines in each corner of the sails for material creases and tension.

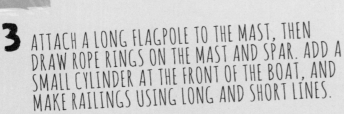

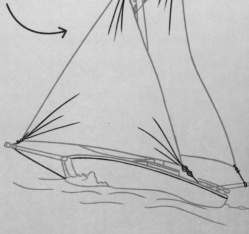

5 DRAW SOME WAVY LINES ON THE SAILS FOR MOVEMENT AND TO SUGGEST WHERE THE MATERIAL HAS BEEN JOINED TOGETHER. SKETCH MORE ROLLING WAVES TO THE FRONT OF THE BOAT.

6 ADD SHORT, WIGGLY LINES ON THE SAILS FOR TIES. NOW PAINT THE PICTURE, APPLYING A LIGHT, FADEAWAY TECHNIQUE ON THE SAILS FOR A 3D EFFECT.

A curved line on the hull or outside of the boat gives the impression of wooden planks.

For the background, use a smooth watercolor wash, so that the boat pops against the soft horizon.

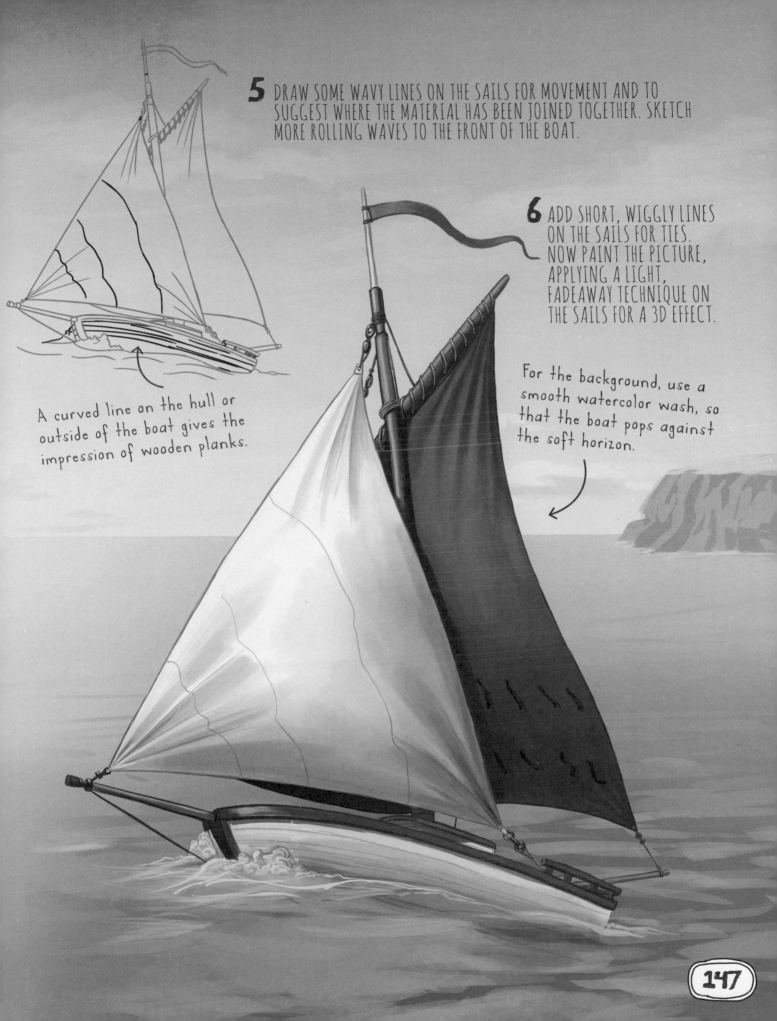

147

CIRCUS
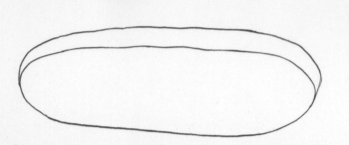

Larger elements at the top of the tent give the scene a sense of scale and depth.

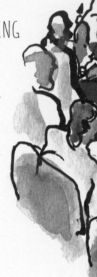

1

TO DRAW A BASIC CIRCUS RING, SKETCH TWO OVERLAPPING OVAL SHAPES USING SIMPLE PERSPECTIVE, AS SHOWN.

2

CREATE PEOPLE IN THE AUDIENCE USING CIRCLES AND SEMICIRCLES. DRAW CURVED LINES FOR THE TOP OF THE TENT, AND ADD A STAR IN THE RING.

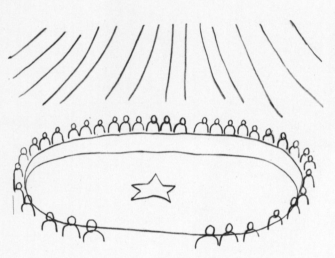

3

SKETCH LOOSER LINES AROUND EACH AUDIENCE MEMBER, AND ADD MORE PEOPLE! DRAW ROUNDED SEMIRECTANGLES AT THE BACK OF THE AUDIENCE FOR SEATING.

Make the audience members in the foreground bigger than those in the background to add to the perspective.

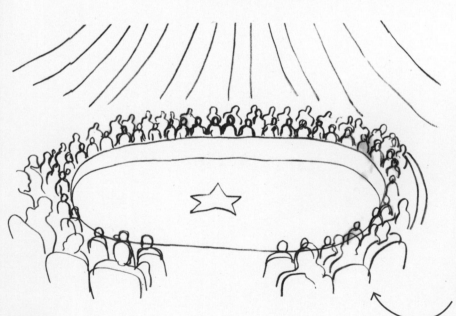

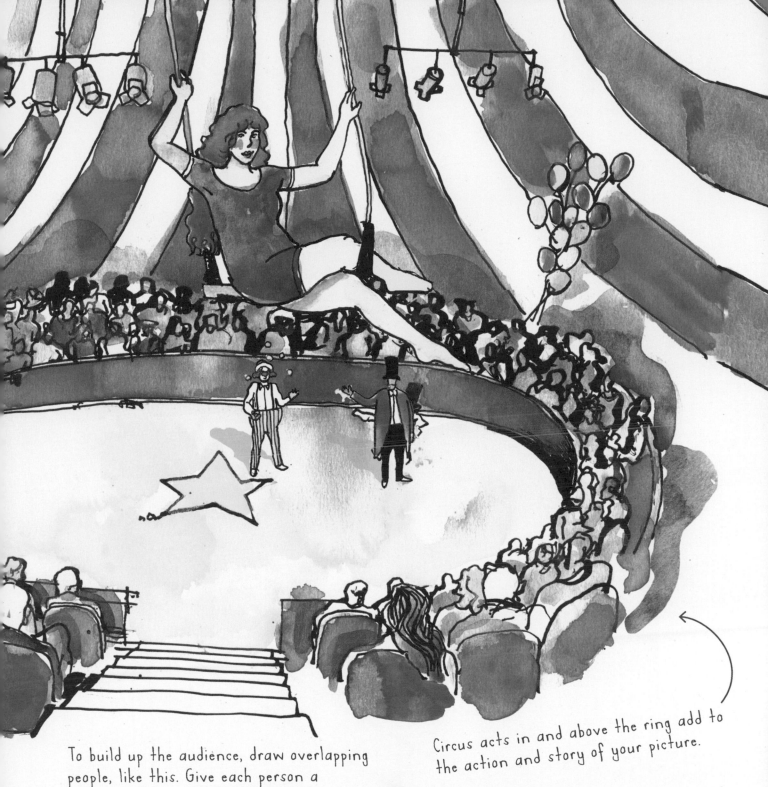

To build up the audience, draw overlapping people, like this. Give each person a different hairstyle for individuality.

Circus acts in and above the ring add to the action and story of your picture.

4

DRAW EVEN MORE PEOPLE IN THE AUDIENCE, AND ADD THE RINGMASTER, CLOWN, AND TRAPEZE ARTIST. DRAW SOME LIGHTS AT THE TOP OF THE TENT AND BALLOONS IN THE CROWD. USE WATERCOLOR PAINTS TO FINISH.

GOLDEN GATE BRIDGE

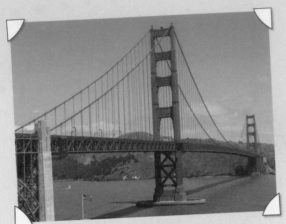

Find a reference photo to help you get the details right.

1

DRAW A HORIZONTAL LINE FOR THE BRIDGE'S ROAD, THEN ADD TWO SLOPING GUIDELINES TO CREATE A TRIANGLE. SKETCH TWO VERTICAL GUIDELINES FOR THE TOWERS.

Always draw your guidelines lightly in pencil, so that they can be easily erased when you've finished.

2

DRAW RECTANGLES FOR THE TOWERS, PLUS STRAIGHT LINES AND CURVES FOR THE SUSPENSION CABLES. NOTICE HOW THE CURVED ONES GET CLOSER TOGETHER, CREATING A SENSE OF DEPTH.

3

START BUILDING UP MORE OF THE BRIDGE'S STRUCTURE. ADD ROUNDED SQUARES ON THE CENTER TOWER AND A CURVE AND RECTANGLE FOR THE ARCH ON THE LEFT.

4

NOW FOCUS ON THE FINE DETAILS. USE ZIGZAG LINES FOR THE SIDES OF THE BRIDGE AND THE ARCH. ADD EXTRA PARALLEL LINES FOR THE VERTICAL SUSPENSION ROPES.

For a greater sense of perspective, add more detail to the areas of your drawing that are in the foreground.

When you're happy with your pencil sketch, go over it again using waterproof inks.

5

ADD MORE CABLES AND TOWER DETAILS TO YOUR DRAWING, THEN START COLORING! USE A BLUE WATERCOLOR WASH FOR THE SKY, AND LEAVE TO DRY. FINALLY, PAINT THE BRIDGE IN STRONG ORANGE AND RED TONES.

Use darker shades for the parts of the bridge that are in the distance. Lighter tones suggest areas that are in direct sunlight.

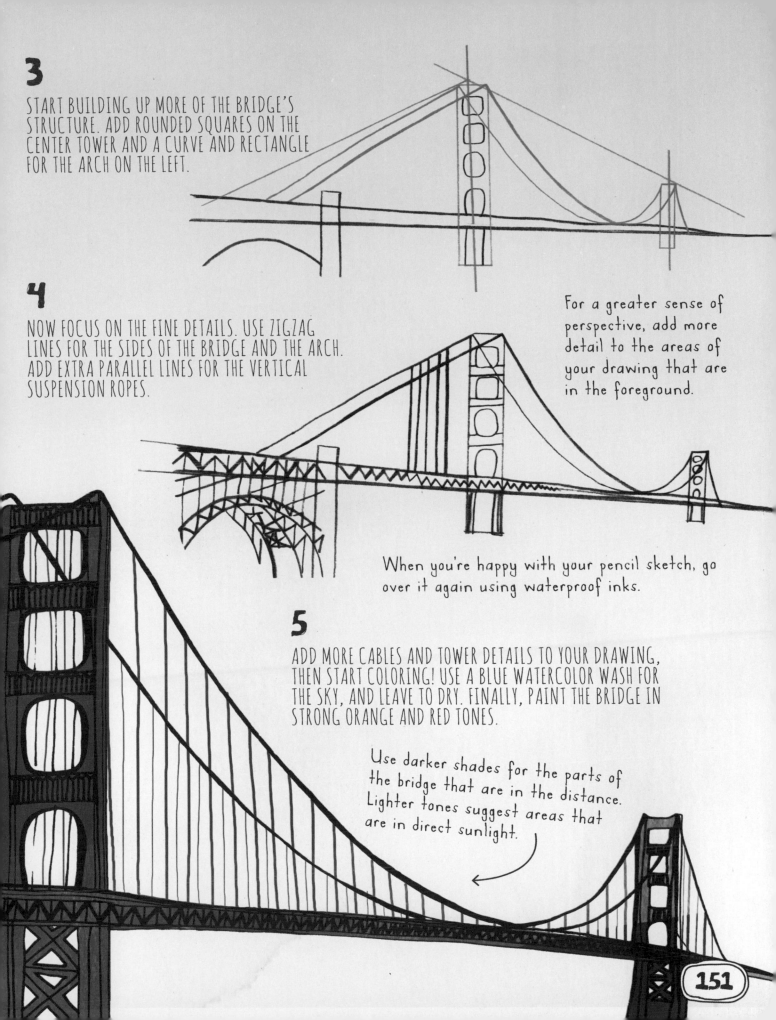

FEATHERS

1 SKETCH THREE OVERLAPPING ROUGH OVALS. THEN ADD A THIN, CURVED STICK DOWN THE CENTER FOR THE FEATHER'S SHAFT AND QUILL.

2 DRAW A WAVY OUTLINE AROUND THE OVAL SHAPES, ADDING GAPS AND SPIKY PARTS FOR A FEATHERY OUTER TEXTURE. ERASE THE GUIDELINES.

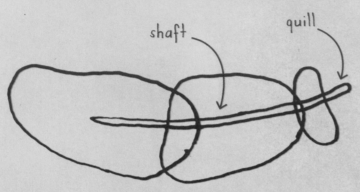

shaft

quill

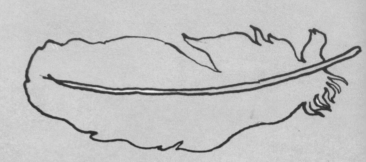

barbs

3 ADD LOTS OF CURVED LINES FOR THE BARBS, LEADING FROM THE SHAFT OUTWARD. DON'T MAKE THEM TOO PERFECT—SOME CAN EVEN CURVE BACKWARD! FINISH WITH COLOR AND SHADING.

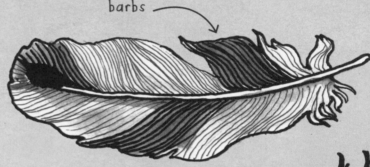

PEACOCK FEATHER
Start with a lollipop shape. Add wavy barbs around the outside and an oval and pie shape in the middle. Color with rich greens, yellows, and blues.

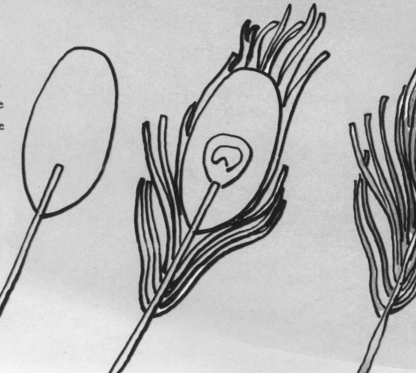

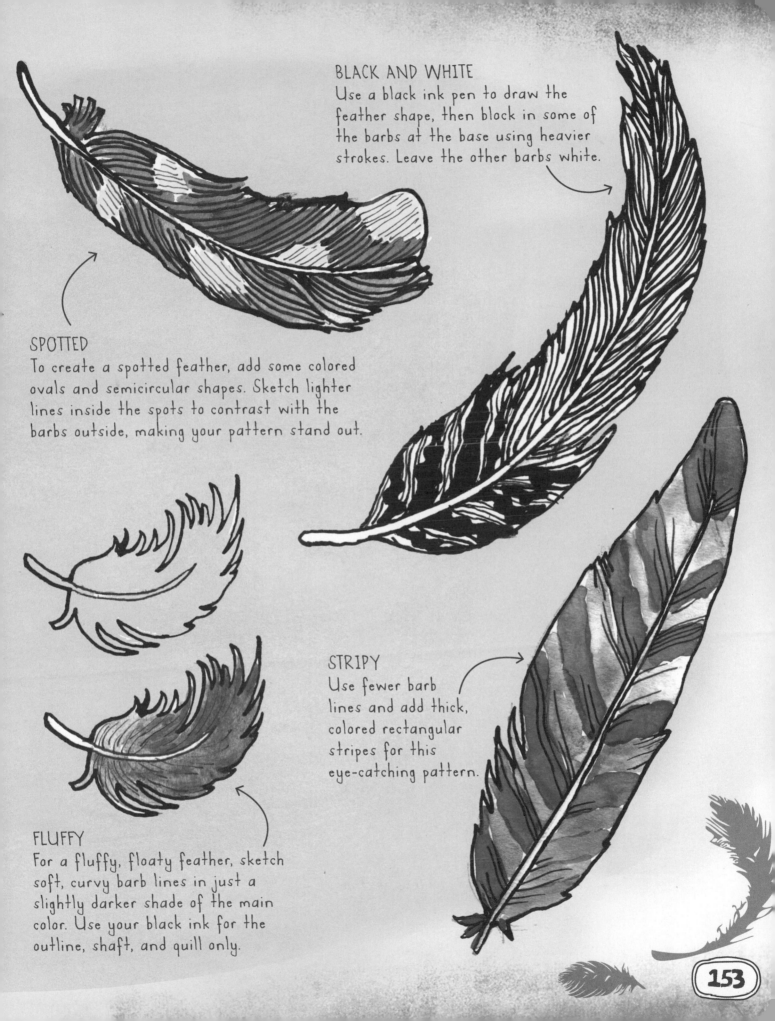

BLACK AND WHITE
Use a black ink pen to draw the feather shape, then block in some of the barbs at the base using heavier strokes. Leave the other barbs white.

SPOTTED
To create a spotted feather, add some colored ovals and semicircular shapes. Sketch lighter lines inside the spots to contrast with the barbs outside, making your pattern stand out.

STRIPY
Use fewer barb lines and add thick, colored rectangular stripes for this eye-catching pattern.

FLUFFY
For a fluffy, floaty feather, sketch soft, curvy barb lines in just a slightly darker shade of the main color. Use your black ink for the outline, shaft, and quill only.

CENTAUR

1

USE STRAIGHT AND CURVED LINES TO DRAW A SIMPLE STICK FIGURE LIKE THIS.

2

DRAW CIRCLES AND OVALS TO BUILD UP THE CENTAUR'S BODY SHAPE. THEN SKETCH IN THE ROUGH OUTLINE OF ITS BODY.

3

USE SAUSAGE SHAPES FOR THE LEGS, AND SKETCH CIRCLES AND OVALS FOR THE VARIOUS JOINTS. USE LONG, WAVY LINES TO DRAW THE TAIL.

Only start adding detail when you're happy with the basic shapes of the different body parts.

4

START ON THE MORE DETAILED AREAS, SKETCHING IN THE HANDS, HAIR, AND FACIAL FEATURES. ADD A BELT, BAG STRAP, HEADBAND, AND QUIVER OF ARROWS.

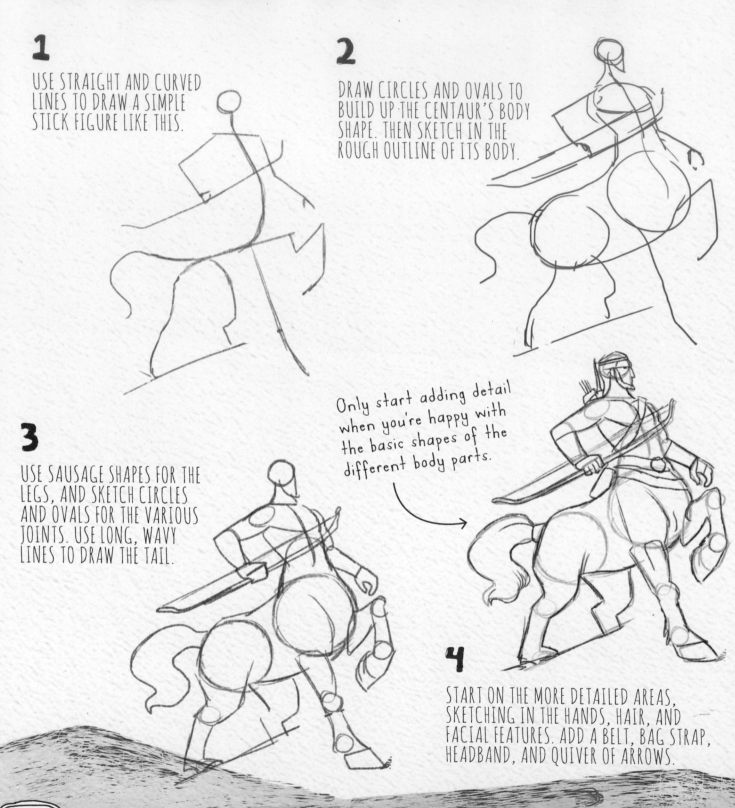

6

TO ADD COLOR, USE A DARK BROWN FOR THE LOWER BODY, WITH LIGHTER SHADES FOR THE HIGHLIGHTS. PICK A SKIN COLOR FOR THE FACE AND CHEST, USING DARKER TONES TO HELP DEFINE THE SHAPES OF THE MUSCLES.

5

ERASE THE GUIDES. REFINE YOUR PENCIL OUTLINES, AND ADD MORE DETAIL TO THE UPPER BODY. USE SHADING TO GIVE THE TAIL AND LOWER BODY A HAIRY TEXTURE.

Use long, wavy, overlapping pencil strokes to create a hairy texture.

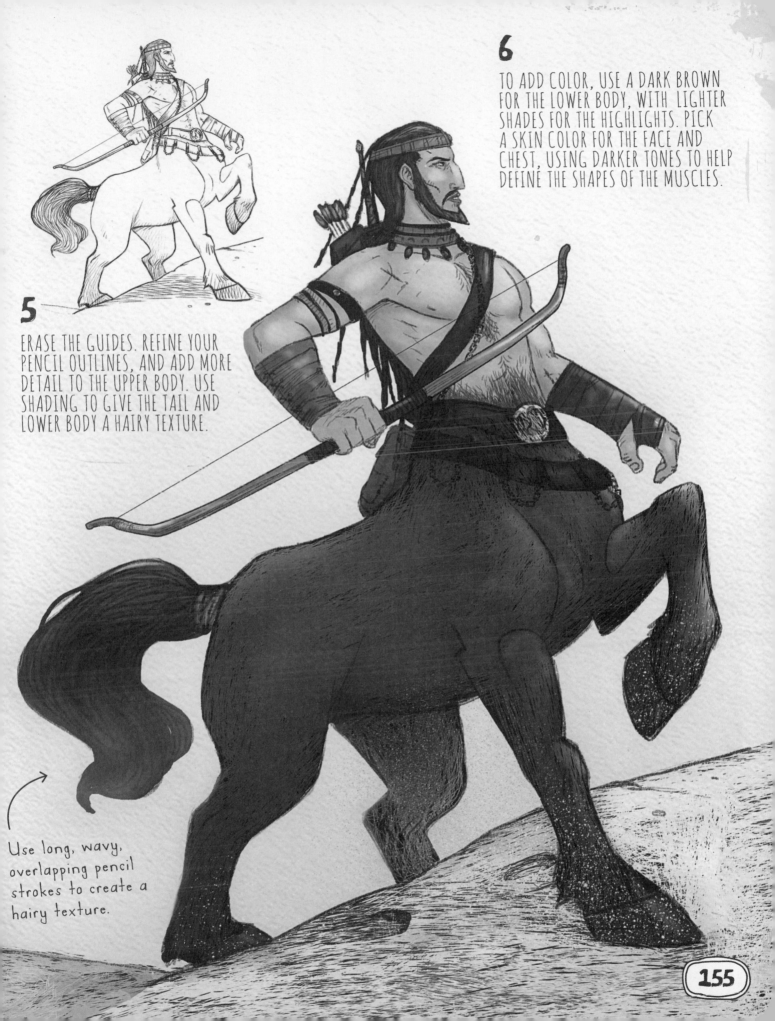

KARATE BOY

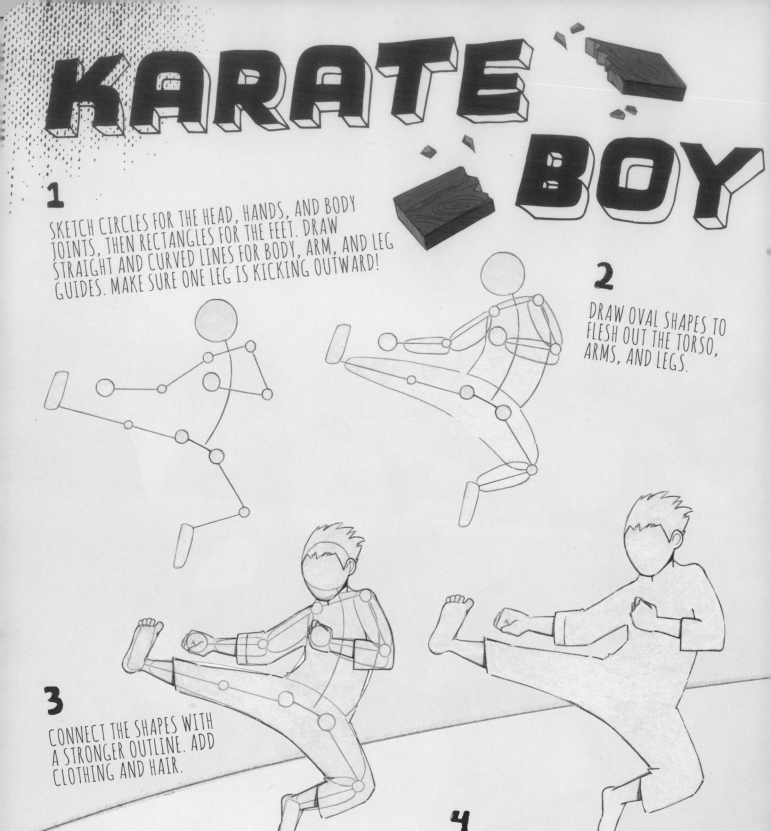

1

SKETCH CIRCLES FOR THE HEAD, HANDS, AND BODY JOINTS, THEN RECTANGLES FOR THE FEET. DRAW STRAIGHT AND CURVED LINES FOR BODY, ARM, AND LEG GUIDES. MAKE SURE ONE LEG IS KICKING OUTWARD!

2

DRAW OVAL SHAPES TO FLESH OUT THE TORSO, ARMS, AND LEGS.

3

CONNECT THE SHAPES WITH A STRONGER OUTLINE. ADD CLOTHING AND HAIR.

4

ERASE YOUR GUIDELINES TO LEAVE THE OUTLINE OF THE KARATE-KICKING BOY.

5

NOW FOCUS ON THE DETAILS OF YOUR DRAWING. SKETCH IN THE FACIAL FEATURES AND WORK UP THE CLOTHING.

Draw the hair and karate belt at angles for movement and action.

Add shading in the skin tone and on the clothing for depth and texture.

6

ADD A JAPANESE BUILDING IN THE BACKGROUND TO SET THE SCENE FOR YOUR KARATE PICTURE. USE WATERCOLOR PAINT TO FINISH.

Use darker shades to give an idea of fabric folds. And make sure you give the boy an expert's black belt!

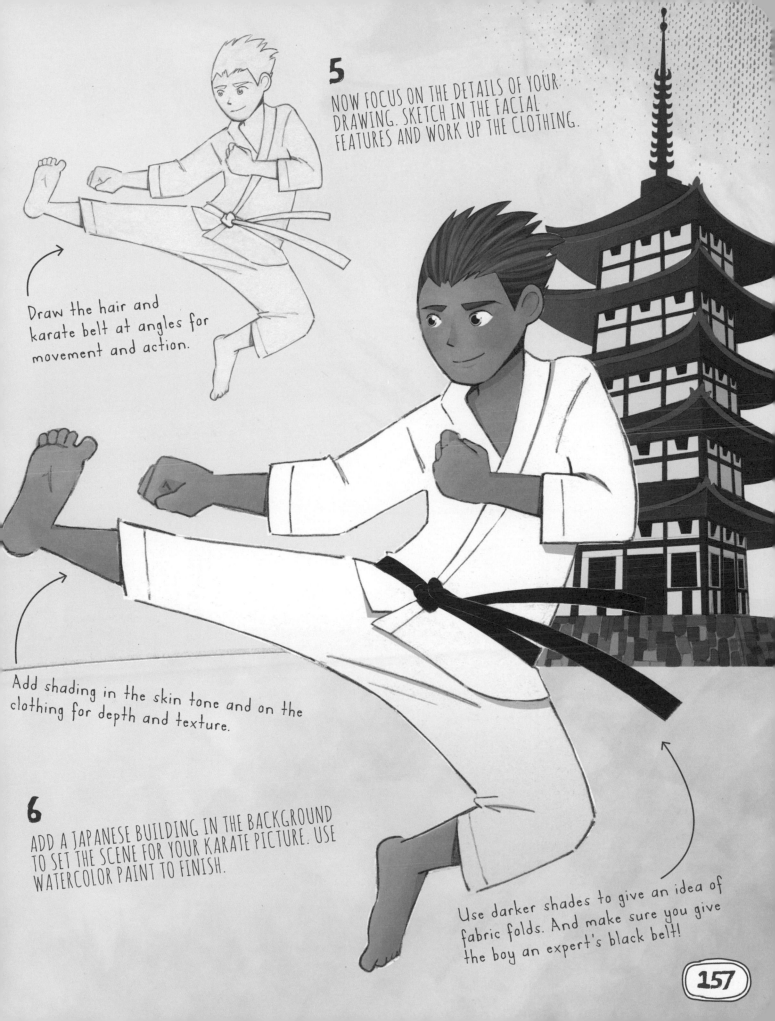

TIME MACHINE

BUILD UP SIMPLE SHAPES TO DRAW A CRAZY-LOOKING
CONTRAPTION THAT CAN TRAVEL THROUGH TIME!

FRAMEWORK

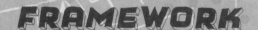

First, use simple shapes such as ovals and sausages
to create the basic framework of your time machine.

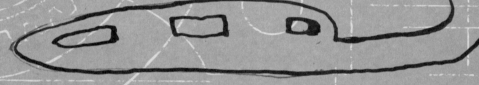

Refine the outline of each section of your
time machine. Start adding surface details to
make it look more mechanical or futuristic.

CIRCUIT

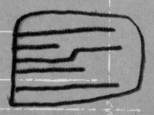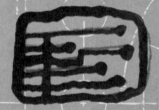

To draw a simple circuit board, sketch a rough rectangle
and add horizontal lines with dots at the ends. Go over
the lines in thick ink pen strokes. Color the board green.

DIGI CLOCK

Design a clock to show the
year your machine has
traveled to! For the display
screens, use simple rectangle
shapes with round edges.
Use circles for side buttons.

1100   1200   1300   1400   1500   160

ONCE YOU'VE DESIGNED EACH PART
OF YOUR TIME MACHINE, PUT ALL THE
DIFFERENT SECTIONS TOGETHER. YOU CAN
USE SIMILAR-SHAPED PARTS TO THE ONES
SHOWN HERE, OR TRY CREATING YOUR OWN!

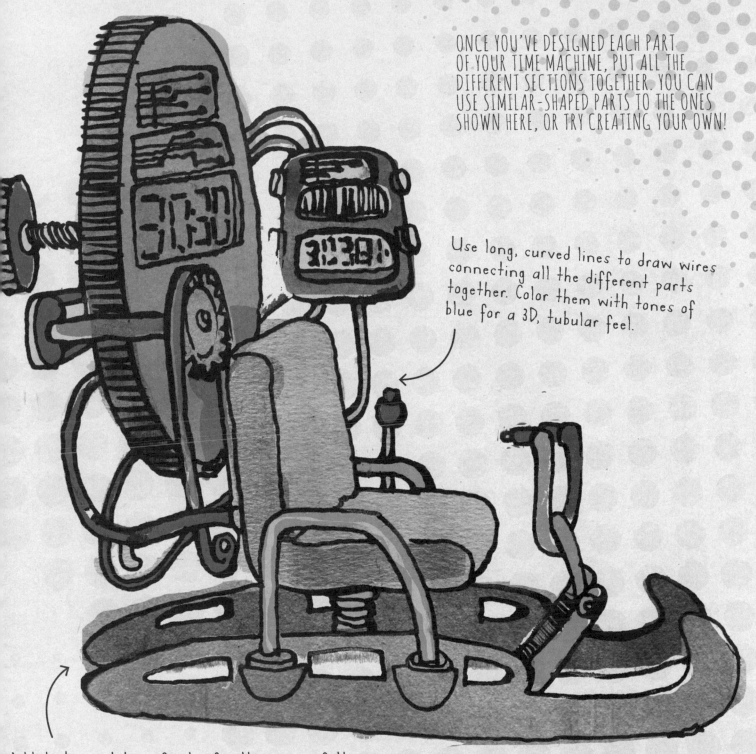

Use long, curved lines to draw wires
connecting all the different parts
together. Color them with tones of
blue for a 3D, tubular feel.

Add darker patches of color for the areas of the
machine that are in shadow. Varying between
lighter and darker shades helps add to the 3D look.

1700   1800   1900   2000   2020   AD

HATS

LEARN HOW TO DRAW ALL KINDS OF HATS, THEN HAVE FUN DECORATING THEM WITH DIFFERENT PATTERNS AND TEXTURES.

WHEN YOU DRAW A HAT, REMEMBER THAT THE WEARER'S HEAD WILL AFFECT ITS SHAPE. IT WILL ALSO LOOK DIFFERENT DEPENDING ON THE ANGLE.

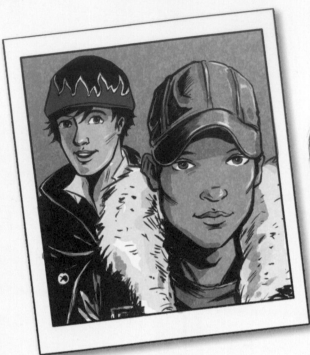

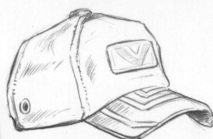

CAP SIDE-ON

Try drawing a cap from the side to see its full shape. This one is vaguely dome-shaped with straight sides.

CAP FRONT-ON

When you draw a cap from the front, the peak-shaped brim is more obvious. Some are curved, while others are flatter.

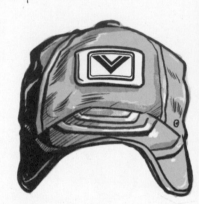

FEDORA STYLE

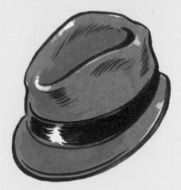

Don't make the top dent in a fedora too deep—remember, there's still someone's head underneath it!

SKI HAT

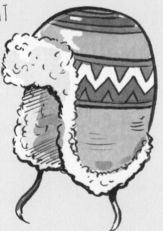

Give the hat trim a fuzzy texture by drawing a wobbly outline first. Then add lots of tiny curls to it.

TOQUE

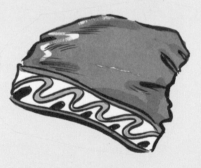

When you sketch a toque, make sure it follows the curved shape of the head, with a little extra material sticking up at the top.

WITH GIRLS' HATS, EXPERIMENT WITH AN EVEN WIDER VARIETY OF SHAPES, PATTERNS, AND TEXTURES.

Hats will tend to flatten a person's hairstyle, but you'll still see some hair sticking out from underneath!

TEXTURE

Keep your pencil lines quite rough and scratchy to suggest the texture of fabric.

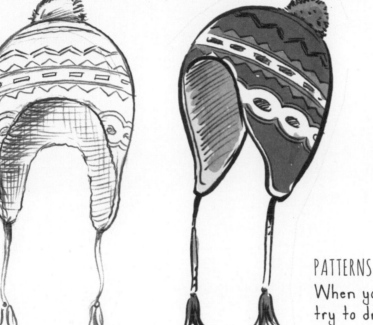

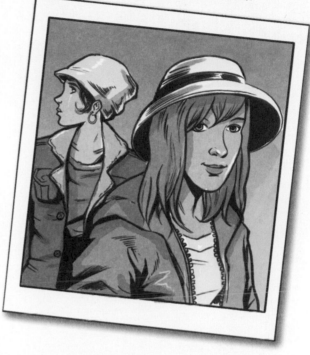

PATTERNS

When you add a pattern to the side of a hat, try to draw it so that it follows the curved shape of the wearer's head.

FLOWER HAT

This rigid-shaped hat is a little like a cone with the top cut off. Add flowers and bands to decorate.

KNITTED

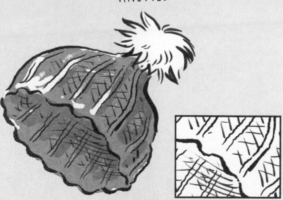

Use short, faint, overlapping lines to make a kind of crisscross pattern that looks like knitted yarn.

NEWSBOY HAT

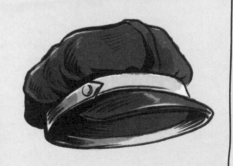

Draw the band first, then used curved lines to draw the puffed shape of the actual hat.

DOT LIZARD

1 USING A RULER, LIGHTLY DRAW A DASHED DIAGONAL LINE. DRAW A SWIRLY LINE ON TOP, AS SHOWN.

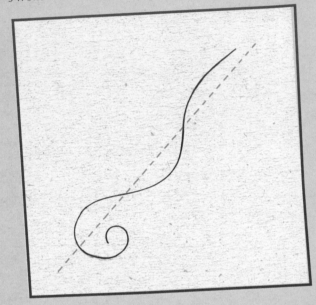

2 DRAW AROUND THE SWIRLY LINE TO CREATE THE LIZARD'S HEAD, BODY, AND TAIL. SKETCH STICK LEGS AND HANDS AT FUN ANGLES.

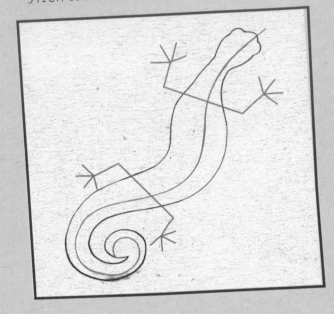

3 DRAW AROUND THE STICK LIMBS TO FLESH OUT THE LIZARD'S STUBBY LEGS AND WIDE TOES AND CLAWS.

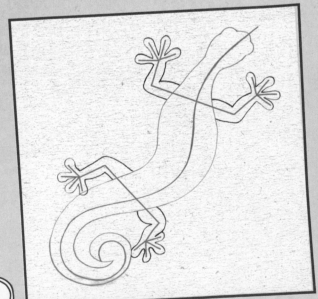

4 ERASE THE GUIDELINES, THEN USE GOUACHE (A THICK WATERCOLOR PAINT) TO COLOR YOUR LIZARD. ONCE DRY, SKETCH WHERE YOU WANT THE DOTS, LINES, AND PATTERNS TO GO.

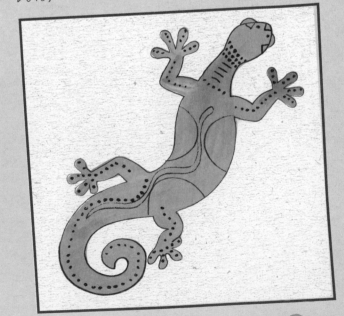

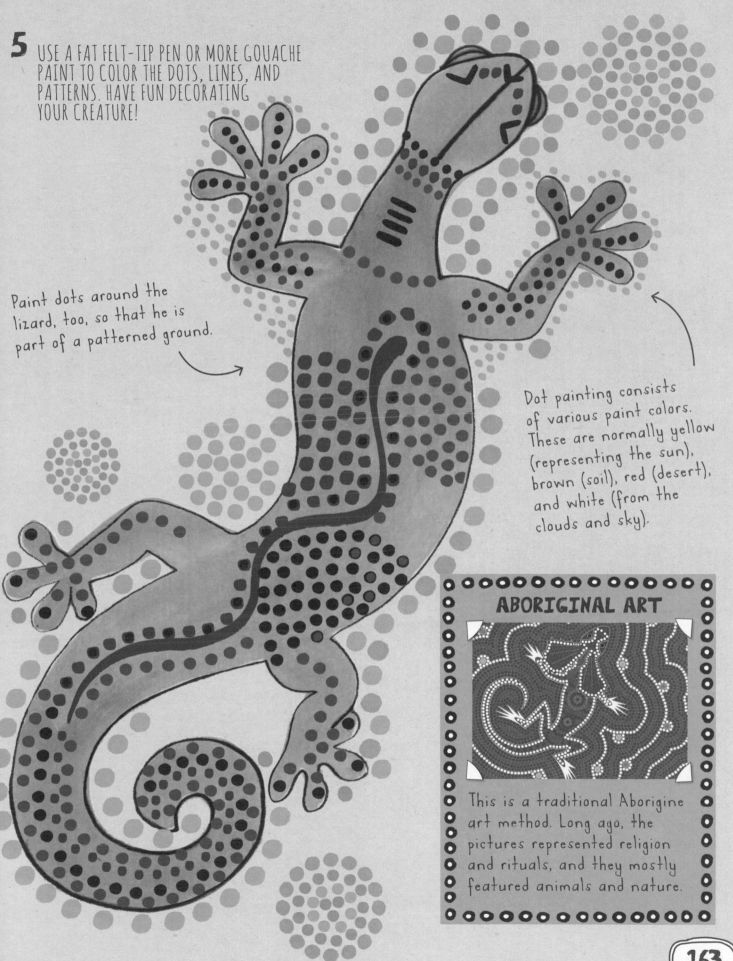

5 USE A FAT FELT-TIP PEN OR MORE GOUACHE PAINT TO COLOR THE DOTS, LINES, AND PATTERNS. HAVE FUN DECORATING YOUR CREATURE!

Paint dots around the lizard, too, so that he is part of a patterned ground.

Dot painting consists of various paint colors. These are normally yellow (representing the sun), brown (soil), red (desert), and white (from the clouds and sky).

ABORIGINAL ART

This is a traditional Aborigine art method. Long ago, the pictures represented religion and rituals, and they mostly featured animals and nature.

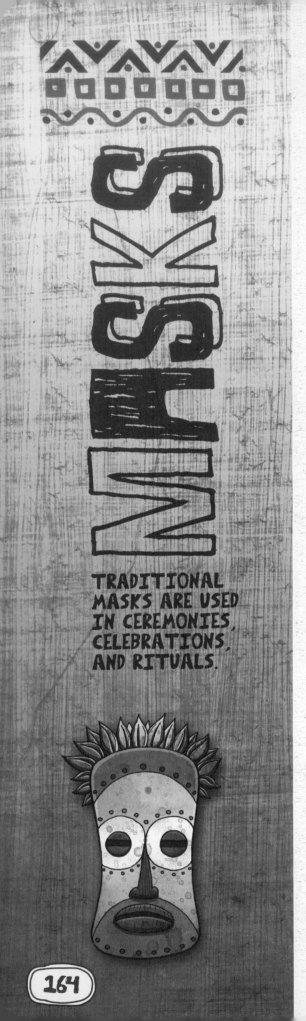

MASKS

TRADITIONAL MASKS ARE USED IN CEREMONIES, CELEBRATIONS, AND RITUALS.

1

SKETCH A LONG OVAL SHAPE, THEN ADD A CURVED, ALMOST SEMICIRCULAR SHAPE ON TOP. ADD A CENTER LINE AS A GUIDE.

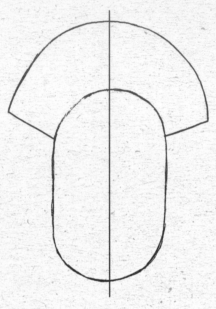

2

DRAW A THIN BORDER INSIDE THE SEMICIRCLE. ADD A NOSE, MOUTH, AND A SMALL MASK ON THE HEAD. SKETCH SOME TRIANGLES AROUND THE FACE.

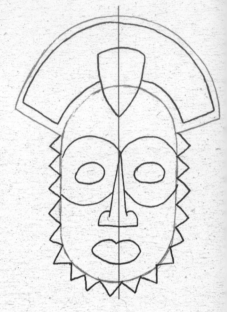

3

DRAW STRIPES ON THE HEADDRESS AND FACE. ADD SPIRALS BENEATH THE EYES, THEN SKETCH A FACE ON THE SMALL MASK.

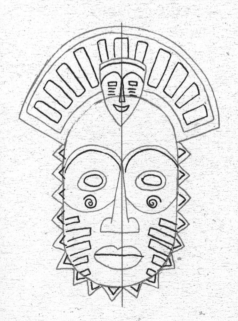

4

COLOR YOUR MASK IN BRIGHT COLORS. USE LIGHT AND DARK SHADES IN VERTICAL LINES TO SUGGEST A WOODLIKE TEXTURE.

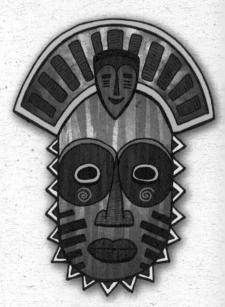

EXPERIMENT WITH DIFFERENT-SHAPED MASKS AND PATTERNS.

SPOTS AND STRIPES
Draw the outline of a mask, then sketch the facial features, making sure each side is symmetrical. Add contrasting patterns, such as spots and stripes.

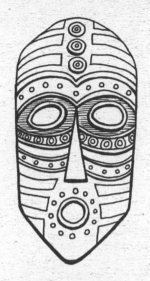
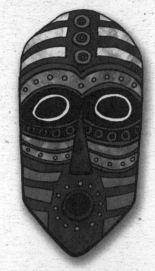

FEATHERS AND DIAGONALS
Sketch a feather shape at the top of your mask and chevrons down the center. Repeat and fan lots of feathers around the top of the mask.

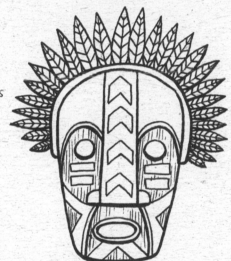
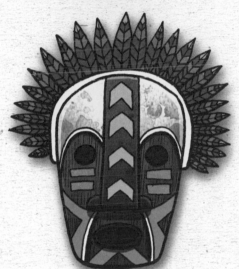

SHAPES AND CROSSES
Create a mask with eight panels, as shown. Decorate the mask with triangles, circles, diagonals, and rectangles.

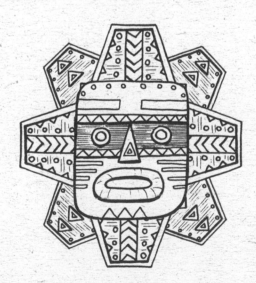
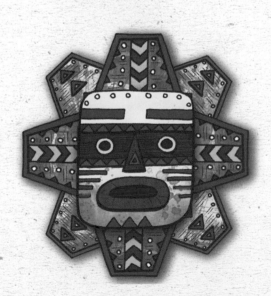

CLOTHES STORE

THIS STORE MIGHT LOOK TRICKY TO DRAW, BUT IT'S MADE UP OF LOTS OF SIMPLER SHAPES.

Draw a clothes rail and add a few hangers. Have fun drawing tops, dresses, or skirts—it's up to you!

Draw someone trying on a trendy outfit. Choose a fun, laidback pose.

Practice sketching each object on its own before drawing it in your scene.

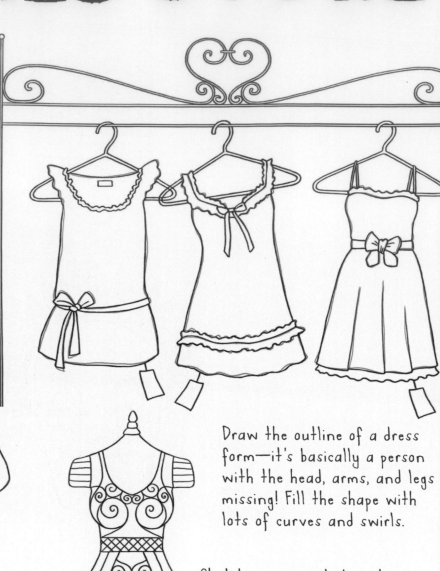

Draw the outline of a dress form—it's basically a person with the head, arms, and legs missing! Fill the shape with lots of curves and swirls.

Sketch some simple box shapes with pairs of shoes perched on top. Take a look at fashion mags for inspiration!

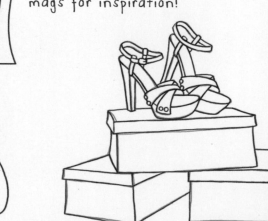

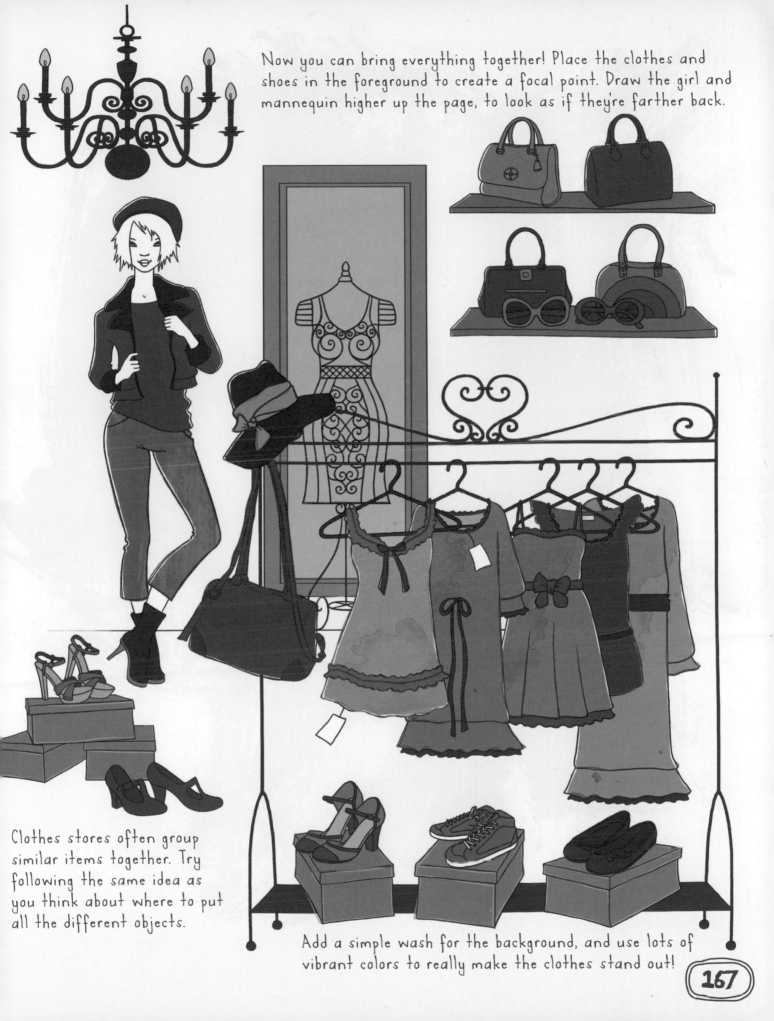

Now you can bring everything together! Place the clothes and shoes in the foreground to create a focal point. Draw the girl and mannequin higher up the page, to look as if they're farther back.

Clothes stores often group similar items together. Try following the same idea as you think about where to put all the different objects.

Add a simple wash for the background, and use lots of vibrant colors to really make the clothes stand out!

MOUNTAIN RANGE

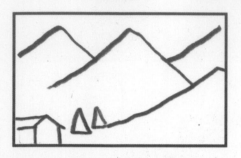

START BY SKETCHING BASIC TRIANGLE AND RECTANGLE SHAPES AS A GUIDE FOR THE OVERALL LOOK OF YOUR MOUNTAIN RANGE SCENE.

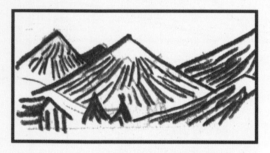

ADD HATCHING LINES, FOLLOWING THE DIRECTION OF THE MOUNTAINS WITH YOUR STROKES. LEAVE THE MOUNTAIN PEAKS WHITE FOR SNOWY TOPS.

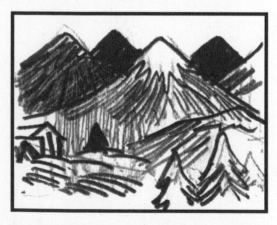

USE LIGHT AND HEAVY SHADING TO CREATE DEPTH. SKETCH SPIKY LINES AROUND THE WHITE MOUNTAIN PEAK FOR THE SNOW.

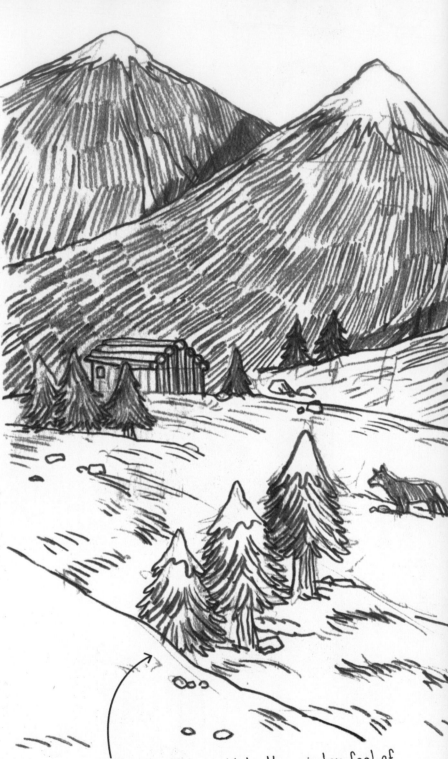

Snow-capped pine trees add to the wintry feel of your drawing. Give the drawing personality with other small details, such as a wolf and log cabin.

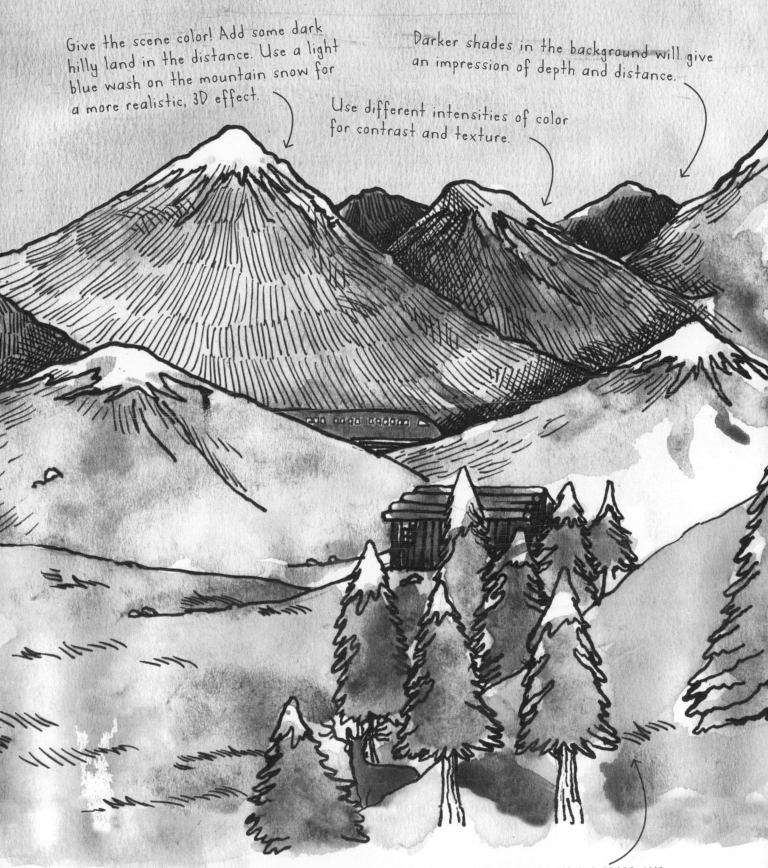

Give the scene color! Add some dark hilly land in the distance. Use a light blue wash on the mountain snow for a more realistic, 3D effect.

Use different intensities of color for contrast and texture.

Darker shades in the background will give an impression of depth and distance.

BEFORE COLORING, SKETCH A TRAIN, DEER, AND LINES TO SUGGEST GRASS AND TEXTURE IN THE TREES AND MOUNTAINS. USE AN INK PEN TO GO OVER ALL YOUR LINES, THEN ADD COLOR. BUILD UP THE SCENE WITH MORE TREES.

BASEBALL PLAYER

1
USE A LIGHT 2H PENCIL TO DRAW A SIMPLE STICK FIGURE. CONCENTRATE ON THE BASIC POSE, MAKING SURE THE FEET ARE PLANTED CORRECTLY.

2
SKETCH THE VARIOUS BODY PARTS, USING YOUR STICKS AS A GUIDE. FOCUS ON GETTING THE OVERALL SHAPE AND PROPORTIONS RIGHT.

3
NOW ADD A LITTLE DETAIL. LIGHTLY SKETCH THE HELMET AND THE SHAPES OF THE CLOTHES. DRAW THE FINGERS, AND ADD ROUGH FACIAL FEATURES.

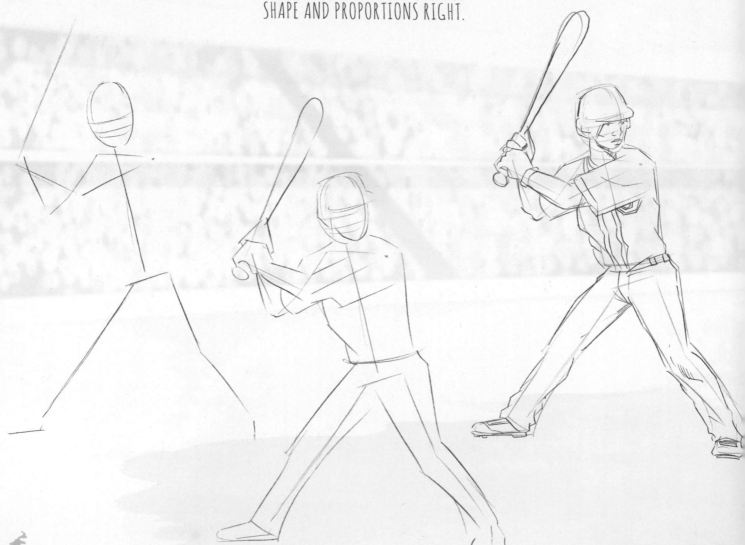

4

USE A 4B PENCIL TO WORK ON THE FINE DETAILS. SHADE IN AREAS NOT HIT BY YOUR LIGHT SOURCE AND THE FOLDS IN THE CLOTHING.

5

GO OVER YOUR PENCIL LINES WITH A BLACK INK PEN. PAINT THE BASEBALL BAT A LIGHT BROWN, AND PICK OUT DETAILS ON THE PLAYER'S CLOTHES IN A BRIGHT, PUNCHY COLOR.

Draw a baseball and add light horizontal lines to show it's moving super fast!

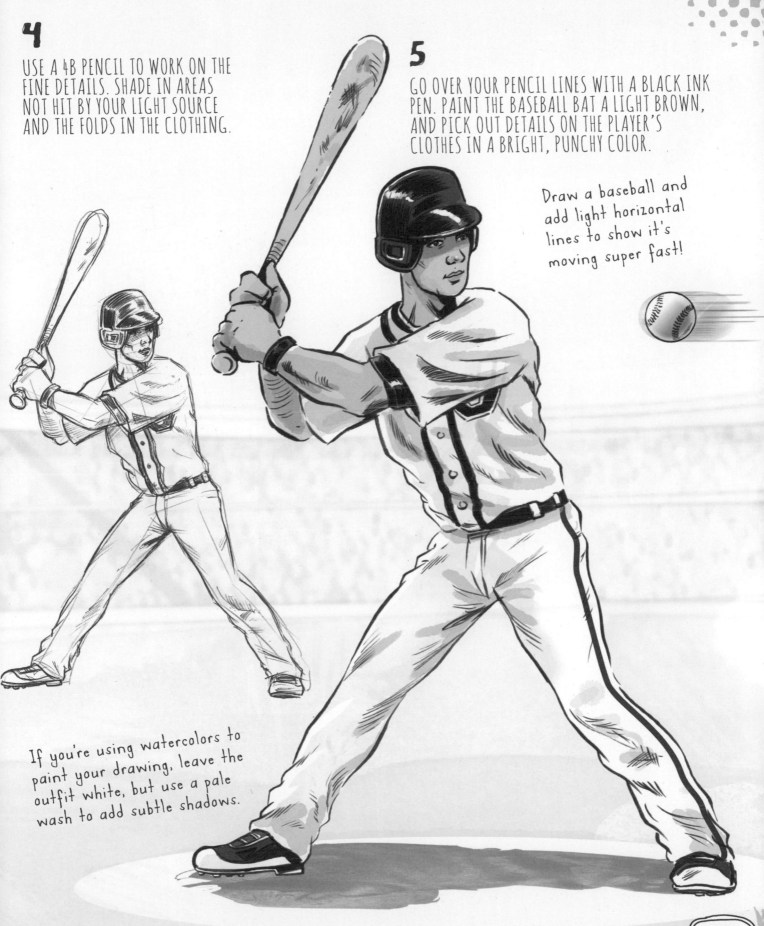

If you're using watercolors to paint your drawing, leave the outfit white, but use a pale wash to add subtle shadows.

SNOWFLAKES

Draw three lines to make a basic star shape. Sketch a smaller star inside it, then add arrow shapes on the bigger star, as shown.

Turn each arrow into a triangle by drawing a line across it. Sketch more arrow shapes, and add some diamonds, too.

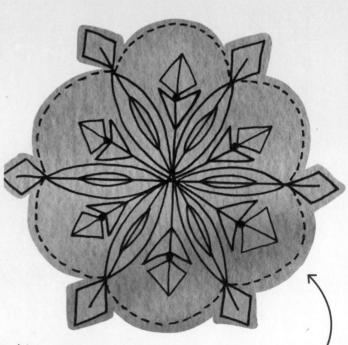

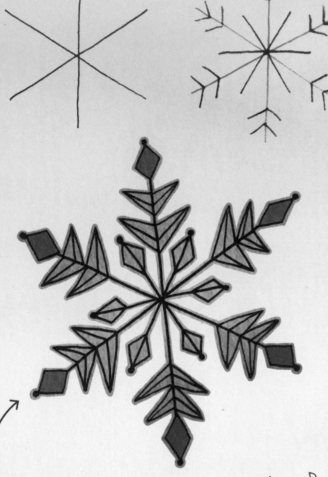

This snowflake is similar to the one above. Don't color exactly in the lines for a soft effect. Use cool colors like purple and lilac for a wintry feel.

The lilac background and dashed line around the outside of this snowflake give it a flowery-looking variation of the other snowflakes.

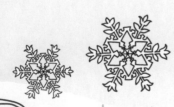

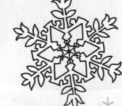

For this spotted design, start with the basic star shape, then add circles to the ends of the spikes.

For another variation, add more circles and gradually lighten the color of them toward the center.

Change the size, position, and number of circles for a more interesting spotted snowflake.

The dots on this snowflake give it a lacy feel. Shade the edges a darker color for depth and delicacy.

After the basic star shape design, draw zigzags around the edge of the snowflake, joining the spikes together. Add a leaf-shaped pattern inside for a heavier flake.

GRIFFIN

1

START WITH SIMPLE OVALS TO SKETCH THE BASIC SHAPE OF YOUR GRIFFIN, AS SHOWN.

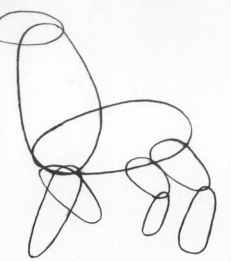

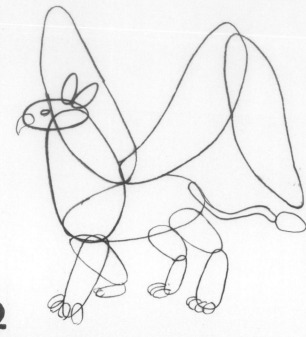

2

DRAW MORE ROUGH OVALS FOR THE WINGS, EARS, TOES, EYE, AND TAIL END. CREATE A HOOKED, EAGLE-SHAPED BEAK AND A THIN, LIONLIKE TAIL.

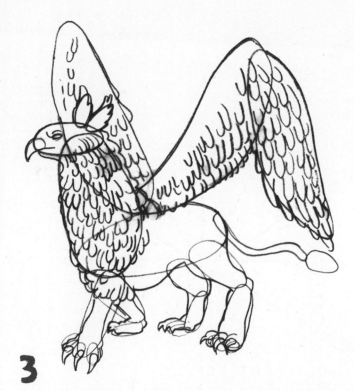

3

REPEAT SIMPLE "U" SHAPES ON THE GRIFFIN'S WINGS AND TORSO FOR A FEATHERY EFFECT. USE A HEAVIER, MORE FLUID LINE TO DRAW AROUND THE EARS, FACE, BODY, LEGS, AND CLAWS, TO CONNECT THEM.

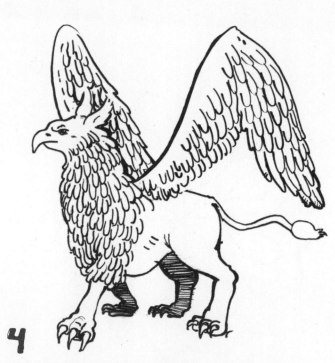

4

OUTLINE YOUR SKETCH WITH BLACK PEN OR INK. ADD SOME SHADING ON THE TWO LEGS IN THE BACKGROUND. FILL IN MORE DETAIL ON THE BEAK, FACE, EARS, AND TAIL. ERASE ANY PENCIL MARKS.

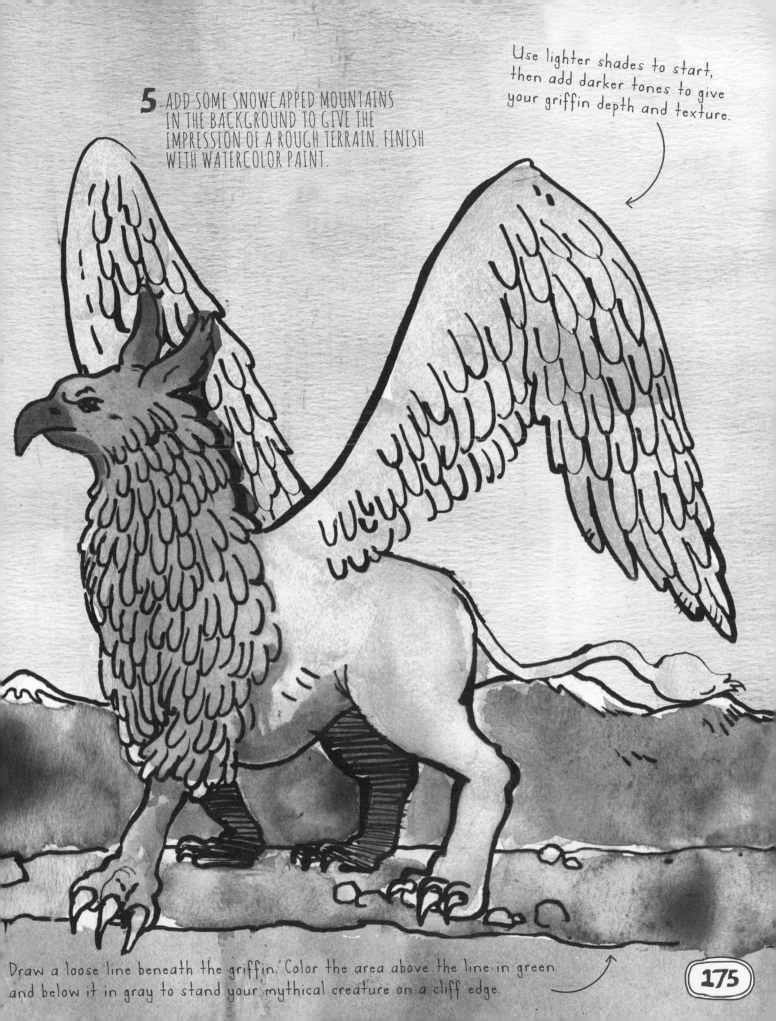

5 ADD SOME SNOWCAPPED MOUNTAINS IN THE BACKGROUND TO GIVE THE IMPRESSION OF A ROUGH TERRAIN. FINISH WITH WATERCOLOR PAINT.

Use lighter shades to start, then add darker tones to give your griffin depth and texture.

Draw a loose line beneath the griffin. Color the area above the line in green and below it in gray to stand your mythical creature on a cliff edge.

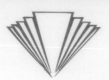

THE 1920S

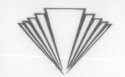

KEEP IT COOL AND CLASSY FOR **THIS DECADE.**

HAIRSTYLES

Use wavy lines to draw this '20s men's hairstyle. Sketch short, straight lines at the sides.

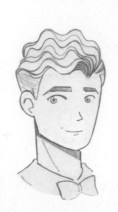

VEST

Draw this vest pattern with rows of fan shapes. Add shaded curved shapes to each one, tapering to a single point.

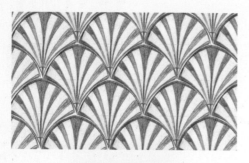

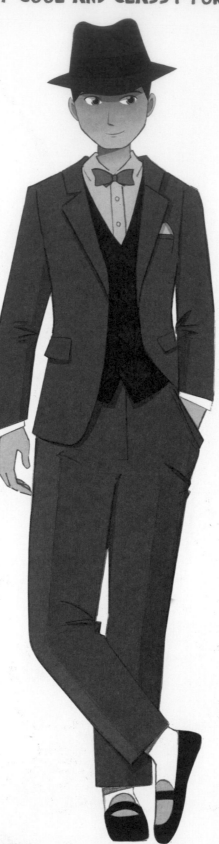

HATS

A straw boater is basically a cylinder attached to a disk shape, with a ribbon and bow. The fedora hat is taller with the top pinched in at the sides.

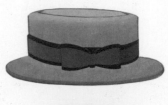

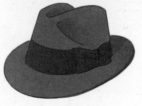

SHOES

Two-tone and laced shoes were trendy in the '20s. Use curved lines for the simple shape of a side-on shoe. Design a pattern using more curves.

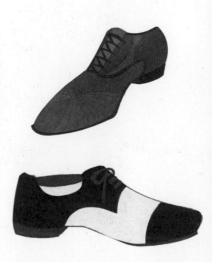

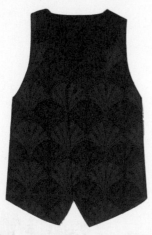

HAIRSTYLES

For a straight bob, keep to the head shape, then define straight bangs. For a wavy style, sketch long, flowing lines ending in neat curls by the mouth.

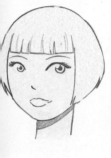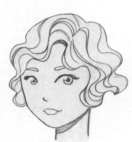

HATS AND BANDS

Women's hats were simple and elegant in the '20s. Add bands and bows to basic hat shapes using curved lines. Color these elements in contrasting tones.

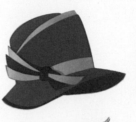

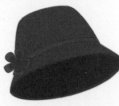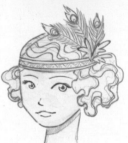

DRESS

For this dress pattern, draw overlapping diamond shapes in different sizes. You can also try overlapping curves and rectangle shapes.

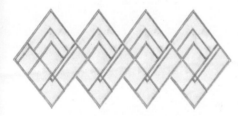

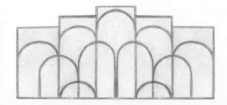

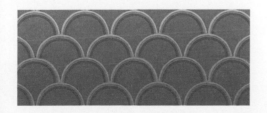

Instead of a hat, try feathers attached to a headband. Use small lines to get the feathery texture.

SHOES

Use curves to draw these chic shoes. As with men's footwear, two-tone styles were all the rage!

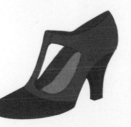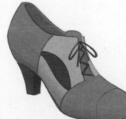

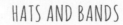

THE 1960S

DESIGN SOME COOL CLOTHES AND HAIRSTYLES—SIXTIES STYLE!

HAIRSTYLES

The famous men's "mop top" style is basically a simple inverted bowl shape. For the shorter rockabilly look, add an upturned section of hair above the forehead. Use wavy lines for long hair.

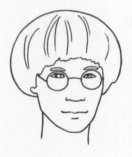
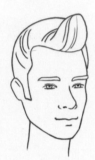

SHIRT FABRIC PATTERNS

Bold, colorful patterns were popular in the '60s. Recreate them using repeating curved shapes or rows of round-edged squares and rectangles.

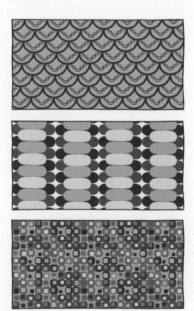

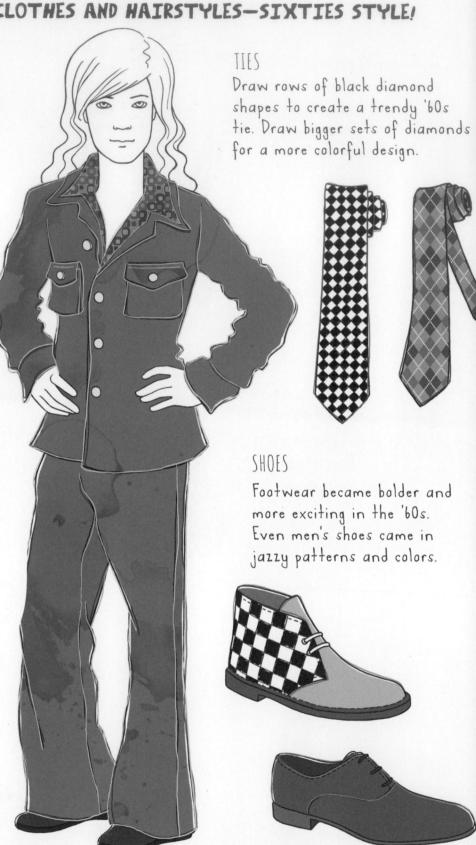

TIES

Draw rows of black diamond shapes to create a trendy '60s tie. Draw bigger sets of diamonds for a more colorful design.

SHOES

Footwear became bolder and more exciting in the '60s. Even men's shoes came in jazzy patterns and colors.

HATS

As hairstyles grew in the '60s, hat styles had to adapt in shape! Draw simple shapes and curves, and decorate with stripes and two-tone patterns.

HAIRSTYLES

Like men, women had short and long hairstyles. Draw the "bob" by sketching waves with small, upward curls at the end.

DRESS FABRIC PATTERNS

Geometric designs were really popular in this era. Design your own by sketching rows of circles or squares. Draw groups of overlapping "C" shapes, and paint them in bright colors for another '60s look.

This typical '60s cut has more volume as the hair is swept up. Use long, wavy lines.

SHOES AND BOOTS

Sketch tall boots and platform shoes, then add bright colors and striking patterns for the perfect '60s design!

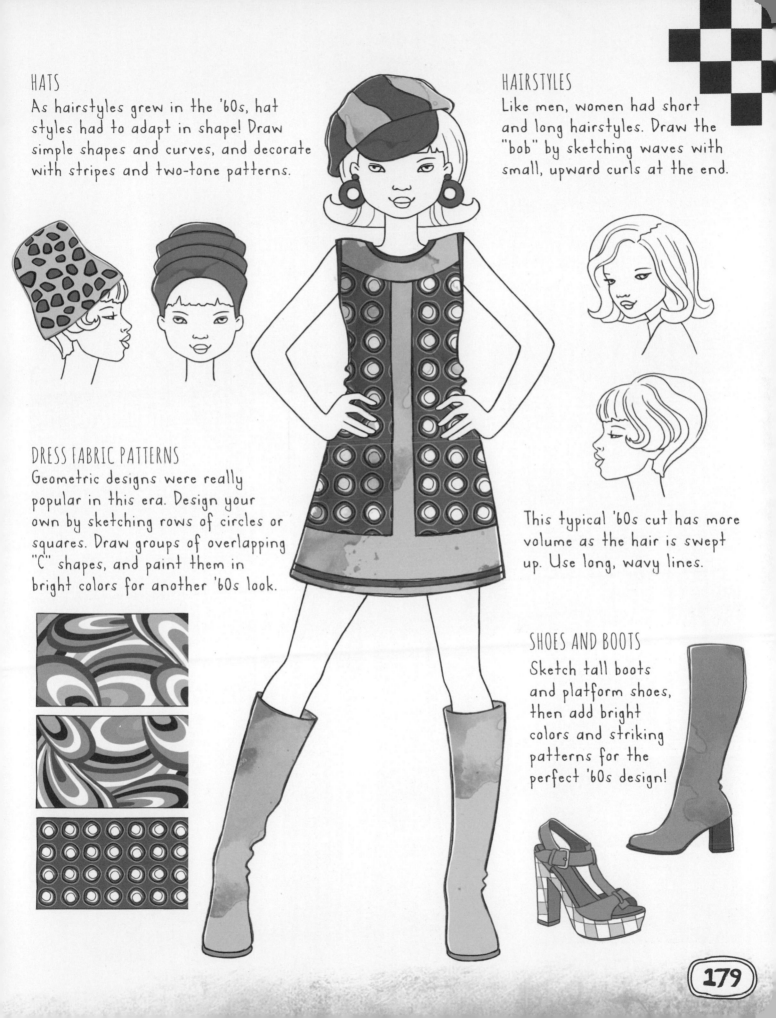

THE 1970S

FLARES, PLATFORM SHOES, AND LONG HAIR ... IT'S THE SEVENTIES.

HAIRSTYLES

Men tended to have long hair in the '70s. Draw the style on the left by sketching long, sweeping curves, starting from the crown. Use fewer lines to draw a neater hairstyle.

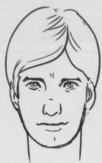

VEST

Create a hippie-style vest by adding rows of tassels and beads. Simple patterns add visual interest, and earthy colors make clothing look leathery.

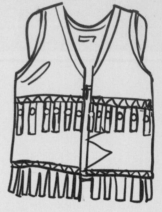

SHIRT PATTERNS

Shirts in the '70s were often bright and gaudy! Recreate these pattens using square, circle, and triangle shapes. Place the shapes inside each other and/or dot them around.

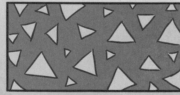

PANTS

Draw pants with high waists and chunky belts. Use long, sweeping lines to sketch flared bottoms.

SHOES

Fashionable men's shoes had thick soles. Draw them using more boxlike shapes than normal shoes. Color them with strong, contrasting tones.

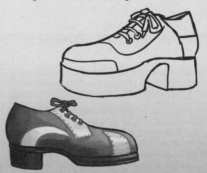

HAIRSTYLES

Women's hair in the '70s was often long and straight like men's. To draw a long, wavy style, use lots of large curves and swirls, building up the different layers.

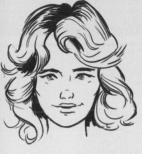 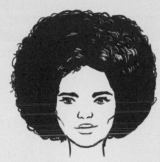

HATS

Hats from the '70s are easy to draw since they are basically dome-shaped. Use curved or wavy lines to sketch the brims, and add bows and ribbons for visual interest.

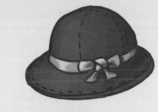

FABRIC PATTERNS

Patterns with wavy lines, swirls, and flowers were big in this decade! Design some yourself using two or more bold, contrasting colors.

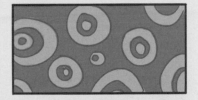

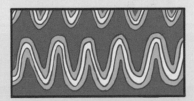

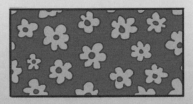

SHOES

The tops of women's shoes tended to look more delicate than men's. When you draw them, use more curves and sharper lines. The soles can look even chunkier and the heels a lot higher!

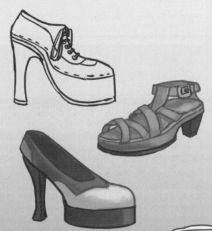

THE 1980s

NEON PRINTS, LEG WARMERS, AND BIG HAIR—IT'S THE EIGHTIES!

HAIRSTYLES
For a mullet (short in the front, long in the back), sketch wavy lines from the center of the head, with more behind the ears. For a mohawk, draw long, upright lines.

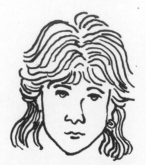

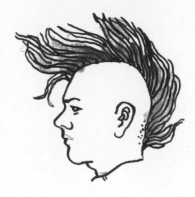

HATS
Draw a cap and decorate with jagged, overlapping shapes. Or, sketch a wide-brim hat shape, and fill it with crosshatch shading.

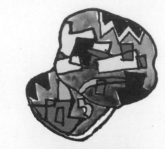

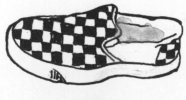

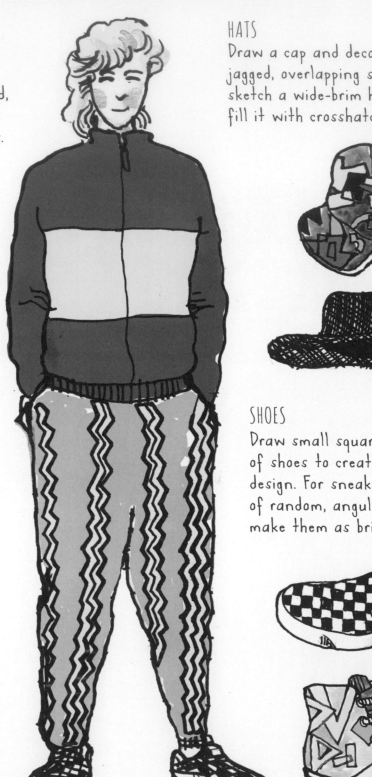

SHOES
Draw small squares on a pair of shoes to create a checkered design. For sneakers, use lots of random, angular shapes, and make them as bright as you can!

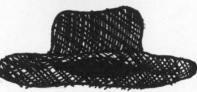

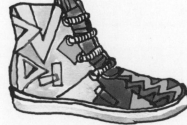

SHIRTS AND PANTS
Use simple zigzag lines for patterned '80s pants. Sketch a sports top with a wide band across the chest. Use two or more colors that really zing!

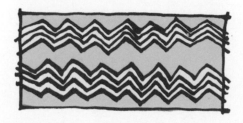

HAIRSTYLES

Use lots of long, wavy lines and "S" shapes to recreate classic '80s big hair. Draw tiny vertical lines on the side of the head to get a shaved effect, with closely packed wavy lines for a gelled-up look.

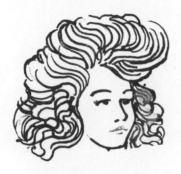

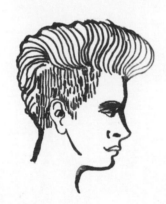

CAPS AND BANDS

Decorate a curved hairband with zigzags and top with a big bow in a clashing color. Make an '80s sun visor look reflective by adding jagged highlights to it.

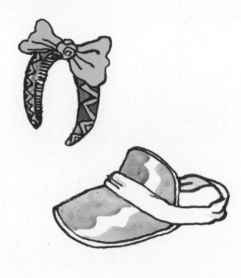

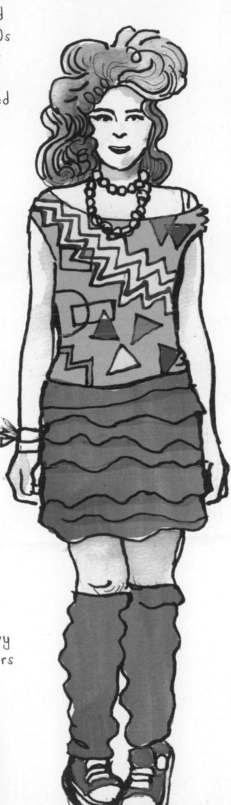

SHOES

Draw circles on a simple pump shape, then color the shoes in a neon shade. Or, add zigzags to pumps and color in vibrant, contrasting tones.

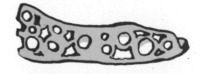

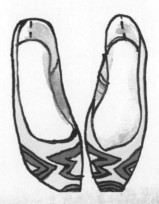

TOPS AND SKIRTS

Draw a simple off-the-shoulder T-shirt, and decorate it with overlapping geometric shapes in neon colors. Use horizontal, wavy lines to draw the different layers on a ruffle skirt.

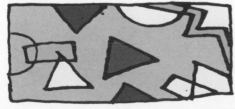

LOGOS

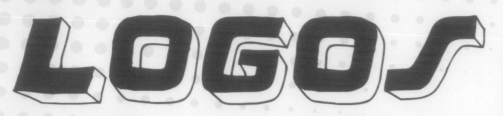

LOGOS GIVE BRANDS AN INSTANT IDENTITY. LEARN TO DRAW YOUR OWN LOGO—FOR A BRAND OR JUST FOR YOU!

SHAPES

THE FIRST THING TO DO IS TO PLAN THE SHAPE THAT WILL HOLD YOUR LOGO. TRY A CIRCLE, TRIANGLE, SHIELD, OR EVEN STARBURST, AND CUSTOMIZE THE EDGES FOR YOUR UNIQUE LOOK.

A basic shape suggests simplicity. Customize with a ribbon or a semicircle pattern for a more ornate effect.

CIRCLE

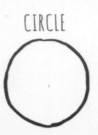

FRAME

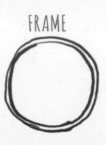

RIBBON

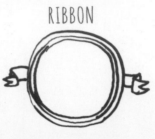

DECORATIVE

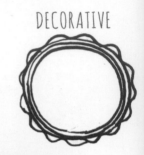

IMAGERY

THEN CHOOSE A FUN PICTURE OR ICON THAT MOST REPRESENTS YOU OR YOUR INTERESTS. KEEP YOUR DRAWING SIMPLE, SO THAT IT IS INSTANTLY RECOGNIZABLE FROM A DISTANCE.

Most of these icons are drawn using basic shapes like circles, triangles, ovals, and curved lines.

MUSICIAN

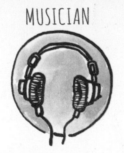

BOXER

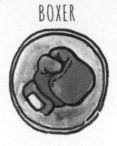

BEST FRIEND

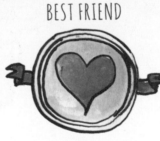

ANIMAL LOVER

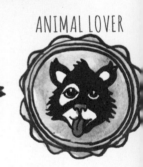

BANNERS

NOW THINK ABOUT WHERE TO PUT THE NAME OF YOUR BRAND, IF YOU WANT TO INCLUDE IT. YOU COULD USE A BANNER TO HOLD YOUR TEXT, AND COLOR IT TO REPRESENT YOU.

Create a banner using curvy lines and triangle shapes. Add your brand name, then color it in.

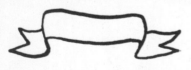

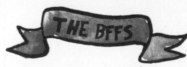

THE BFFS

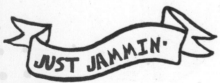

JUST JAMMIN'

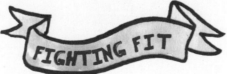

FIGHTING FIT

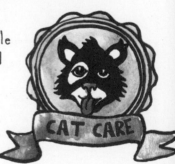

CAT CARE

SPORTSPERSON

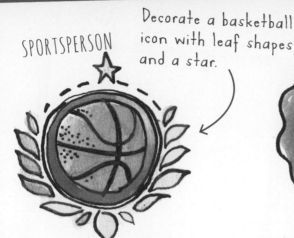

Decorate a basketball icon with leaf shapes and a star.

CHEF

Draw some wavy edges, such as a cupcake wrapper, to hold a baking logo.

GAMER

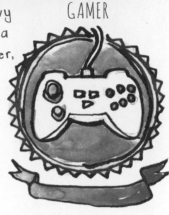

Give a gaming logo a banner and a cool name.

ARTIST

Draw a simple shield shape and add some flappy wings to hold artists' tools.

TOP OF THE CLASS

NAME

Use curvy lines to create a school crest. Add your name or a book icon.

PHOTOGRAPHER

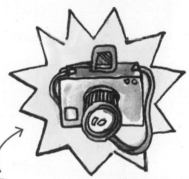

This star-shaped logo looks like a camera flash. Snap!

ROCK STAR

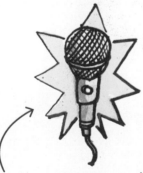

Use crosshatching lines for a microphone. Add a starburst shape behind.

MUSICIAN

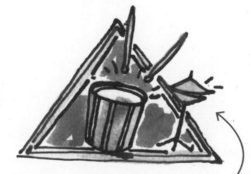

Use short lines to show noise—like around this banging drum and clanging cymbal.

Try whirling cogs to suggest a scientific brain at work!

SCIENTIST

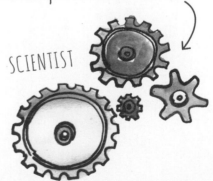

POP ART

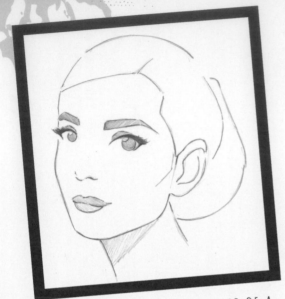

1 FOR A POP ART FACE, START WITH A PHOTO OF A FACE WITH A STRONG CONTRAST BETWEEN DARK AND LIGHT AREAS. USE A PENCIL TO TRACE THE OUTLINES OF THE HEAD AND FACIAL FEATURES.

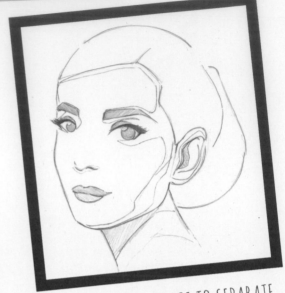

2 DRAW MORE OUTLINES ON THE FACE TO SEPARATE THE MAIN AREAS OF LIGHT AND DARK. TRY TO KEEP THESE SHAPES AS SIMPLE AS POSSIBLE.

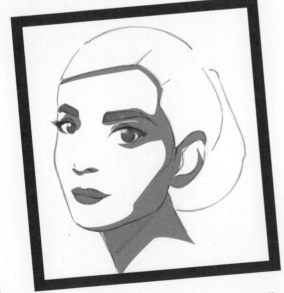

3 LEAVE THE LIGHT AREAS WHITE, THEN USE GRAY PENCILS OR PAINTS TO ADD SHADING TO THE AREAS THAT LOOK SLIGHTLY DARKER OR ARE IN SHADOW.

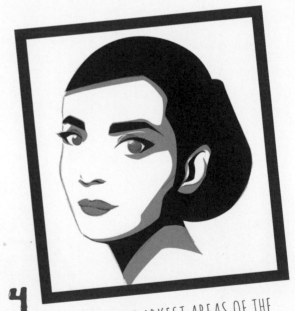

4 USE BLACK FOR THE DARKEST AREAS OF THE PORTRAIT, SUCH AS THE HAIR, EYEBROWS, AND UPPER NECK.

5 PAINT YOUR PICTURE WITH STRONG, VIBRANT COLORS. THE SECRET IS TO CREATE A SHARP CONTRAST BETWEEN THE LIGHTEST AND DARKEST TONES. HAVE FUN EXPERIMENTING WITH DIFFERENT COLORS, AND DISCOVER WHICH COMBINATIONS WORK BEST FOR YOUR IMAGE!

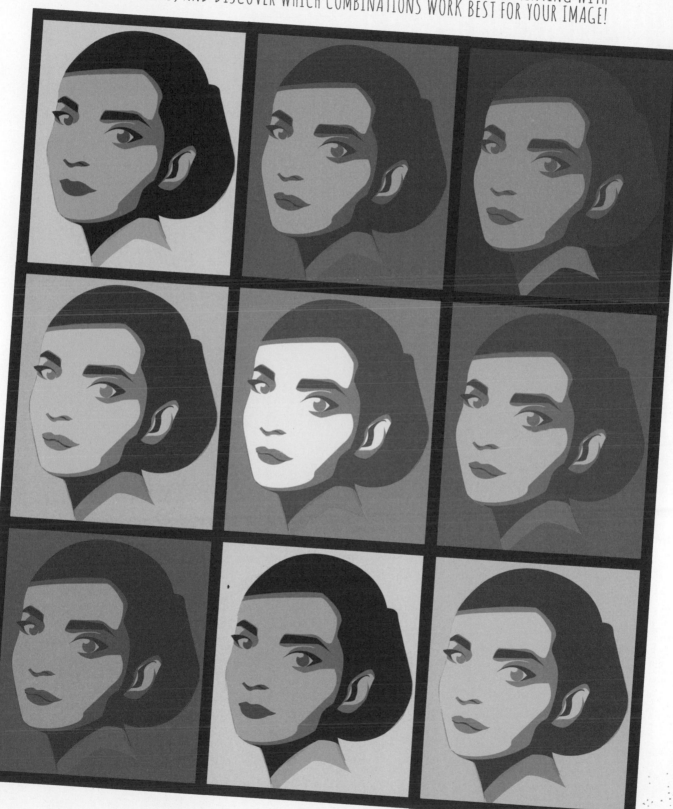

ALIEN PLANET

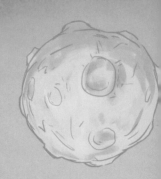

TEST THE LIMITS OF YOUR IMAGINATION BY CREATING A WORLD FULL OF SLEEK SPACESHIPS AND AMAZING ALIENS!

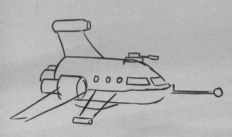

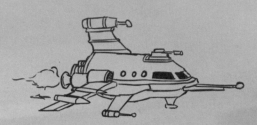

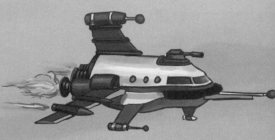

1

FOR A SPACESHIP, START WITH THE BASIC SHAPE. USE A MIX OF CURVES AND STRAIGHT LINES TO DRAW THE HULL, FINS, AND ROCKET BOOSTERS.

2

BUILD UP THE SURFACE DETAIL USING EXTRA LINES AND SMALL SHAPES. SHADE IN THE WINDOWS, AND ADD FLAMES AT THE REAR.

3

CHOOSE A SIMPLE COLOR SCHEME FOR YOUR SPACESHIP, AND ADD HIGHLIGHTS AND SHADED AREAS TO MAKE IT LOOK 3D!

This alien ship is based on the body of a shark! Use similar sleek and smooth shapes to make your own spaceship look like it can glide through air or water!

Try combining parts of different animals to create an alien. This one is part bird, part spider, and part butterfly!

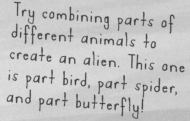

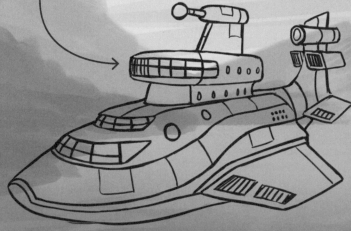

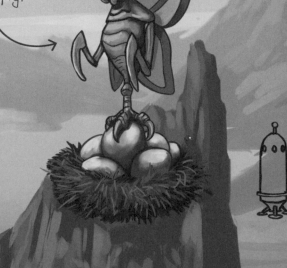

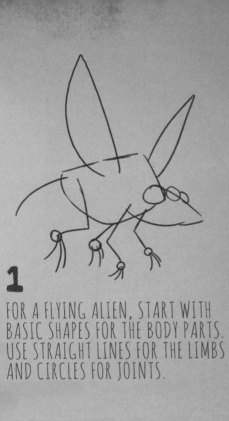

1

FOR A FLYING ALIEN, START WITH BASIC SHAPES FOR THE BODY PARTS. USE STRAIGHT LINES FOR THE LIMBS AND CIRCLES FOR JOINTS.

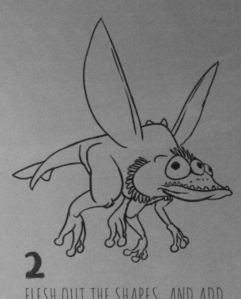

2

FLESH OUT THE SHAPES, AND ADD CURVES FOR THE MUSCLES. WORK ON THE FACIAL FEATURES, ADDING LOTS OF TEETH AND SCALES!

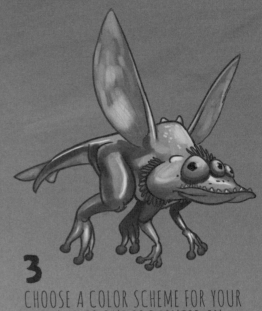

3

CHOOSE A COLOR SCHEME FOR YOUR ALIEN. THIS ONE IS PAINTED IN VIVID TONES, SUGGESTING IT'S LIKE NOTHING FOUND ON EARTH!

Create alien buildings using simple shapes such as cones, cylinders, and domes. Decorate with more complex shapes.

Think about how the locals look on your alien planet. Are they fierce or funny? Let your imagination go crazy!

Create a strange alien landscape using watercolor washes in lots of different shades.

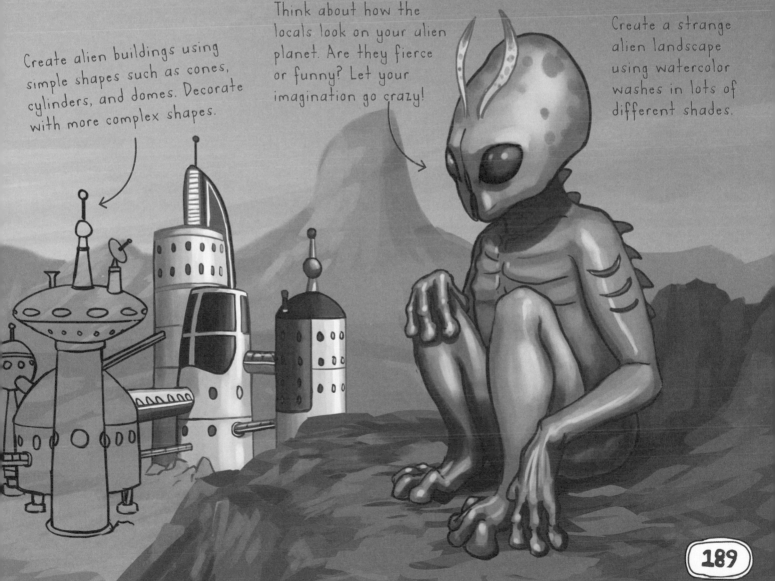

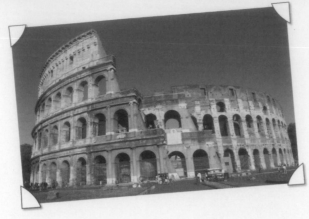

The Colosseum is a famous amphitheater in Rome, Italy. It's not as tricky to draw as it looks! Start with a photo for reference.

1

USING A LIGHT PENCIL, SKETCH THE TWO MAIN BASIC SHAPES OF THE COLOSSEUM, AS SHOWN, REFERRING TO YOUR PHOTO AS YOU GO.

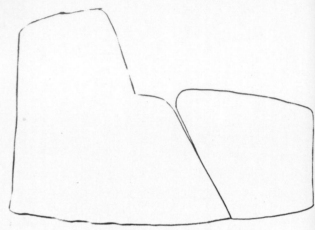

2

LOOSELY DRAW HORIZONTAL LINES WITHIN THE SHAPES, CURVING THEM SLIGHTLY TO FOLLOW THE FRAME OF THE COLOSSEUM.

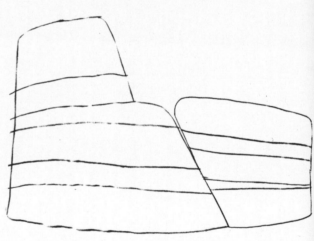

3

NOW ADD VERTICAL LINES TO CREATE A BASIS FOR THE WINDOWS.

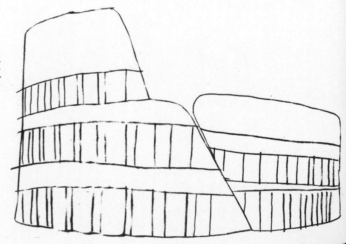

4

START FILLING IN THE DETAILS. CREATE THE ARCHED SHAPE OF THE WINDOWS AND ENTRANCEWAYS, THEN ADD IN SOME BRICKWORK FOR TEXTURE AND DEFINITION.

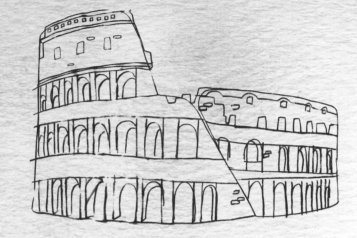

5

GO OVER YOUR OUTLINES IN PEN AND INK, THEN ERASE THE PENCIL LINES. KEEP THE LINE WORK LOOSE AND IMPERFECT TO CREATE THE FEEL OF A PARTIALLY RUINED BUILDING.

Draw jagged edges around the building to further suggest ruin and damage.

6

COLOR WITH LIGHT WATERCOLOR BRUSHWORK, AND ADD SHADOWING IN THE WINDOWS TO CREATE DEPTH. DRAW AND PAINT SOME SMALL PEOPLE AT THE BOTTOM TO GIVE AN OVERALL IMPRESSION OF SIZE AND GRANDEUR.

DESERT ISLAND

MIX DIFFERENT TECHNIQUES TO CREATE THIS FANTASY SCENE.

Start with simple outlines for the trunks and leaves of palm trees. Use a bristly brush when you paint the leaves.

Draw a pencil outline of a raft, then go over it in ink. Don't worry if your line work looks rough—that's authentic!

Find some reference images online to help you draw different kinds of fish.

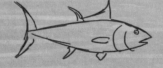
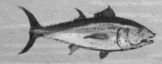

Use subtle blues and greens for the sea. Add white highlights on top to give the effect of light reflecting on the rippling water.

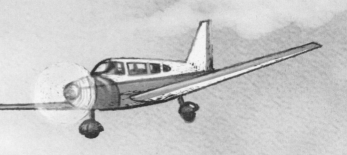

Draw a plane flying overhead to give the scene more of a story. What other vehicles or objects could you add?

For the shrubbery, use the end of a brush to dab greens and yellows onto the paper.

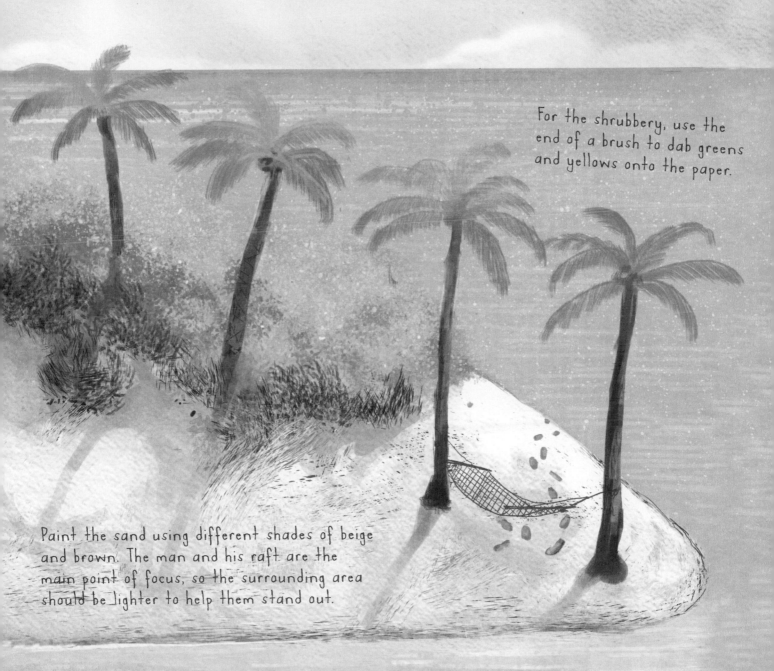

Paint the sand using different shades of beige and brown. The man and his raft are the main point of focus, so the surrounding area should be lighter to help them stand out.

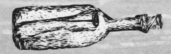 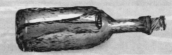

How about a message in a bottle in your scene? Add ink marks to make it look old, plus highlights to make the surface look like glass.

193

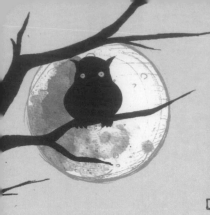

PUMPKIN PATTERNS

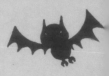

DRAW PUMPKINS, THEN PRACTICE SPOOKY PATTERNS INSIDE. TRY THESE ON REAL PUMPKINS AT HALLOWEEN AND IMPRESS YOUR FRIENDS. MWAH-HA-HA!

1 DRAW AN OVAL, THEN SKETCH ANOTHER ONE AROUND IT. ADD A TRIANGULAR SHAPE ON TOP, AND GIVE IT A FLAT BASE, LIKE THIS.

2 SKETCH CURVES ONTO THE PUMPKIN SKIN, AND DRAW A HAUNTED HOUSE SHAPE USING RECTANGLES AND TRIANGLES.

3 DRAW OVALS, TRIANGLES, RECTANGLES, AND CYLINDERS FOR THE TREE, GHOST, DOOR, AND WINDOWS, AS SHOWN.

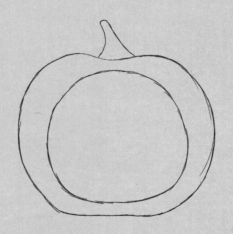

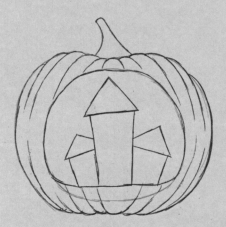

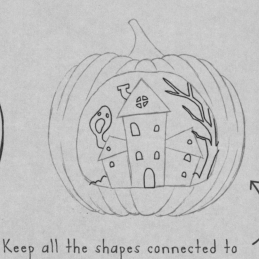

Keep all the shapes connected to each other, so nothing floats around.

4 DRAW LINES AROUND SOME OF THE ELEMENTS OF YOUR PICTURE TO ADD DEPTH AND GIVE IT A "CARVED OUT" EFFECT.

5 ADD SHADING TO THE STEM AND SKIN, THEN COLOR THE PUMPKIN. MAKE THE BACKGROUND BRIGHT, AS IF THERE'S A CANDLE INSIDE.

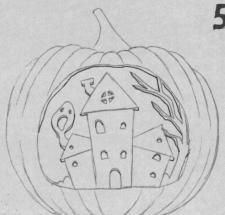

CARVE YOUR DESIGN

SPIDER

Draw a spider shape using ovals for the body, triangular shapes for the fangs, and cylinders for the long, spindly legs. Make sure the legs are touching the rest of the pumpkin.

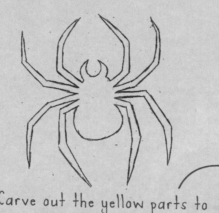

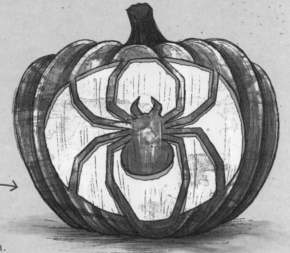

Carve out the yellow parts to leave the spider in the pumpkin.

wITCH

Use pointed lines to draw a witch. Add a moon around her. Then connect the witch's broomstick and dress to the moon, so that the witch stays in place when you carve out the gaps.

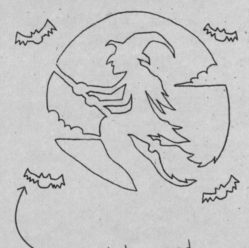

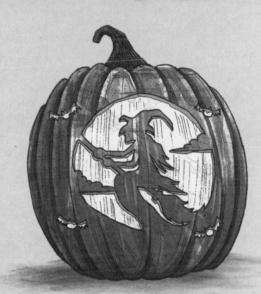

Carve out some bats around your main witch piece.

GRAVEYARD

Sketch a creepy graveyard with tombstones and a curved tree. Erase the lines connecting the tombstones and tree to the pumpkin.

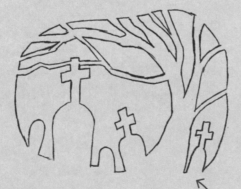

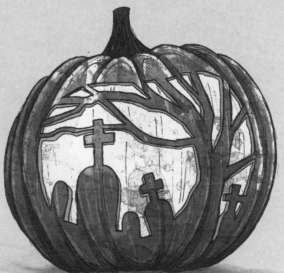

Cut out the sections between the tree branches very carefully.

ASTRONAUT

1

SKETCH A CIRCLE FOR YOUR ASTRONAUT'S HEAD, OVALS FOR HER HANDS, AND STRAIGHT LINES FOR HER BODY, ARMS, AND LEGS. DRAW AROUND YOUR GUIDELINES, AS SHOWN.

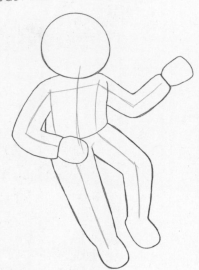

2

WORK UP THE SPACESUIT, AND ADD A HELMET AND SOME GLOVES. ERASE YOUR GUIDELINES FROM STEP 1.

3

FINISH THE HELMET AND HANDS, THEN CREATE CREASES IN THE SPACESUIT USING CURVED LINES.

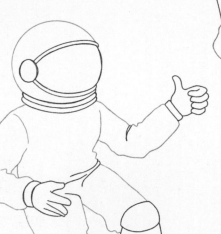

4

GIVE YOUR ASTRONAUT A FACE AND HAIR. ADD CIRCLES ON HER TORSO AND A RECTANGULAR OXYGEN TANK ON HER BACK.

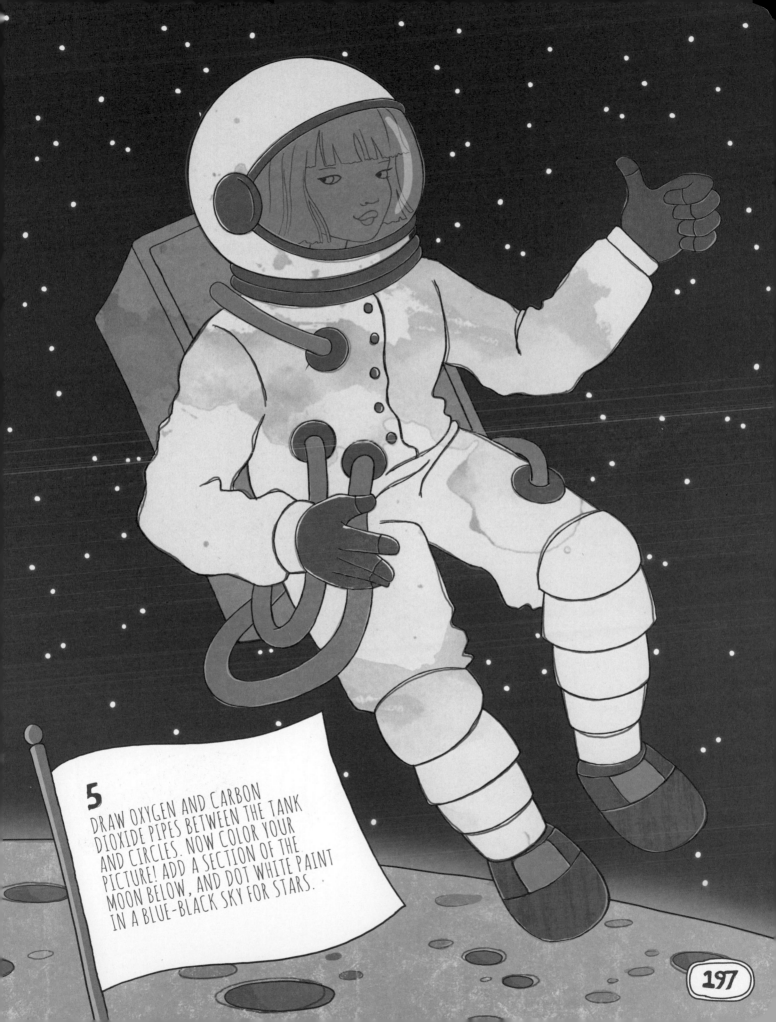

5
DRAW OXYGEN AND CARBON DIOXIDE PIPES BETWEEN THE TANK AND CIRCLES. NOW COLOR YOUR PICTURE! ADD A SECTION OF THE MOON BELOW, AND DOT WHITE PAINT IN A BLUE-BLACK SKY FOR STARS.

HOVER CAR

DESIGN YOUR VERY OWN CAR THAT FLIES THROUGH THE AIR!
HERE ARE A FEW IDEAS TO INSPIRE YOU ...

BODY SHAPE

Start with the outline of your car. The bodywork is roughly a box shape, with two arches cut out from the side. It's up to you whether or not your car has a roof!

INVERTED WHEELS

Think about how your car will hover. This hover car has special wheels that change into rocket boosters— they flip downward and the thrust lifts the vehicle into the air.

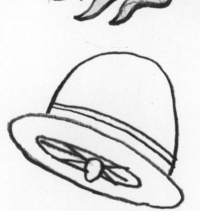

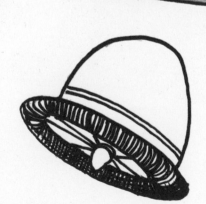

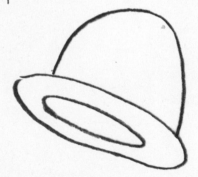

To draw a simple rocket booster, sketch a hat shape with a broad oval brim at the bottom.

Add spokes at the bottom of the rocket booster, plus any extra design details you like.

Finish off by adding lots of short, curved lines to the brim to make it look like tubing.

WINDSHIELD AND DRIVER

Draw a rectangle with curved corners for the windshield. Build up the driver's body shape using curved lines and ovals.

Add more details to the driver, such as his hair and facial features. Add the seats!

Add the finer details. A few angled lines on the windshield make it look like glass.

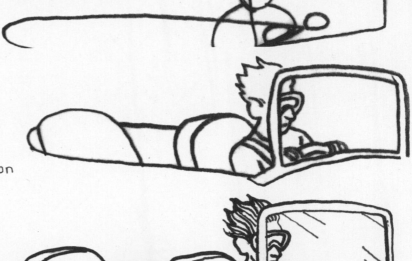

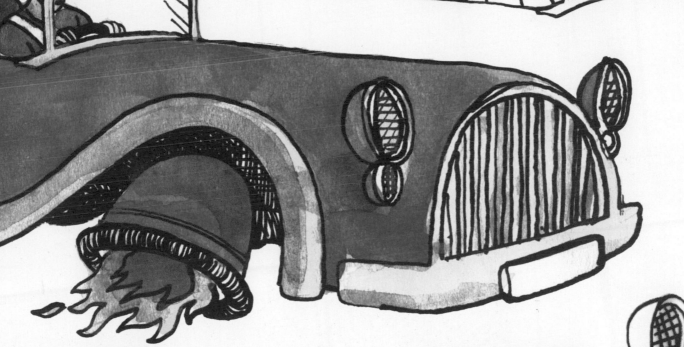

FIERY THRUST

Rocket flames make this car look really exciting. If you like, you could also draw smoke blasting out from underneath. What other cool features could your hover car have?

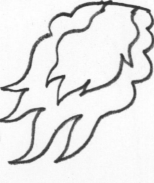

HEADLIGHTS

All cars need lights. This car has two big oval-shaped headlights with smaller signal lights underneath. Make yours retro like this, or give übermodern a try!

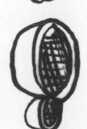

WRAPPING PAPER

USE PRETTY PATTERNS TO TURN ROLLS OF PLAIN PAPER INTO GORGEOUS GIFT WRAP!

ZIGZAGS

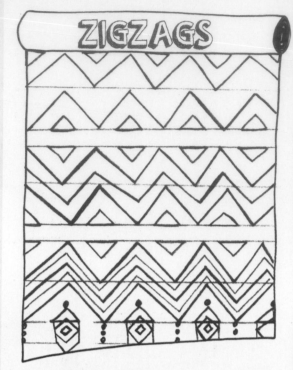

USE A PENCIL AND LONG RULER TO DIVIDE YOUR PAPER INTO HORIZONTAL STRIPS. DRAW ZIGZAGS AND DIAMOND PATTERNS BETWEEN THEM.

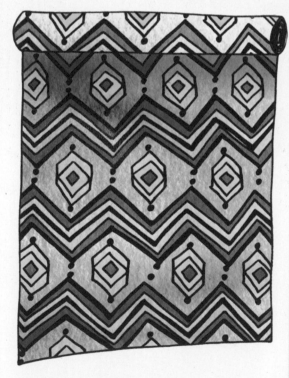

GO OVER YOUR DESIGN WITH WATERPROOF PENS, VARYING THE LINE THICKNESSES FOR IMPACT. THEN ADD SOME COLOR! PURPLES AND GREENS WORK WELL TOGETHER.

CIRCLES

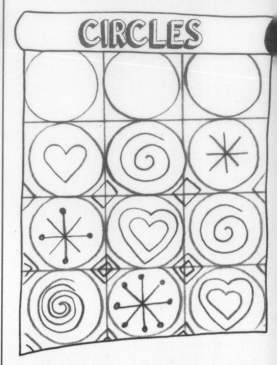

DIVIDE YOUR PAPER INTO LARGE SQUARES. SKETCH A CIRCLE IN EACH SQUARE AND A PATTERN IN EACH CIRCLE. DRAW DIAMOND SHAPES WHERE THE SQUARE CORNERS MEET.

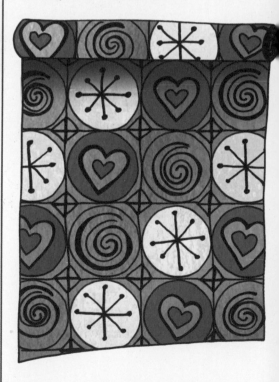

PAINT THE WHOLE BACKGROUND IN A SINGLE COLOR. WHEN IT'S DRY, PAINT THE CIRCLES AND SHAPES IN CONTRASTING COLORS.

FESTIVE

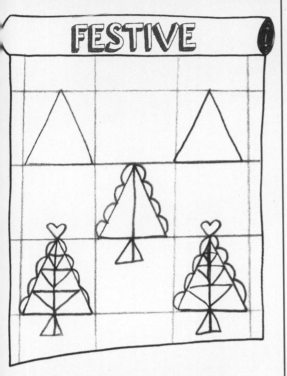

ONCE AGAIN, DIVIDE THE PAPER INTO BIG SQUARES. ADD A TRIANGLE TO EVERY OTHER ONE. ADD MORE TRIANGLES TO EACH SHAPE, AS WELL AS SOME DECORATIONS.

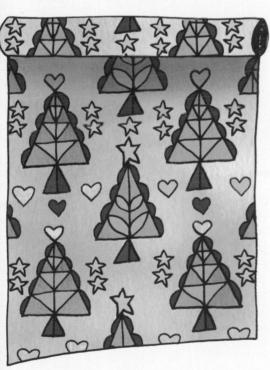

PAINT THE BACKGROUND A PALE GREEN, AND LEAVE TO DRY. USE DARKER SHADES FOR THE TREES, WITH CONTRASTING COLORS FOR THE DECORATIONS.

BIRTHDAY

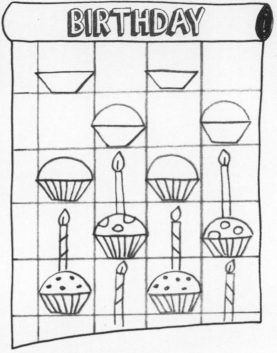

FIRST DRAW YOUR GRID, THEN SKETCH A CUPCAKE BASE IN EVERY OTHER SQUARE. DRAW A CURVE ON TOP OF EACH BASE. ADD CANDLES AND OTHER DETAILS.

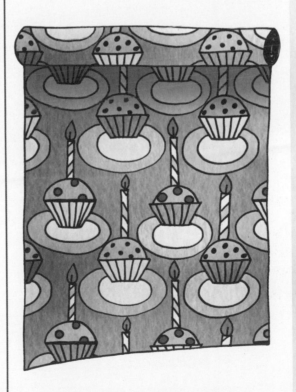

USE A PALE WASH OVER THE WHOLE PAPER. THEN, FOR INTEREST, PICK OUT DETAILS SUCH AS THE CUPCAKE CUPS AND DECORATIONS IN DIFFERENT COLORS.

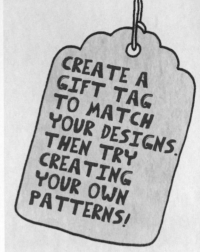

CREATE A GIFT TAG TO MATCH YOUR DESIGNS. THEN TRY CREATING YOUR OWN PATTERNS!

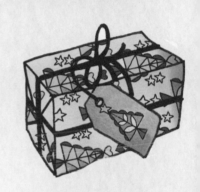

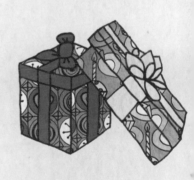

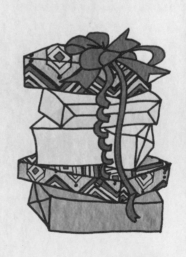

3D TREASURE MAP

1 START WITH A TRAPEZOID SHAPE (A RECTANGLE WITH THE SIDES SLANTING INWARD). ADD RIPPED EDGES FOR AN OLDER, WORN-AND-TORN LOOK. DRAW A CURVED ISLAND SHAPE IN THE MIDDLE.

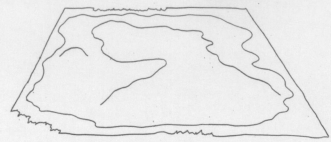

2 SKETCH RIPPLING LINES AROUND THE ISLAND FOR THE SEA. SHADE IN SOME CLIFF EDGES TO RAISE THE ISLAND OUT OF THE WATER. ADD A PATHWAY WITH A BIG "X" AT THE END.

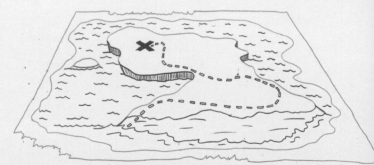

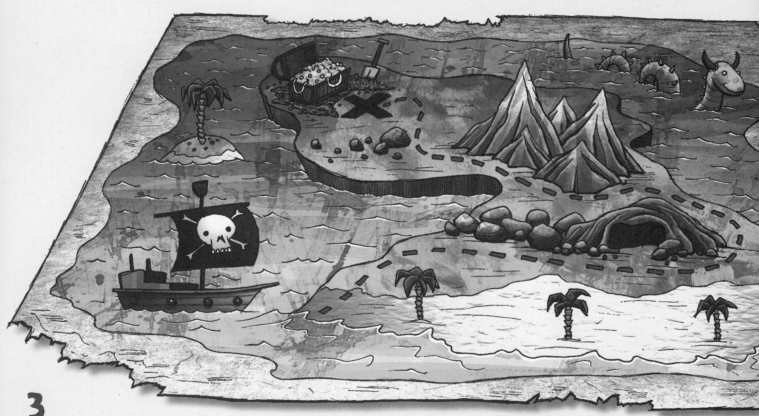

3

ADD MORE DETAILS, SUCH AS A PIRATE SHIP, TREASURE CHEST, CAVE, SEA MONSTER, MOUNTAINS, AND TREES, TO GIVE YOUR MAP MORE CHARACTER AND INTEREST. GET CREATIVE WITH THIS! COLOR AND SHADE YOUR MAP.

MAP FEATURES

MOUNTAINS

Draw jagged triangle shapes. Add smaller triangles and lines inside your basic mountains, then shade them for a 3D effect.

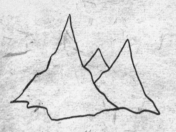 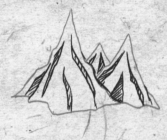

CAVES

Start with a rough semicirle for the cave. Draw a smaller semicircle for the opening. Add shading in and around the cave for depth.

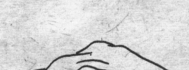 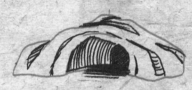

PIRATE SHIP

Sketch curved lines and rectangles to create the ship, mast, and flag. Add wavy water lines, and don't forget the skull and crossbones!

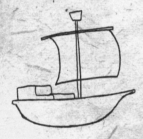 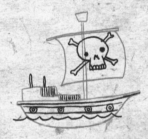

PALM TREES

Repeat small, upside-down trapezoid shapes for the trunk. Then draw droopy, pointed leaves on top. Add shading to the trunk and leaves.

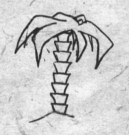 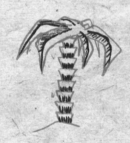

SEA MONSTER

Draw an oval-shaped head and two curved lines for the neck. Sketch semicircles for the body, then triangles for the tail, spikes, and horns. Add the eyes, mouth, and water lines.

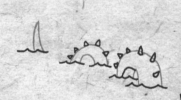

TREASURE CHEST

Start with a basic cuboid shape, then draw a rectangular lid with two semicircles on either side. Add lines to the chest for texture, and sketch circles and semicircles for the treasure!

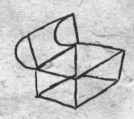 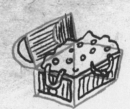

MERMAID

1 SKETCH CIRCLE GUIDES FOR THE HEAD AND JOINTS, STRAIGHT LINES FOR THE BODY AND ARMS, RECTANGLES FOR THE HANDS, AND TRIANGLES FOR THE FISH TAIL.

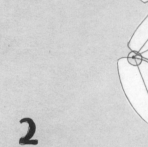

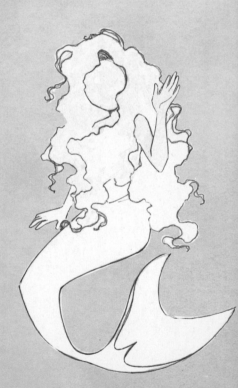

2 ADD BASIC OVAL SHAPES AROUND THE ARMS, BODY, AND TOP THREE SECTIONS OF THE TAIL.

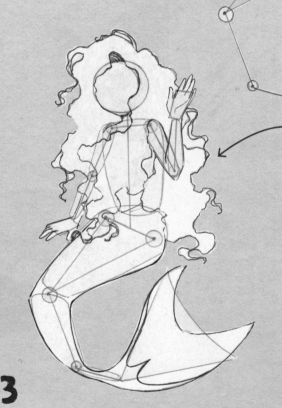

Wavy lines create long, flowing hair and suggest movement under the sea.

3 DRAW AROUND YOUR GUIDELINES WITH A HEAVY, FLUID LINE. ADD HAIR, FINGERS, AND A FLIPPY TAIL.

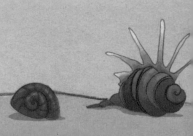

4 ERASE YOUR GUIDELINES TO LEAVE YOUR BASIC MERMAID DRAWING.

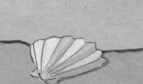
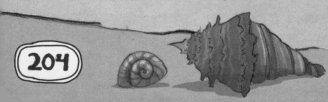

5

NOW DRAW IN YOUR MERMAID'S FACIAL FEATURES, AND ADD MORE DETAIL TO THE FISH TAIL.

Create the illusion of thick hair with different shades of the same color.

6

PAINT YOUR MERMAID! ADD SIMPLE "U" SHAPES ON HER TAIL TO CREATE FISH SCALES.

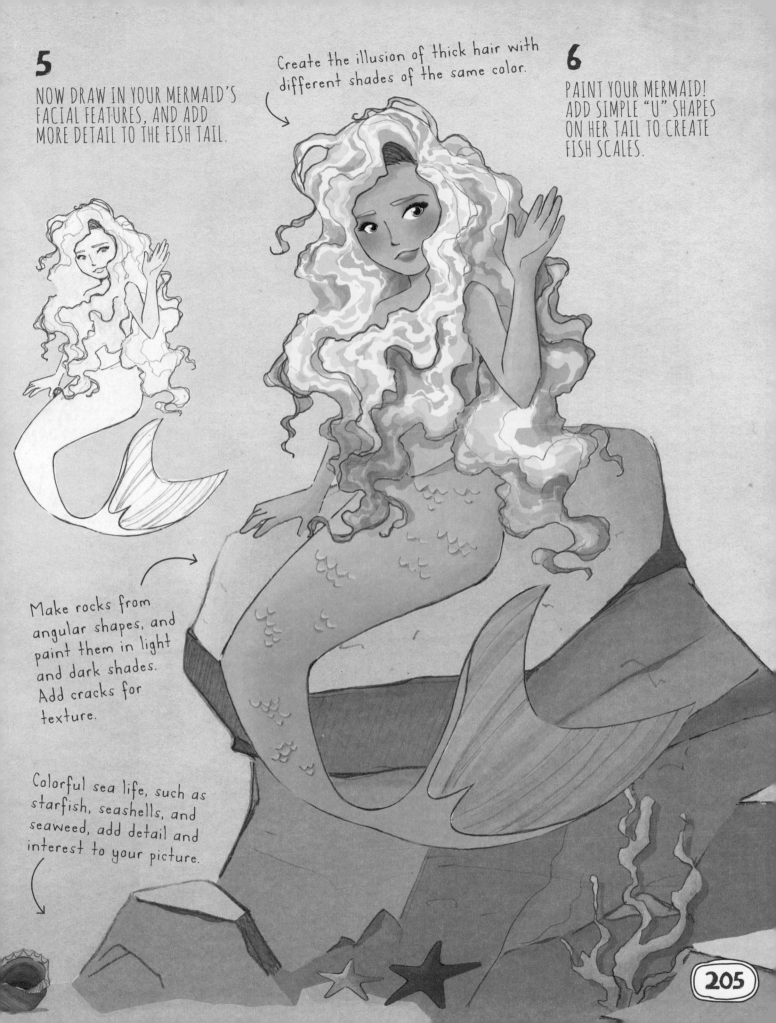

Make rocks from angular shapes, and paint them in light and dark shades. Add cracks for texture.

Colorful sea life, such as starfish, seashells, and seaweed, add detail and interest to your picture.

WEREWOLF

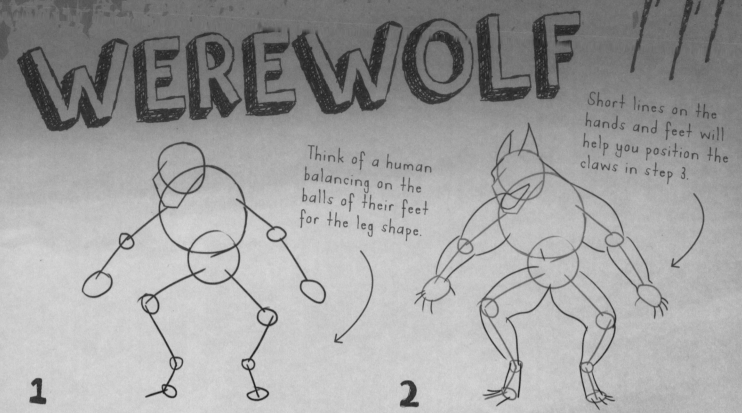

Think of a human balancing on the balls of their feet for the leg shape.

Short lines on the hands and feet will help you position the claws in step 3.

1
SKETCH CIRCLES FOR THE HEAD, BODY, HANDS, FEET, AND BODY JOINTS, AND STRAIGHT LINES FOR THE ARMS AND LEGS, AS SHOWN. ADD A RECTANGULAR-SHAPED SNOUT.

2
DRAW FLUID LINES AROUND YOUR GUIDES TO SUGGEST BULKY MUSCLES. SKETCH TWO TRIANGLES FOR EARS, AND ADD IN THE MOUTH.

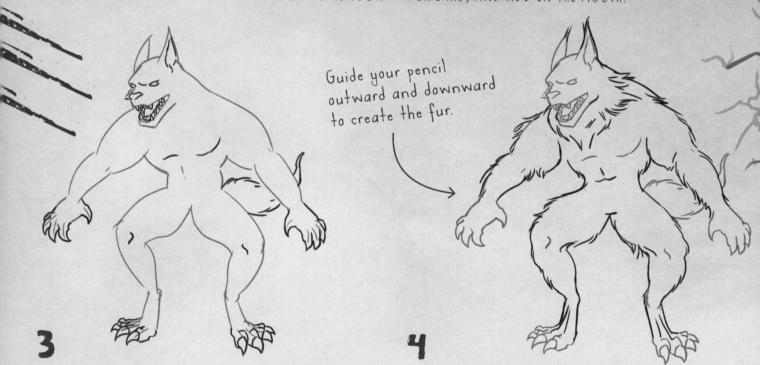

Guide your pencil outward and downward to create the fur.

3
ADD CLAWS, EYES, AND A DOGLIKE NOSE. SKETCH A SCRUFFY TAIL USING SHORT, FLICKY LINES. DRAW SMALL TRIANGLES FOR TEETH AND CURVED LINES ON THE CHEST AND KNEES. ERASE THE LINES FROM STEP 1.

4
APPLY THE SAME FLICKY LINES YOU USED FOR THE TAIL TO ADD IN THE WEREWOLF'S FUR. STRAIGHT LINES ON THE FEET WILL GIVE THE IMPRESSION OF STRETCHED TENDONS. ERASE THE ROUGH LINES FROM STEP 2.

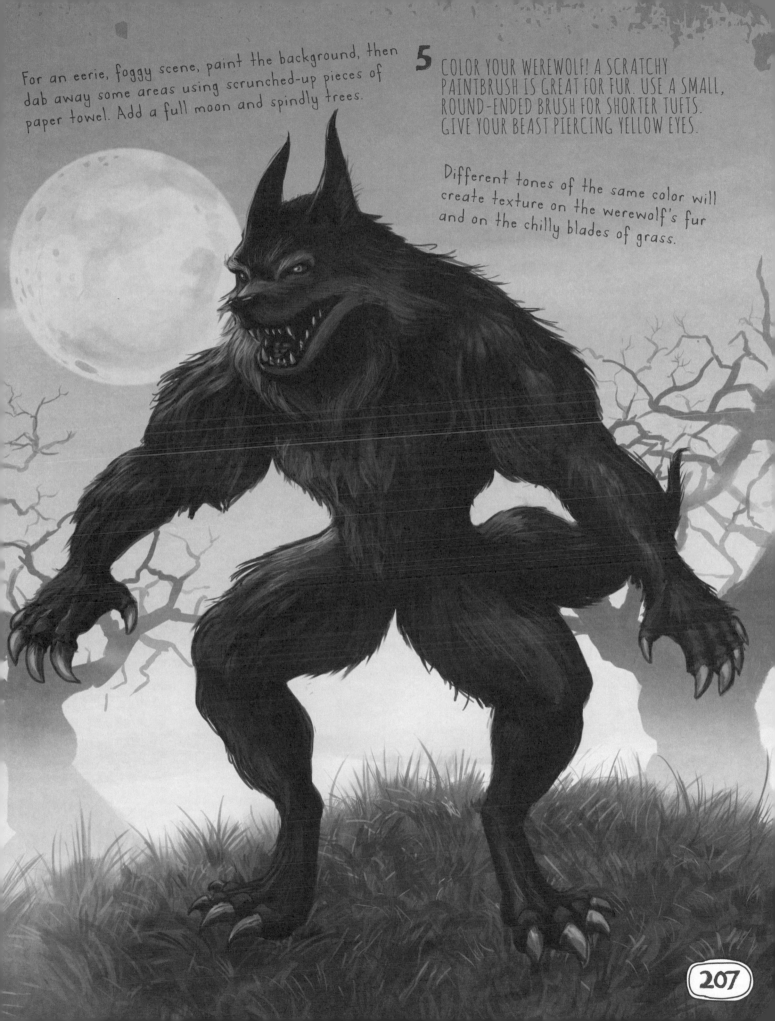

For an eerie, foggy scene, paint the background, then dab away some areas using scrunched-up pieces of paper towel. Add a full moon and spindly trees.

5 COLOR YOUR WEREWOLF! A SCRATCHY PAINTBRUSH IS GREAT FOR FUR. USE A SMALL, ROUND-ENDED BRUSH FOR SHORTER TUFTS. GIVE YOUR BEAST PIERCING YELLOW EYES.

Different tones of the same color will create texture on the werewolf's fur and on the chilly blades of grass.

COMIC STYLE

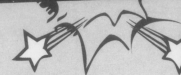

1 SKETCH PERSPECTIVE LINES TO HELP YOU DRAW A SUPERHERO COMING STRAIGHT AT YOU OFF OF THE PAGE. ADD AN OVAL SHAPE FOR THE HEAD WITH A HORIZONTAL CURVED LINE BELOW IT.

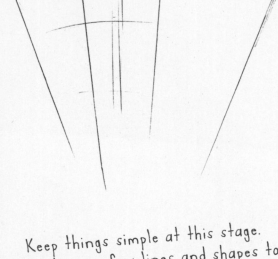

Keep things simple at this stage. Just use a few lines and shapes to help you think about the pose.

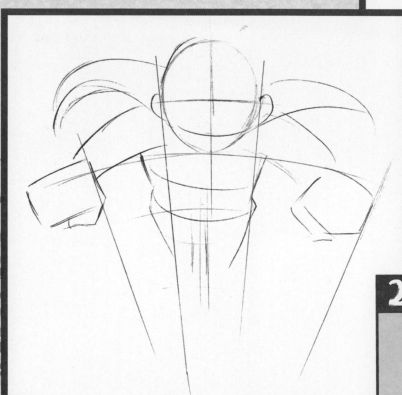

Comic style is about exaggerated elements and simple features. Once you've mastered your character, try drawing a whole comic strip!

2 DRAW THE ROUGH SHAPE OF YOUR FIGURE WITHIN YOUR GUIDES, PAYING CAREFUL ATTENTION TO THE PERSPECTIVE. THE FISTS ARE NEAR TO US, SO THEY NEED TO LOOK VERY BIG. THE LEGS AND FEET ARE FARTHER AWAY SO SHOULD APPEAR MUCH SMALLER.

3

ADD MORE DETAIL. SKETCH IN THE SHAPES OF THE HAIR AND FINGERS, AND GIVE YOUR SUPERHERO A SIMPLE, SILLY COMIC EXPRESSION. TO ADD MOVEMENT, DRAW A FLOWING CAPE USING CURVED LINES.

4

USE A HEAVIER PENCIL TO ADD EVEN MORE SURFACE DETAIL AND SHADOW. GO OVER THE DRAWING IN BLACK INK, THEN PAINT YOUR SUPERHERO IN BRIGHT, COMIC-BOOK COLORS.

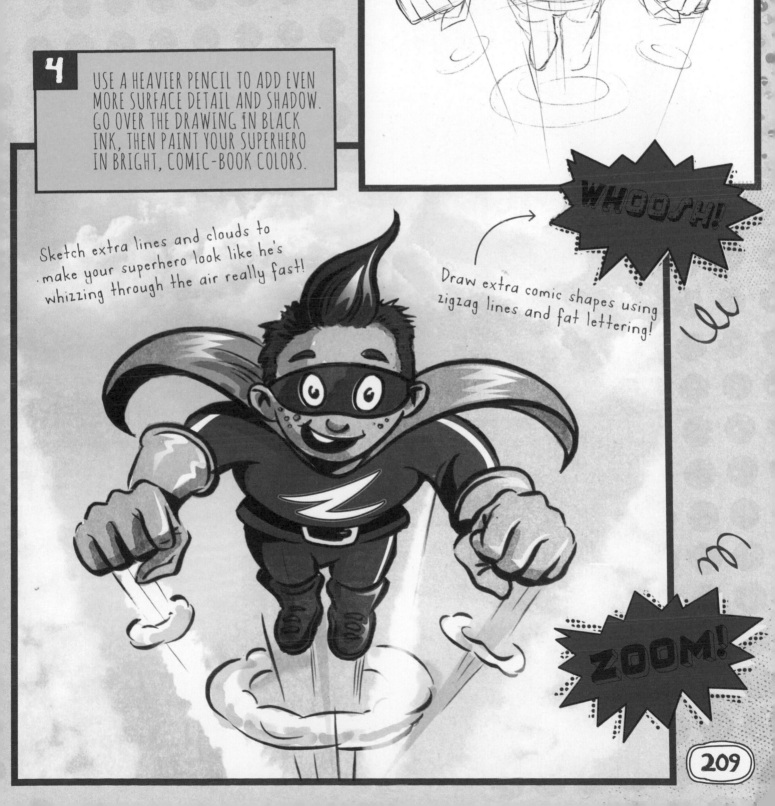

Sketch extra lines and clouds to make your superhero look like he's whizzing through the air really fast!

Draw extra comic shapes using zigzag lines and fat lettering!

WHOOSH!

ZOOM!

209

MOSAIC

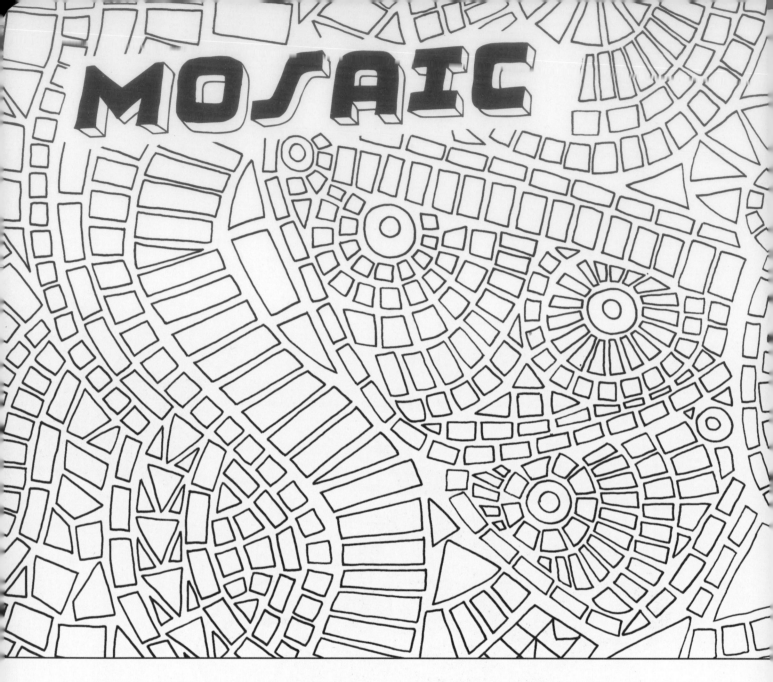

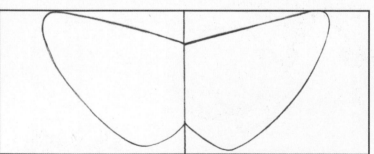

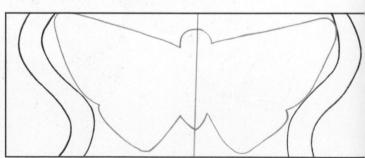

1 START WITH A BASIC SHAPE TO BUILD YOUR MOSAIC AROUND. FOR A BUTTERFLY, SKETCH A VERTICAL LINE, THEN DRAW A SIMPLE WING ON EACH SIDE.

2 DRAW WAVY LINES AROUND THE BUTTERFLY WINGS, READY FOR THE MOSAIC PATTERN LATER ON. ADD A SEMICIRCULAR HEAD AND A POINT FOR THE BODY.

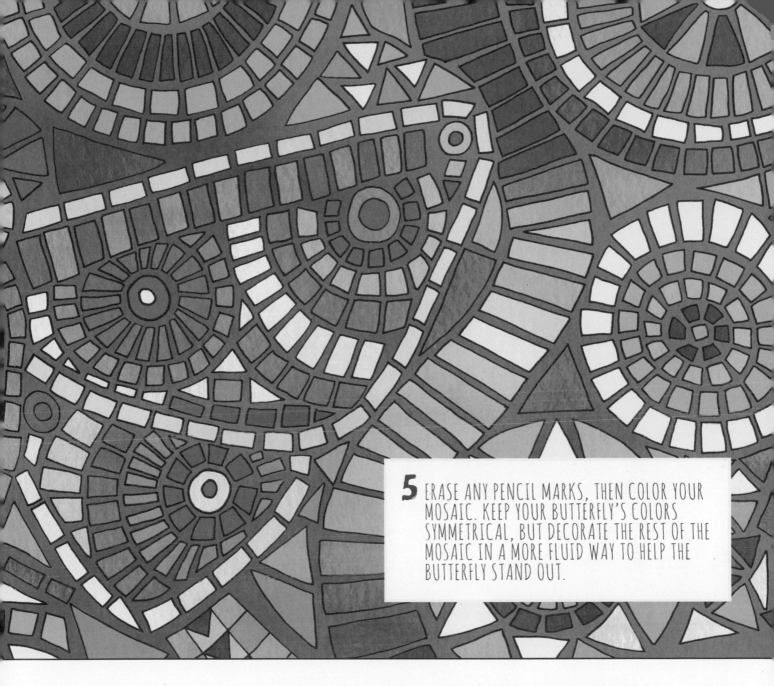

5 ERASE ANY PENCIL MARKS, THEN COLOR YOUR MOSAIC. KEEP YOUR BUTTERFLY'S COLORS SYMMETRICAL, BUT DECORATE THE REST OF THE MOSAIC IN A MORE FLUID WAY TO HELP THE BUTTERFLY STAND OUT.

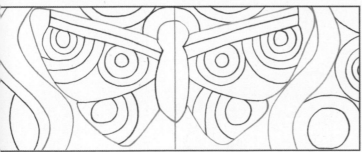

3 SKETCH A SYMMETRICAL PATTERN ON THE WINGS AND A MIXTURE OF SHAPES AROUND THE BUTTERFLY. THESE DON'T NEED TO MIRROR EACH OTHER.

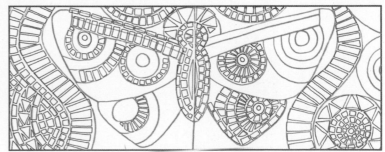

4 DRAW THE INDIVIDUAL MOSAIC PIECES USING TINY RECTANGLES, SQUARES, CIRCLES, AND TRIANGLES. GO OVER YOUR OUTLINES WITH AN INK PEN.

211

PILOT

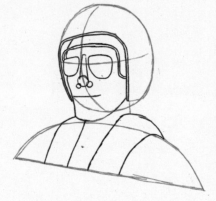

Use stars, circles, and wing shapes to design your own air force badges.

1

DRAW AN OVAL FOR THE HEAD. ADD HORIZONTAL AND VERTICAL CURVES AS GUIDELINES, AS SHOWN. DRAW A CURVED SHAPE FOR THE SHOULDERS.

2

GIVE THE SHOULDERS A LITTLE MORE SHAPE, AND SKETCH IN THE OUTLINE OF THE HELMET. ADD A CURVED SHAPE FOR THE CHIN.

3

USING YOUR GUIDELINES, SKETCH IN THE FACIAL ELEMENTS—NOSE, MOUTH, AND SUNGLASSES. ADD LINES FOR THE SHOULDER STRAPS.

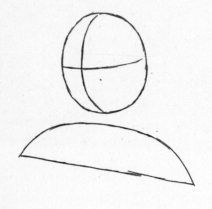

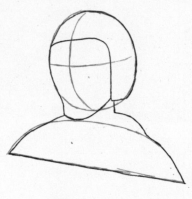

4

REFINE YOUR PENCIL LINES, AND CONTINUE ADDING DETAIL TO THE FACE AND STRAPS. DRAW A ROUNDED-OFF TRIANGULAR SHAPE FOR THE FACE MASK.

5

NOW ADD THE FINER DETAILS. DRAW SMALL CIRCLES AND LINES ON THE HELMET, AND SKETCH AN EARPIECE ON ONE SIDE. ADD TUBING AND OTHER DETAILS TO THE FACE MASK.

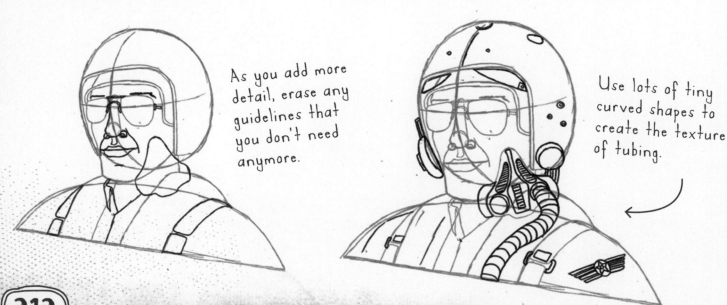

As you add more detail, erase any guidelines that you don't need anymore.

Use lots of tiny curved shapes to create the texture of tubing.

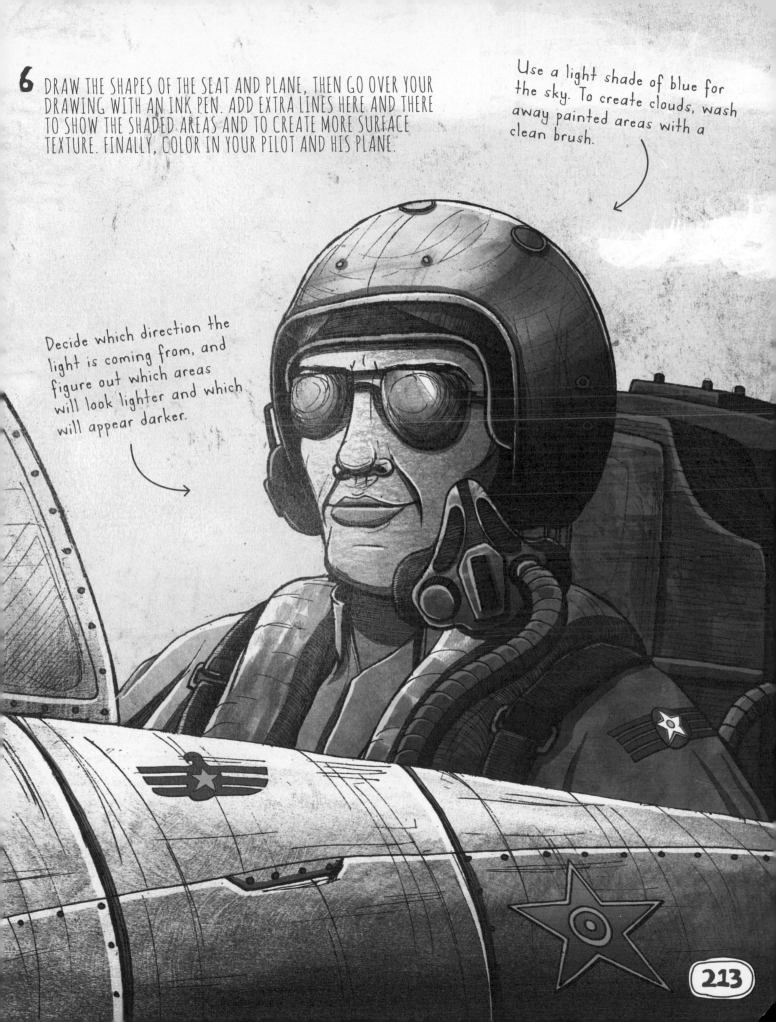

6 DRAW THE SHAPES OF THE SEAT AND PLANE, THEN GO OVER YOUR DRAWING WITH AN INK PEN. ADD EXTRA LINES HERE AND THERE TO SHOW THE SHADED AREAS AND TO CREATE MORE SURFACE TEXTURE. FINALLY, COLOR IN YOUR PILOT AND HIS PLANE.

Use a light shade of blue for the sky. To create clouds, wash away painted areas with a clean brush.

Decide which direction the light is coming from, and figure out which areas will look lighter and which will appear darker.

EGYPT

LEARN TO DRAW THE ELEMENTS OF ANCIENT EGYPT AND DRAW LIKE AN EGYPTIAN!

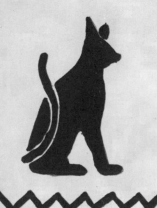

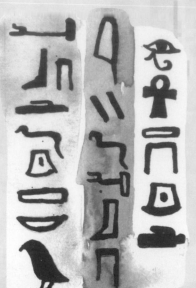

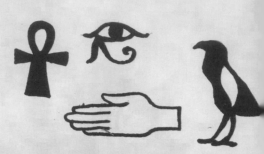

HIEROGLYPHICS: Ancient Egyptians used pictures of objects, people, and animals as a writing system. Draw bold, black lines and curves to create your own hieroglyphs.

ANCIENT EGYPTIAN WOMAN: Try drawing this figure with long, smooth lines. Use a limited color palette of bright yellows, oranges, and blues to give your painting authenticity

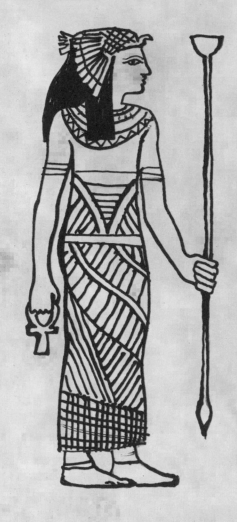

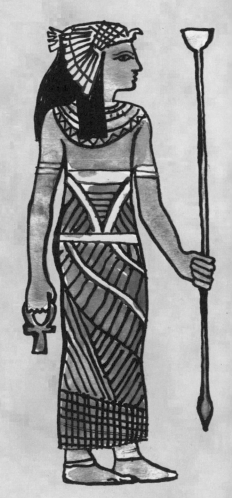

SPHINX: Draw this human-lion hybrid statue in bold, simple lines. Keep the facial features simple, using curved lines for the eyes, nose, and mouth.

Color your sphinx with a mix of yellow watercolor and yellow ocher for a sandy, desertlike wash. Add a little brown shading to give your picture more depth.

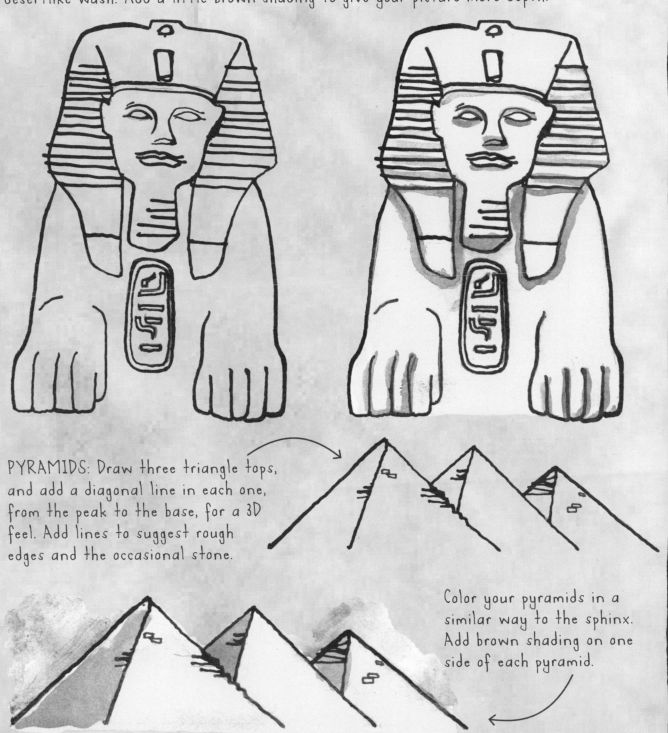

PYRAMIDS: Draw three triangle tops, and add a diagonal line in each one, from the peak to the base, for a 3D feel. Add lines to suggest rough edges and the occasional stone.

Color your pyramids in a similar way to the sphinx. Add brown shading on one side of each pyramid.

Find photos of Egyptology online or in books to help inspire your drawings!

WEDDING DRESS

1 SKETCH GUIDELINES FOR THE HEAD, ARMS, SHOULDERS, TORSO, AND BOUQUET. USE A ZIGZAG FOR A POSE WITH PERSONALITY. THEN DRAW THE OUTLINE OF THE DRESS.

2 FLESH OUT THE SHAPES OF THE HEAD, SHOULDERS, ARMS, AND HANDS. ADD THE BRIDE'S HAIR, AND SKETCH THE UPPER PART OF HER DRESS WITH CURVED LINES.

Add a rough patch of color to make the pale dress stand out.

3 USE LONG, SWEEPING CURVES FOR THE VEIL. DRAW THE FLOWERS AND USE WAVY LINES TO SKETCH THE RIBBONS. ERASE GUIDELINES.

4 PAINT THE DRESS A PALE COLOR, ADDING DARKER TONES FOR THE SHADOWY AREAS. PAINT THE BRIDE'S SKIN AND HAIR, AND USE A BRIGHT COLOR FOR THE FLOWERS.

DESIGN A DRESS

Create your own wedding dress designs by experimenting with different shapes, patterns, and textures.

Dab the end of your brush onto the paper to give this faint, stippled texture.

Choose a simple motif, then repeat it all over the dress to create an elegant pattern. Keep the colors simple and feminine.

Roses are easy to draw. They're just groups of rough-edged circles painted pink.

For an original look, add an accessory in an eye-catching color.

Add extra details to the hem of your dress for that finishing touch. You could add a simple colored border, or draw layers of wavy lines for a more dramatic look.

Draw lots of overlapping bands to create this beautiful bow!

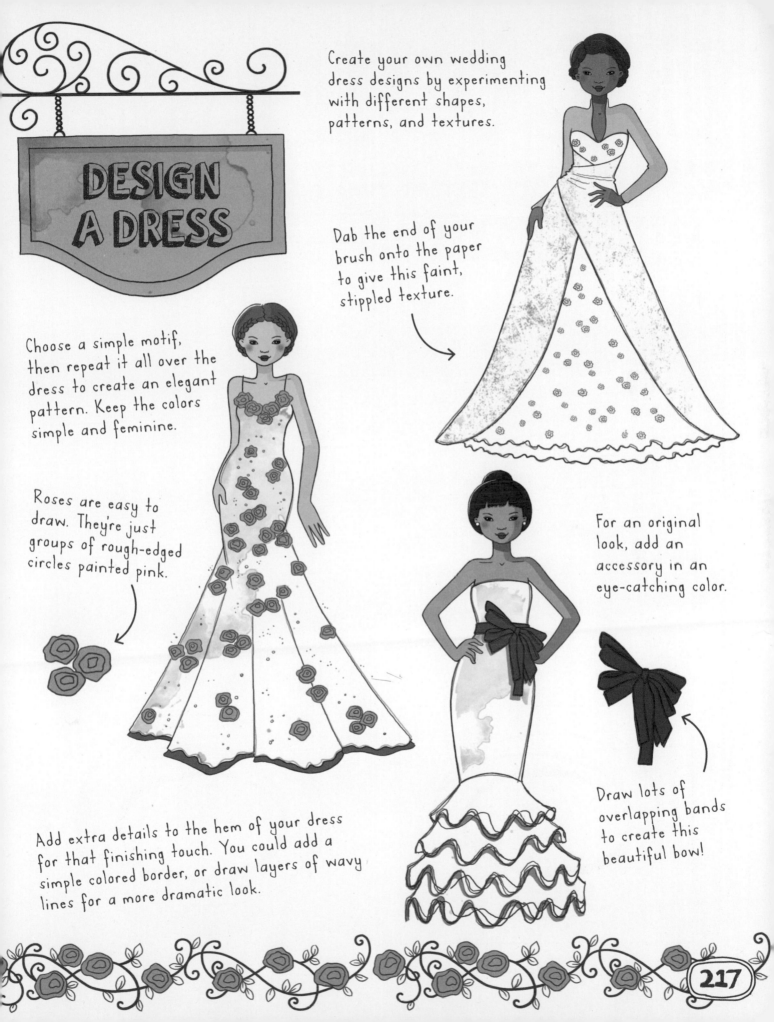

ILLUSIONS

IT'S FUN BREAKING THE RULES OF PERSPECTIVE TO CREATE IMPOSSIBLE OBJECTS. YOU CAN EVEN CREATE PICTURES THAT LOOK LIKE THEY'RE MOVING

IMPOSSIBLE OVAL

1

USING A PENCIL, SKETCH A HORIZONTAL GUIDELINE. THEN DRAW AN ARC ON EITHER SIDE TO FORM A SYMMETRICAL OVAL SHAPE.

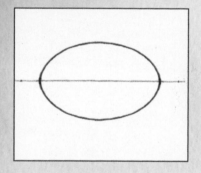

2

ADD A LARGER CURVE ATTACHED TO ONE END OF THE OVAL. DRAW ANOTHER CURVE UNDERNEATH, ATTACHED TO THE OPPOSITE END.

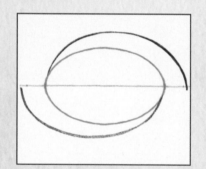

3

DRAW A LARGER OVAL AROUND ALL THE SHAPES YOU'VE SKETCHED SO FAR. LOOK CLOSELY AT THE PICTURE BELOW FOR ITS POSITION.

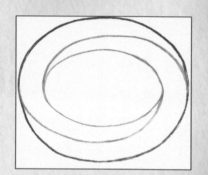

4

GO OVER YOUR DRAWING WITH A WATERPROOF PEN. TRY VARYING THE LINE THICKNESSES TO CREATE A MORE 3D EFFECT OVERALL.

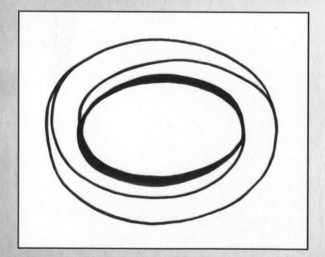

5

ADD COLOR WITH WATERCOLOR INKS. MAKE ONE SIDE DARKER THAN THE OTHER TO ADD TO THE 3D FEEL. YOUR DRAWING IS DONE, BUT THE CRAZY THING IS THAT THIS OBJECT CAN'T ACTUALLY EXIST—LOOK HOW IT TWISTS!

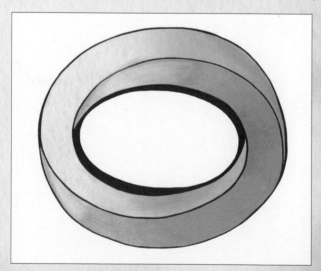

THE FAKE FORK

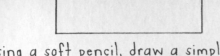

Using a soft pencil, draw a simple rectangular shape as a guide.

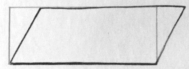

Add diagonal lines to the rectangle to start creating a box shape that looks 3D.

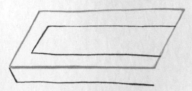

Draw a parallel horizontal line at the bottom and a short, slanted vertical one. Add extra lines to create a big "C" shape.

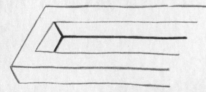

Sketch extra lines in the middle of the "C" shape to add extra depth. Erase the guideline on the right-hand side.

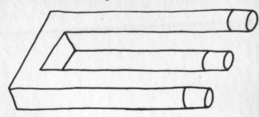

Draw a cylinder shape at the end of each pair of lines. Add color, but notice how the middle and bottom poles come from nowhere!

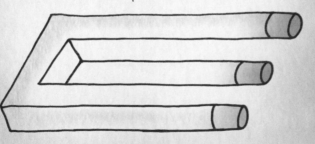

HYPNOTIZER

Draw a large cross with a ruler. Using the central point as a guide, draw two circles with a compass.

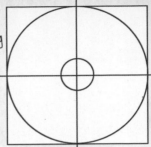

Add three more circles as shown, keeping the point of the compass at the same central point.

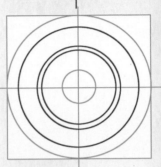

Using your ruler again, draw six lines across the diameter of the big circle. You should now have 12 triangular segments.

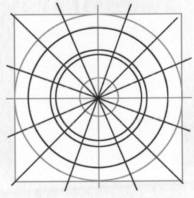

Color alternating sections in black. Stare hard, and watch the shapes move!

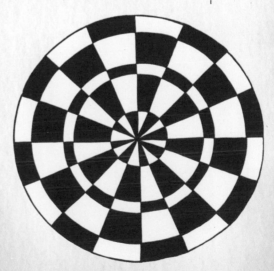

INDEx

ABOUT THE ARTISTS

PAULA FRANCO is a children's book illustrator and graphic designer. She enjoys creating new characters and detailed backgrounds. Paula lives in Argentina with her two rescue dogs, Mora (which means blackberry in spanish) and Mizzy.

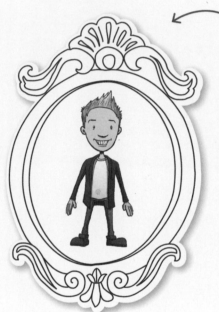

SI CLARK is an illustrator and animator. He grew up in the countryside but now lives in London. He started drawing at a very early age and has pretty much been drawing every day since then. Si is obsessed with drawing trees and cities, as well as finding strange textures to scan into his drawings!

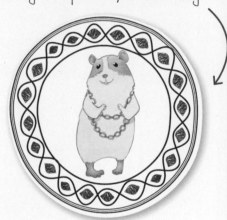

YASUKO has developed a graphic illustration style, mixing ink work, brush strokes, and digital textures. She loves Japanese fashion and sometimes makes her own clothes. Yasuko lives and works in Paris and loves to spend time drawing in the Louvre art museum.

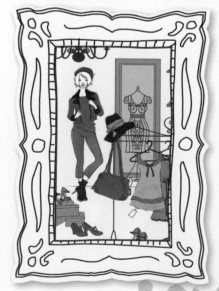

ALEX HEDWORTH works as an illustrator for an animation studio. He has been drawing for as long as he can remember—his first drawings were copies of comic books, and he is now working on a graphic novel of his own.

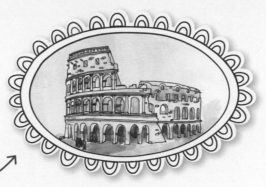

JULIE INGHAM is an illustrator and designer who lives and works by the sea in West Sussex, England. Her favorite things to draw are skyscrapers and all things decorative!

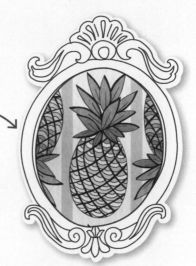

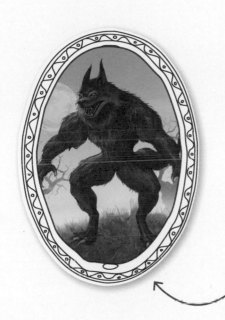

TOM MCGRATH'S work is inspired by artwork he has seen, books he has read, movies he has watched, and even occasionally by real life. He is obsessed with clouds, fish, and airships.

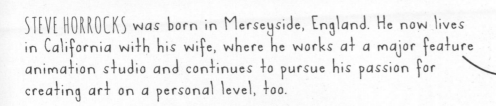

STEVE HORROCKS was born in Merseyside, England. He now lives in California with his wife, where he works at a major feature animation studio and continues to pursue his passion for creating art on a personal level, too.

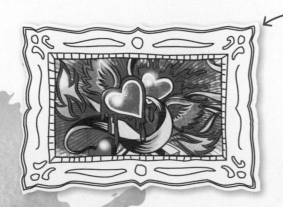

DAVID SHEPHARD is a children's book illustrator and designer. He lives in the shadow of a Norman castle in Sussex, England, with his wife, children, and several pets. He loves drawing people and faces, and works best in his attic, where his family slides his supper under the door!

now go make your mark!

You know the materials. You know the techniques.
You've mastered fashion, patterns, people, and even aliens.

So go sketch, practice, doodle, and draw these ideas and more ...

And go DRAW IT ALL!